TECHNOLOGIES
OF CRITIQUE

INVENTING WRITING THEORY

Jacques Lezra and Paul North, series editors

TECHNOLOGIES OF CRITIQUE

WILLY THAYER

Translated by John Kraniauskas

Fordham University Press *New York*   *2020*

This book was originally published in Spanish as Willy Thayer, *Tecnologías de la crítica: Entre Walter Benjamin y Gilles Deleuze* © 2010 Ediciones metales pesados.

Fordham University Press gratefully acknowledges financial assistance and support provided for the publication of this book by the Fondo Nacional para el Desarrollo Cultural y las Artes (FONDART), Chile.

Fordham University Press has no responsibility for the persistence or accuracy of URLs for external or third-party Internet websites referred to in this publication and does not guarantee that any content on such websites is, or will remain, accurate or appropriate.

Fordham University Press also publishes its books in a variety of electronic formats. Some content that appears in print may not be available in electronic books.

Visit us online at www.fordhampress.com.

Library of Congress Cataloging-in-Publication Data available online at https://catalog.loc.gov.

Printed in the United States of America

22 21 20   5 4 3 2 1

First edition

CONTENTS

TRANSLATION HAS ALWAYS ALREADY BEGUN: TRANSLATOR'S INTRODUCTION

If all writing constitutes a worlding of worlds of sorts, then translation—another writing—arguably involves a reworlding, an "afterlife" in Walter Benjamin's words, providing text with new spatiotemporal coordinates.[1] Conceived as such a process, translation would not just be a technical "encounter" of languages and its administration as such—including its moments of conjuncture (equivalence in translation) and disjuncture (difference in translation)—but a practice of transculturation. This means, in other words, that via the recontextualizing effect of translation (that may even include, as in this case, shifts in the publishing economies of the academic fields into which each version is inscribed, and their respective readerships), this English-language version of Willy Thayer's *Tecnologías de la crítica*, originally published in Spanish in Chile in 2010, is in many ways another work.

At the same time, however, as Benjamin clearly recognizes—and *Tecnologías de la crítica* is in large measure a brilliant reading of Benjamin's oeuvre—that the novelty of the afterlife of a text in translation cannot and does not involve the abstract negation, the erasure, of the "original." In an ethico-political tradition that may begin with Friedrich Schleiermacher but that passes through Benjamin and culminates more recently in Jacques Derrida's reflections on the hosting and welcoming of one language by—and in—another, the latter, host language is itself also transformed in the labor of translation as it wrestles with and internalizes the untranslatable, largely inadvertently, as its secret cargo (in the form, for instance, of the pressure that certain flexibilities of Spanish grammar put on the English sentence). As Pierre Macherey reminded us many years ago, no utterance or text comes to us alone.[2] It is this materiality of language—its constitutive sociality—that makes translation a practice of transculturation (rather than, for example, of imperial acculturation or mere technical interculturation, however self-assured their administered equivalences may be).[3] For example: Thayer belongs to a dynamic radical intellectual milieu in Chile that was linked with the emergence of an experimental and avant-gardist artistic and literary scene during the 1970s and 1980s (neoliberalism and military dictatorship) and after (neoliberalism and postdictatorship) that is most often associated with novelists such as Diamela Eltit, painters such as Eugenio Dittborn, critics such as Nelly Richard, and publishers such as Cuarto Propio and Metales Pesados, the publisher of *Tecnologías de la crítica* as well as previous works by Thayer. There are of course others, too, some of whom are mentioned in the endnotes and references of the main text, below. And several of these interlocutors form part of a fairly longstanding and intensely focused critical culture of Benjaminian thought in Chile, which includes the translation of his works. Beginning with the efforts of Ronald Kay, such reflection and translation continues today with those of Pablo Oyarzún, Elizabeth Collingwood-Selby, and Federico Galende, all important Benjamin scholars, philosophers, and critics in their own right. I am sure that *Tecnologías de la crítica* would be a very different text without the conversations, agreements, and disagreements, the debates within (and outside) this group and that, although I am not exactly sure how, are nevertheless present in the book's words and compositional preferences as a condition and whose traces may still be spectrally present in this English-language version.[4]

In this sense, one might say of *Tecnologías de la crítica,* a critique of critique, that the work of translation as transculturation has always already begun, such that this reworlding just adds one more layer that potentially brings it to the attention of new readers and milieus. Indeed, *Tecnologías de la crítica* may be thought of as a cognitive mapping of "critique" via its constituting and instituting technologies (which Thayer refers to as the "organism," the "theater," and "singularity") and its discursive history—that is, of its many translations and travels—from its Greek and Latin "ruins" (Thayer's word) to its Spanish-language present, as mediated by its versions and transformations in both the German and the French. English does not play a major bibliographical role in this history—although the work of Danto, Jameson, Kuhn, Poe, and others is briefly mentioned—except now, here, as one more translation.

As soon as the Spanish word *crítica* is thus welcomed into English, however, it is confronted with a problem—that is, the possibility of its translation as either "critique" or "criticism." Arguably, it is the latter, "criticism," that is the more widely used. In his *Keywords,* for example, Raymond Williams has an entry for "criticism" rather than "critique," and as he sets out his account of its uses and his criticism of them (that is, criticism's decontextualized and ideological foregrounding of *judgment*), he fails to mention the alternative "critique"—as, for example, an account of the conditions of possibility of judgment—at all (despite this being Williams's own main point in his account: he performs a more or less conventional ideology-critique of the term).[5] From Thayer's perspective, such a use of the term "criticism" privileges the discursive history of *crítica*'s Latin ruin, while partially erasing the significance of its translation, as *cerno*, from the Greek word-ruin *kríno*, and its constellation of meanings—that include to dis*cern* (in the English) as well as *kestrel* (*cernícalo* in Spanish) and thus, also, to loom or to hover (*en ciernes* in Spanish). As announced in his short prologue-epigraph, below, this image of criticism is part of Thayer's critical strategy of deconceptualizing the concept of critique, opening it up (in a Derridean "pedagogic" vein) to its textuality and—as in this image of the hovering kestrel—interrupting "criticism," resulting, as he writes, in a "vacillation that does not follow the rhythm of the argument—of judgment—and remains balancing without making a decision, in a state of indecision."[6] Such an image of criticism is, I believe, fundamental to Thayer's critique of critique, of the overlapping—constellated—transcendental, juridical, and sovereign orders that inform it, especially in the Chilean context of dictatorship and postdictatorship at the time, as well as, differently, in its English-language version as "criticism." The ethico-political mark of this version's hosting of Thayer's deployment of the term in translation, therefore, involves foregoing the use of the English term "criticism"—thus torqueing the juridical art of its judgment—to insist on translating *crítica* as critique throughout (while following Thayer as he eventually pulls the term critically—with the help of both Benjamin and, equally importantly, Gilles Deleuze—toward the idea and image of "*a* critique" with which the book concludes).[7]

In the process of translating *Tecnologías de la crítica,* a number of changes have been introduced into the text: a combination of the author's unfulfilled original intentions and more-recent revisions that have been incorporated into the present version to improve on the way in which the flow of his argument is presented.[8] What are the more substantive changes introduced by the author for the present edition?

First, the elimination of a second epigraph by Jacques Derrida that, alongside Thayer's own, arguably overplayed the idea that it was Derridean deconstruction that might occupy that "between" Walter Benjamin and Gilles Deleuze that is suggested in the text's original Spanish-language subtitle ("Between Walter Benjamin and Gilles Deleuze"), and that thus framed its reading along deconstructive lines.[9] What does happen in this "between"—apart, that is, from the arguments mentioned above? In fact, many writers and texts occupy this space, several of whom are associated with the "technologies" that Thayer describes and their critique: Heidegger, as well as Kant, Hegel, and Marx, even Descartes, Leibniz, and Aristotle (the latter in particular insofar as, in Thayer's view, he may be conceived as the inventor of the idea of the "aura"—*qua* idealized distance—that later, in its bourgeois form, Benjamin will destroy).[10] This also includes the all-important

images associated with them—for example, Marx's *Jenny*. Second, Thayer has
rewritten the two fragments that are dedicated to George Sorel's *Reflections
on Violence* and Benjamin's critique of it: he thus strengthens and develops
the critique of sovereign, militant art, justice, and politics that characterizes *Tecnologías de la crítica* as a whole. And, in this particular regard, he does so in
ways that resonate with the late Ernesto Laclau's account of the abstract metaphoricity of Sorel's reflections—which, paradoxically, in their militant blindness
to particularity (although Thayer might insist here rather on "singularity"), actually depoliticize. In this sense, Sorel cannot occupy the space of the "between"
(because he cannot "hover").[11] Third, Thayer has eliminated a division that made
Tecnologías *de la crítica* a work in two parts. It now only has one, as befits another image that Thayer mentions in conversation when describing the book:
that of sliding down a toboggan. The elimination of the divide thus restores
the all-important sense of flow that the reader is to experience, a certain loss of
control as she is taken along by words (which is why the book is organized into
fragments rather than divided by chapters, enhancing thus the experience of a
bumpy flow). What is more, dividing the book in two is, for Thayer, reminiscent
of the introduction of a *pit*, which defines the theater as a technology of critique
and which separates out, while producing, subject and object, action and contemplation. Again, such a theatrical technology comes under attack from a "mechanical" Benjamin, the social logic of whose critical language—as with Marx's—
has been reconfigured along industrial lines without being subsumed by them.
Finally, I think it is worth mentioning a change that has not proved possible: It
was the author's and translator's intention that this version of *Tecnologías de la
crítica* have footnotes rather than endnotes. Many of these notes are, however,
of considerable length, which has meant that such a reformatting was not technically possible for this edition (as indeed was the case for the Spanish-language
one). It should nevertheless be borne in mind by readers, since in many ways it
was crucial to the composition of the text: such an experience of reading would
interrupt (rather than halt) the flow, slowing down the ride and shifting the
gaze, in the tradition of collage, montage, and assemblage, providing it with a
moment of counterpoint. Thayer's intended montage is not to be conceived,
however, as being in the Eisensteinian tradition that suggests the dialectical overcoming of two images with a third but as a way of producing moments of waver-
ing (hovering)—or stuttering—that are so important to the Deleuzian Benjamin
whom Thayer suggests in his book. Here, the footnotes would not constitute a
site of authority but rather, I think, an attempt to introduce a radical democratic
nonfounding interruption and pedagogy into philosophy—as a means, in other

words, of forestalling what both Lukács and Adorno suggest is the necessary arrogance of the essay form..

Such amendments made for translation[12] also echo another of Thayer's arguments and images: that both citation and translation break down the idea of originary authenticity. This translation is thus not quite the translation of an original. What we have here, in *Tecnologías de la crítica* (and its translation), is one of the foremost works of Benjamin-and-Deleuzian scholarship, a critique, in the form of a re- and de-constructed, *Frankenstein* text.

I would like to thank Paula Barría at Metales Pesados in Santiago de Chile and the editors at Fordham University Press in New York—especially Jacques Lezra, Paul North, and Tom Lay as well as E. W. Maxwell Meyer and Eric Newman—for their enthusiasm and, especially, their patience. I would also like to thank Carol Watts for hers. Finally, I would like to thank Willy Thayer for his generous help in completing this translation.

London, November 2018

Critique needs to touch the limit, to make it visible, and so discontinue it. In this regard, it is crucial above all that critique's own limit not remain behind it, so that it does not proceed blindly, incautiously, or dogmatically. Insofar as critique, in each and every case, succeeds in exorcising the immanence in which it is exercised, its name is translated into a constellation of terms that trace its virtuality. The polychronic coexistence of such terminologies constitutes the figure, the image of critique.

1

CRITIQUE AND LIFE

When critique is regularly exercised it is done so—consciously or not, and for whatever the immediate reason may be—with regard to life. As if the vocation, the desire for critique (that unrealizable something that in its eagerness and multiple tasks moves and concerns it), were always life, its affirmation and potentiation, as if, that is, the virtuality and possibility of life were the *invisible hand* that governs the virtuality and possibility of critique. As if critique and life always, in each and every case, belonged to the same side or band and, in every instance, the potentialities of life opened up a path, eroding away all barriers in a manner analogous to the procedures in which critique either opens its own way amid closed paths (*aporos*) or in the vertigo of open roads (*pantoporos*). As if critique and life did not aspire to conservation at all, undermining themselves in an erosion without origin or presupposition, without point of departure or of arrival, *unworking* thus, in their pure affirmation and becoming without being, riverbeds and banks, identities, and positions,[1] without, however, proposing to do so—that is, without erecting themselves into a critique *of . . .* , an affirmation *of . . .* , the life and becoming *of . . .* ;[2] without opposing or coercing, without, that is, vestiges of negativity: *swelling like a spring and proceeding through the middle* of containments, contracts, and blockages (Deleuze and Guattari) and gaining in speed of erosion, however blocked the narrow strait may be,[3] but extinguishing itself, too, at times, in the mortification that blocks and disempowers it.

Critique, however, has not always seconded life's currents, nor has life—its virtuality—always been welcomed by critique. According to Georg Lukács, for example, critique and life must be strictly kept apart.[4] But when Lukács highlighted this divorce, what he was really separating was not simply life from critique but the understanding of life and of critique as they had been a-critically immersed in and explained by the so-called "philosophies of life."[5] Lukács opposed *his own* historical-dialectical-materialist understanding of critique—that is, *his* understanding of critique, revolution, and life as negation—as the production of a knowledge without lacunae (of an absolute system of the world), to the undialectical, nonnegative, and purely affirmative understanding set out by the *philosophies of life* (some philosophies of life—Nietzsche's above all, especially his notions of life, critique, and revolution),[6] insofar as they provided for the opening of a gap, a difference, an event that is irreducible to the system of negative representationality—an understanding, writes Lukács (referring to the philosophy of life), that contains sufficient indices of irrationalism, mysticism, and mythology to nourish fascism's blindness, blindness as fascism. But even in conjunctures such as Lukács's, in which critique and life are strictly distanced from each other, such a distancing remains relative to a particular deployment of the understanding of life, an understanding that attempts to universalize or immunize itself with regard to another with which it is in conflict. In this sense, we might conjecture that this may always be the case, that the affirmation and potentialization of life in a specific case simultaneously constitutes the weakening of life in another. This would imply that life is never exercised simply as life, but rather that it does so from within a frame, a form, a mode, according to certain technologies of life as compared to others. "As all sorts of different perspectives maintain, neither power nor life exist separately. Thus, any inquiry into life will not posit it as a separate object of reflection in its own right—as if a life might exist that is free from all power, or a power free from the dynamics proper to life—but rather refer to the economies of power which life institutes with regard to itself."[7]

If life, therefore, is not exercised simply as life but is exercised in the context of a frame, a form, a mode, certain technologies of life, then what we have initially suggested about critique (that its vocation, its zeal, that which definitively moves and concerns it, is the potentialization and affirmation of life) will need correcting. We will now have to affirm that critique is not exercised, occupied, or preoccupied with simply supporting life in general,[8] but that it always does so in particular, in relation to technologies or forms of life that, in each case, are currently in course and dominant, and that in each case critique is exercised in the midst of particular forms or technologies—eroding their blockages and containments and thereby potentializing itself as a virtuality that exceeds them,[9] and that on being exercised to unwork such technologies (attempting always to open itself up to life in its own moment, in its pure, absolute, unfounding, nonnegative affirmation, free from technologies and forms), its unconditioned becoming makes visible, as if in its own trail (the tail of a comet or aerolite), the frames, rules, modes, forms, the containments, and closures in the midst of which it is exercised as a *real state of emergency*,[10] as if, that is, in searching for the unconditioned character of life, critique always found forms, technologies, and regimes of life. In this sense, the attempt to free life into its own moment, rather than achieving a thematization of life in its pure eventfulness, thematizes and makes visible the technologies, the regimes that block and obstruct it. Life present to its very own moment, that impossibility, is only possible by way of an obstruction that blocks it, and is achieved only when it has passed: as the remains of a regime of life rather than of life as such. Deleuze attempts to describe life in its moment, in its continuous affirmation, and when he does so he describes an ensemble or montage.[11] This is because, as an assemblage, life is irreducible to the differences between presence and representation, conditioned and unconditioned, spontaneity and law, exception and rule, the mediate and immediate. It is rather in the hiatus, the intermittences, the vacillations, and strata of that montage—at its borders, its shores, and termini—that life vacillates and functions. And it functions in the hiatus as a hiatus, as flow-cuts or folds that are defined by a *severing*.[12] The latter is not, however, a simple cut that creates binary poles, representational differences; it is rather, writes Deleuze, a question of "a severing by which each term casts the other forward, a tension by which each fold is cast into the other," infecting them mutually such that they are born, now, without the possibility of constituting themselves as *self-same*—dislocated from identity or the *presence of self to itself*. Each of the places made possible in the inflection (starting from the inflection itself) thus blurs its own topological profile such that it no longer "refer[s] to coordinates: it is neither high nor low, neither right nor left." They rather grow and distribute themselves on the edge and over the edge, according to a *law of disjunction*, with "the latitude to always add a detour by making each interval the site of a new folding."[13] (We will return to this again below, toward the end of the book.)

But if, in the plurality of its forms, critique moves and, in each case, is exercised and constituted within a movement that is already given, blocked by a technology, a regime or a form that regulates it, then the movement of critique will be essentially a-critical, depotentialized, dogmatic with respect to the regime that, a priori, marks its course; the regime rather than critique would then be the (principle) critic. And the same thing might be said of life. This is why for critique it was always important to touch the limit (*limes, peras*) to make it visible, beginning with its own, as the only means of not proceeding, in this respect, blindly, incautiously, dogmatically. This is why critique, its movements and applications, cannot simply be exercised in the context of a frame or technology of life without questioning it, touching and drumming (*tympaniser*) on it, making it visible while exercising it without transcending it.

But to emphasize the relationship between *life* and *form of life*, between *critique* and *critical frame*, underlining the importance of form and frame, would seem to privilege the primacy of *form*—of *technology*, of the *frame*—such that it dominated critique as pure affirmation, erosion, and potentiation, which without technology *grows through the middle* (Deleuze) of technologies. Life, critique, before life, and before critique would then be form-of-life or form-of-critique. Form permanently exceeded, deferred by the potentialities of life and of critique; potentialities systematically immunized, blocked by the forms of life and critique: "Apollo and Dionysius. If the Apollonian constitutes the point at which life is immunized, the Dionysian displays the place of absolute life, that is, the point at which the latter expands and reveals its lack of principle, of identity, and of substantive propriety or property. Life (*bíos*) would be nothing less than the *munus común* whose process consists in potentializing itself (Dionysius) and, at the same time, containing itself (Apollo). But all immunizing containment is always provisional because life is, over and over again, redirected beyond itself."[14]

Stated as if from the side of the frame, then, technology (the mode or the form), the performance of critique and the exercise of life, would seem to remain dominated by negativity, as the deferment and excess of technology or of form. And however much such deferment, excess, or potentialization may by said to have no topological goals or origins—that it emerges from the tremor of permanent excess—negativity still dominates the scene. It is the pitfalls of negativity that contemporary critique attempts to destroy/deconstruct. The following fragment of Nietzsche's contributes to such a deconstruction: "Form is considered to be something that lasts and is thus of value. But form is simply our own invention. And although we may frequently invent the same form, this does not mean, however, that it *is* the *same* form. Rather, *something new always appears*. It is only we, who compare, that, insofar as it resembles the old, integrate the new into the unity of 'form.'"[15]

2

CRITIQUE AND WORK

The relation between critique and life may be less abrupt if we consider it from the perspective of the more conventional link that is often established between critique and work, and work and life, in such well-worn clichés as the *life of the work*, the *living* or *live work*,[1] *life as work*,[2] *a life's work*;[3] its unity and sustainability, its organicity and structure, its elements and rules, the dynamic of parts and whole, its stability, relationality and economy, its condition, the tenor of its fulfilment,[4] its style (of life). Similarly, as regards the levels of its dispersion, its disaggregation, the lack of control of its hyperboles, the loss of its center, the crisis of its dynamic.[5]

But, perhaps, the relation *critique/life* might also become less abrupt if we looked at it, as is more common today, from the perspective of the connection between critique and unworking, between virtuality and life, life and deconstruction,[6] life and becoming,[7] life and montage.[8]

In each case, the criteria and possibilities according to which critique is exercised would depend upon the frames, categories, and regimes of understanding—or the tensions, clashes, or crossings between such frames, categories, or regimes—in which (in each case) life is heterogeneously precomprehended. It is these frames, or modes of life, or the clashes between them (these very *clashes* being just one more technology) that, in each case, precede critical behavior, while the latter is passively applied on their basis without being actively applied *to* them.

Among (between) such regimes or technologies in which processes of life, work, and critique are carried out, one must, before anything else, consider the no-less diffused understanding of life as *life and nothing more*, *life in itself, as such*: pure life, unpolluted, without mediations, bare, undressed and uncloaked, without disguise and representation, frameless, in a frankly natural state, authentic, true, confessed, without secret or reserve, paradisiacal, *a dog's life*, with nothing to hide, without history, without shame, without sin, immune, sacrosanct, virginal but also, at the same time, barbaric, savage life, a life without consideration: primary, anomalous, insalubrious, vile.

A supposed *life in itself* emerges as a referential illusion or centering function, however vicarious, in the clash, the tension, comparison, or encounter between regimes of life (or work). A centering function is inclined to detain the undefined proliferation of frames, life's verisimilitudes, such as *life and nothing more, true (or real) life*.

Immediate life has rarely been caught sight of—naked, without a frame or a stitch (stark naked), lawless, with neither voice nor writing, reduced to the mere state of a frightened animal, as biology—without such immediacy being the result of material mediations, those of the economy, the alphabet, metaphysics, for example—and their taxonomies, their made-to-measure grammars, classification, and hierarchization; their markets and zoos; their farms, fields, and parks, neighborhoods and ghettos, photographs and albums; their air-conditioned museums, their shantytown racism, as well as their "white" pornography. Only in the *mise en scène* of such a classificatory power—of an Aristotelian cinematographer of genera and species announcing their substantivizing snapshots—can animals, men naked to the bone, lost souls without instincts, anomic, be glimpsed in fear, their desire radically contained, vegetative (*threptiké*[9]), like matter to be transplanted or experimented upon. On other floors of this columbarium, tamely complacent animals wander about as if unhindered by any power or ghetto.

If *life in itself* is to consist of anything, its figure—its image—will not be found in any of the technologies, frames (or interframes) in particular, but rather in the *constellation*, the montage, the virtuality of technologies, frames, and interframes: a constellation that is irreducible to a sum or general synthesis that mediates or transcendentalizes terms and virtualities into a general category.[10] If a mediation or general synthesis were to subsume the multiplicity into a totality, this synthesis would itself be incorporated into the montage as one more element or marker without, thereby, becoming fetishized as transcendent. The montage does not preexist but rather circulates as one more remainder, residue that produces a fold in the montage, in the virtuality that emanates from its crossings and relations:[11] diverse, heterochronic, and heterotopic regimes, precipitating and relaunching one another, dizzyingly transforming themselves, coupling, clashing with each other. Montage ignores the distinction between its production and its functioning. It does not constitute a previous plane of encounter and gathering, a mé*dium*, a territory in common, a surface to which technologies arrive so as to delimit each other.

A radiating constellation flowers at the crossing of the heterogeneous, without establishing itself in the same (*ipseity*)—without being assimilated into the other and without immunizing itself from the other—translating itself, infecting itself without becoming ill, because if we are to understand anything by *life* in this work and, consequently, by critique, then such an understanding will be closer to the play and the movement that, in Fragment 48, Heraclitus proposes between *bíos* (life) and *biós* (arc/arch/bow): *the bow (biós) is called life (bíos); but its work is death.*[12] And so, what follows from this: no understanding, no style, no frame—life. None exist outside it (its figure, its multiple performance, its march, its parade, the constellation of its regimes, its potential or virtuality, its polymorphous, polychronic, polytechnic imagination). The figures of these errant and inexact regimes, their becoming, are analogous to the electric arc of multiple lightning bolts, the strings of a lyre or the chords of a violin, the many-stringed bow and arrows—one of which is the curved rod, another the stretched gut, others still the straight arrows—not to mention the arcs that arrows trace in flight, or the rainbow—the messenger of the gods that figures in the many drops and refractions shimmering in the rays of the sun the pact between the earth and sky, the human and the divine.[13] This tense figure of life (*bíos*) cannot be dialectically stabilized into a totality or a synthetic process but rather vacillates in its multiplicity.

It is probably with this in mind that Walter Benjamin named his fragmentary Arcades Project—which thinks life and justice as a tense relation of multiplicity, far from representation and judgment. *Passagen*, that is, *Arches*, alludes to the architecture of the passages—not only the tunnels of heterochronic and hetero-topic commodities that the arches open onto but also to the flying buttresses and arches themselves as opening, tension, movement, vacillation, and multiplicity.

The name of life (*bíos*)—we are now inverting the terms—is bow or arc(h) (*biós*): tension, vigor, as in the tense bow of the many-stringed violin, tense as testified to by the word *zoé*,[14] that other name for life that also speaks of tension, vigor, and movement.[15] Life (*bíos*) as a tightened bow (*biós*) has its contrary in the slack bow (*biós*), the unravelling threaded rope, death. The name of the bow or arc(h) (*biós*) as life (*bíos*) is the tense relation of elements. In this way, the bow (*biós*) becomes one of the primary allegories of life as a tense organism or structure, and of death as *agregatum*, unravelling, distension.

But this life (*bíos*)/death (*biós*), tension/distension, belongs to the organism only while there is a relation to a center. We must also consider the tensions and distensions of a scenario without such a function, in which the virtuality of life is not relative, in either the first or last instance, or a general mediation, or an irreducible ground around which it vacillates. Rather, the virtuality of life is to be considered as a coexisting constellation of technologies, a coexistence that is irreducible to any one of them.

All technologies of life belong to the virtuality of life, but the virtuality of life cannot be reduced to any technology of life in particular. Nor can virtuality be reduced to an "outside" that exceeds the coexisting technologies. Life, its virtuality, is not reducible either to a privileged technology or to the outside of these technologies, or to a synthesis of them. Such an outside, a synthesis or privileged technology, would just constitute one more technology, another moment of virtuality, a vicarious outside. In this sense, we cannot share such affirmations as "life can take on a multiplicity of forms." This is better: "Life is not anterior nor posterior; it does not preside nor precede the forms, the technologies, of life." It is immanent to them. Nor are the technologies—each existing in tension with the others—stabilized in a general mediation or synthesis. This is also the case with the concept of virtuality: virtual is the life that grows within (immanently) the technologies. Virtual, too, are the technologies themselves in their becoming— far from having any one identity but in the crossings of many.

3

THE *KRÍNO* CONSTELLATION

In each and every case, the possibility of critique, its criteria with regard to perception and action, its features and range, will usually depend on the regime of understanding under which life and work are precomprehended, including, within these regimes, a *naturalist* understanding that comes from the nonthematization of the frame, whatever it may be, in which life, critique, and work unfold. Critique is regularly exercised according to the understanding of a specific case or to the clashes and tensions between different understandings— according, that is, to a variety of hostilities, hospitalities, parasitisms, tensions, and refuges.

Each critique, each crisis, takes place in particular sites of production on the basis of their technologies and modes of existence.[1] The latter are already announced in the etymological constellation of the word *kríno*, its derivatives, and idiomatic translations and also in the survival of its Greek ruin, which added to the ruins that are used to translate it, to populate languages, and in writings—a constellation that is also found in etymological dictionaries that always refer to meanings of specific, practical usage according to languages, dates, and cartographies.

Thus, for the Greek word *kríno*: (1) The action of separating, picking, ex-

cluding, sieving, examining, opening, distinguishing, differentiating, a simultaneously analytical-contemplative and manual task. In Latin, these actions are
properly gathered under *cerno*, the ruin with which Latin translates these actions directly from *kríno*—hence expressions such as *cribum*, "to pass through
a sieve" (Pliny), or *cerne*, "you will sift through thick holes" (Ovid)—a ruin that
we also find in the Spanish [and to some extent in the English—Trans.] in *dis-
cernir* (to discern), *discernimiento* (discernment), which is related to "criticize"
in the sense of "to analyze," "separate," "to look at the detail of," "to contemplate
carefully," like the kestrel (cernícalo) that is looming (en ciernes), immobile,
flapping its wings, hypnotizing its prey so as then to swoop (cernirse) down
on it. If we widen the frame, it may be applied to the drunk who stumbles and
fails to advance, to loom (en ciernes), to the vacillation that does not follow the
rhythm of the argument—of judgment—and remains balancing without making
a decision, in a state of indecision. (2) The medical use of *krisis*, which links
together two levels of significance: (a) the performative, in which the critical day
of the illness or of the patient resonates, the objective critical instant, the point
at which the illness breaks; and (b) the speculative, the moment of observation,
of medical diagnosis, and the judgment as to the unfolding of the illness, the
decision concerning diets, the calendar of symptoms leading to the critical day,
the calculation of the days ending in either the death or life of the patient, from
which the performative resonance of *crisis* as a line of rupture or frontier, the
instant in which one gets better or worse, wins or loses: perfect crises (without
relapses), imperfect crises that do not end well. Crisis in the passive sense, as
in *to be in agony*. (3) The juridical and political use of *crisis* with reference to
decision and determination by the law, to the foundation of the constitution
through whose mediation individuals are joined together; the political arrangement of the civic community (the state),[2] the creation and establishment of the
law. *Crisis* as with the decisive tilting of the balance, when deliberation comes
to a halt (and the kestrel awakens to fall on its prey), or as the suspension of
right, the *state of exception* as political sovereignty, the decision as to war and
peace, the crisis most necessary for the existence of the political community.[3]
In *kríno*, both moments are gathered: the performative of crisis, as the breaking point, and the subjective of critique as analysis and discernment. Judgment,
too, in *diakrino*, which should not be confused with the judgment of *dikatho*,
which comes from *diké* (justice) and opens up a register that is different from
the theoretical-contemplative, apathetic, devout, or melancholic, more proper
of the *kríno* constellation. *Dikatho* involves a dramatic register of condemnation
and salvation, of absolution and punishment, truth and lies. (4) The theological

use of *crisis* that, in the *Septuagint*, the Greek version of the Old and New Testaments, announces the beginning of a world government that is attributed to the Holy Alliance. God, lord and judge, contains the promise of justice, harmony, connection, *self-presence*, according to his judgment. Here crisis (and critique, too) becomes disconnected from the apathetic, theoretical-contemplative register that breaks down and unravels in infinite detail, without searching for synthesis, the modality proper to *kríno*, and connected rather to the plaintive justice (*diké*) that saves and condemns, the wisdom of God as a knowledge with moral implications and concerning judicial sentence (*katadiké*), and that will flower when the awaited final world crisis, the final judgment, arrives and true justice, now the hidden hope, apocalyptic respite, "the unshakeable certainty," the final moment of revelation, is revealed.[4] (5) In tragedy, *crisis* announces the knot (in the story), conflict, and corresponds to the *epítasis* (tension) of tragedy that immediately precedes the moment of catastrophe and dénouement, as well as the moral and psychological crisis of the protagonist.[5] The *hupokrisia* or simulation, or the *mise en scène*, in presentation, the *hupokrisia* that masks, plays a role in declaiming, interpreting a piece of theater or music, reading a poem, in the grain of its metrics (its noise). (6) The modes of existence of critique apparent in the Latin constellations of *jus* and *cerno*, in the corresponding philological dictionaries that host other of its modes of existence and translate many others.[6] Constellations visible, finally, in the reception and translation of the Greek and Latin into modern European languages in their respective state and imperial cartographies.[7]

TECHNOLOGIES OF CRITIQUE

ORGANISM

By *technologies* of critique, I refer, in particular, to two or three regimes that are transversal to the various modes of existence of critique and crisis (of life as well as of work). In the first place, it is a question of *organic structure* and of *theater*, which, although not the same, are not essentially different regimes either, superimposing themselves on one another and even substituting the one for the other. In his *Dictionnaire philosophique*, Lalande notes that the concept of *structure* designates, in opposition to a simple aggregate of *elements*, a whole in solidarity with itself, such that each of its elements depends on the others and can only be what it is *in and through* its relation with them.[1] In various of his writings, Aristotle, above all toward the end of Book 7 of his *Metaphysics*—and we are paraphrasing Agamben here[2]—tracks the metaphor of *structure* in the aporias that provide it with its tone. A structure, he writes, is irreducible *to the simple sum of its parts*; it is *something more* than the simple combination of its elements, such that the structure as a whole is not dissolved in their *agregatum*.

However, from where does that *something more* that transcends the simple sum of parts and makes possible the unity of the *aggregate* as an organic, tense, living totality come? That *something more*, the unity that the organism gathers together, must be something other (*héteros tí*) than a mere part, than the combination or sum of parts. Otherwise, the structure would not be constituted, because its unity would be one more addition to the *agregatum*. For Aristotle, that *something more*, that *other thing*, has—exceptionally—to be *another thing*. It is never just one more element in the simple sum of parts but something that only becomes significantly something else if it has abandoned the terrain of the *infinite aggregate* and entered the dimension that he refers to as the *cause of being* (*aitía tou eínai*) and *substance* (*ousia*), the principle that channels and maintains any thing in/as presence. This element, for Aristotle, is *form* (*morfé Kay eídos*).

To reiterate: this *other thing* (*héteros tí*) on which organic unity rests—and becomes present in it such that it unifies and gathers together the multiplicity of its parts in an organism—has to be radically *something else*, found only in the abandonment of the divisible terrain, elevating itself into the dimension of the *cause of being*, the indivisible unity that maintains any thing in its unity, in its presence *to itself*. Aristotle thus invents the aura: "the unique phenomenon of a distance, however close it may be."[3] He invents, or reinvents, the strange, the unfamiliar, as a principle of familiarity, the sublime, the hyperbole, the *exception*, the exceptionality of *héteros tí*, as a founding principle.

- With regard to the metaphor of the organism as a structure made up of parts (counterposed to the *agregatum*, the elemental, unformed matter, the unarticulated, irreducible substrate, lacking all rhythm, and that cannot be changed)—that is, of its capacity to generate copies of itself, to increase the number of parts that make it up and/or their size; of the relation between the parts and the whole and/or between each other; of the behavior required for it to adapt to the environment in which it develops;

of the possibility of it absorbing energy so as to maintain its own internal environment constant, its homeostasis, the regeneration of its elements, the regulation of the wear and tear of its pieces, its components, its tropisms and shifts, its internal network processes; of the potential of maintaining its unity, the functionality of the whole, its soul or anima, its motor; of its control processes (centralized or not), its center(s), its life principles, its autonomy, its separation; of the crisis or of its rupture with respect to the apparatus in which it is located, its finality; of the modes of its composition or decomposition, generation or corruption, its creation and annihilation, its provenance and metamorphosis; of its rhythm, harmony, dynamic, its health, its "truth"; of its critique and crisis, etc. (it is necessary to distinguish mechanical technology from organicist technology—whose further exposition we halt at this point).

It is the metaphor of the organism, of the living or centered structure, of the unitary, structured whole, that has ordinarily been posited as the muse, model, and rule of the work, of life, of their functioning and, therefore, of their critique and their crisis, and not only of the work of art, of painting, sculpture, music, of tragedy and its fable,[4] theater,[5] of discourse[6] and argument, of poetics,[7] but also of the Constitution of the State, of the work of politics,[8] of governments,[9] the military, of the city,[10] language, the work of theology and cosmology,[11] the work of literature and history, of the universe and the relation between its elements,[12] of the university.[13]

There are, thus, certain technologies that have acted as the dominant model or muse for the understanding of work, life, their potentiality, their mode of composition or decomposition, their functioning, their *rhythm* and harmony, their shine and eloquence, their balance, their "truth" or plenitude, their waning, their critique, their crisis and their failure. It has been the organic matrix as well as its shaking that have regularly stamped the framing of critique and of crisis, configuring the parameters of its exercise, its effective performances, its aesthetic, medical, political evaluations, diagnoses, and diets.

THEATER

The theater, for its part, has often been understood as a living structure, be it under the guise either of a verisimilitude that is mechanical or of an organicist verisimilitude of life. In its turn, the organism has been understood as theater and as a garden, too.[14] What the structure of theater adds to the metaphor of the organism is the making explicit of a *point of view* (*theatron*), a *voyeuristic,* perspectival doubling that the organism does not necessarily imply (although it may be structurally prefigured in the *héteros tí*). Before anything else, the term *theatron* names the moment "in which a public contemplates an action from a distance, such that this public now constitutes a point of view with regards to the event."[15] Religious and shamanistic rituals do not provide the space for any point of view, distance, or discernment. In them, the proffered word "is not that of an individual will, but rather that of a preestablished code . . . which is imposed for the time to come . . . it commands, repeating itself according to an imperious model which demands to be received in the way it is ennounced, even when opaque, fixed for once and for all." A ritual has no spectators, only "the faithful, unequally initiated but all obedient."[16] The origin of theater is to be found in *separation*, the irruption of the pit: the instant, or instance in which cult value in its degree zero of exhibitionism or exposition, its degree zero of exchange and distance from itself, sprouts an exhibitionary and exhibitionist vector,[17] a crisis in which the cult, with no distance with itself, exceeds itself, estranging itself from *itself*, opening, producing, in this estrangement, a significant difference in kinds of places: a sacred space and time proper to its ministers that is different from that of its faithful, stage and stalls, the role of actors and of spectators, "a place to which the public comes to look and be moved at a distance by a myth that is familiar and made flesh by actors,"[18] a crisis of the ritual that on breaching its immanence unfolds as spectacle, introducing a division of labor between the action and its anticipation, the event and its reception, opening up the time of *sacrilege*. The possibility of critique emerges in that separation, in the sacrilege of ritual, the technology of theater.

SINGULARITY

The other regime of critique and crisis (of life as well as of the work), transverse to various modes of its existence, is that of singularity.[19] Unlike structure and organism, which are irreducible to the immanence of their parts and presuppose *something more* that transcends the mere combination of elements—*something more* that makes it possible that the *aggregate* is unified in an organic, living totality gathering and tensing the multitude of elements around a center, *something more* that has to be something other (*héteros tí*) than a mere part, and only possible to find abandoning the terrain of the *aggregate*, in another strata— unlike, then, both structure and organism, singularity does not unfold (*desdoblar*) into a double. None of its elements transcends the exact construction, the rigorous montage of immanent elements that constitute it. Singularity, fold, the finite figure of infinite virtuality and testimony—which does not organize or structure its predicates around a center (present or absent) or dialecticize them into an integrating synthesis—does not make a totality, a unity, or identity, although it does not dissolve them either, nor does it dissolve itself as mere *agregatum*. Rather, it is constituted as an exact ensemble that lacks nothing, has no leftovers, and in which nothing is out of place—but without thereby founding topologies, identities. Instead, it always testifies, in each and every framing, to something other than what it testifies to. Singularity is nothing less or more than the relational emplotment of its materials, its form being—undecidedly—its content and vice versa, coinciding thus with its *thing* that is always something else. Its movement, its activity is never teleological. Nor is it figurative or metaphoric. Its flow is not characterized by changes in usage; rather, as a becoming without links, it spreads, erodes, makes tremble, and folds.[20] Singularity's regime—of the infinite fold of infinite distribution and testimony—unworks, destroys, deconstructs the mechanical/organic theater as well as the closure, the immanence of the ritual. What might critique or crisis mean here, amid what singularity proposes as pure erosion of the virtual exercised on the real? And what would "work" mean, and what would life name?

Be it as a centered, mechanical, or organic structure, or as an a-centric *patchwork*, these regimes share a dimension that is both a manual and performative dimension, an arrangement of elements. In the first case, the arrangement corresponds to strong topologies, binarisms, functions that are totalizing, finalizing, centering, or to disaggregates that disperse into what Aristotle referred to as *proton*, the primary as a continuum that absolutely lacks structure, irreducible to form, causality, rhythm, and finality.[21] In the other, it corresponds to fragmentary atopisms and turbulences, vacillations that in-decide, spectralize, that virtualize places, totality, identity, homogeneity, interrupting both the organic structure and the *proton*.

5

THE WORD "CRITIQUE"

Anyone can confirm the regular variations suffered in language dictionaries in the definition of its terms. I am not referring to the variation observed between one dictionary and another but rather to those set out in the same dictionary across successive editions. And in particular, those proposed by the *Diccionario de la Real Academia Española* (RAE), which through different symbolic mechanisms circulates as the lexical bible that in the last instance dictates the meaning of the use of terms (in Spanish). Despite being only one among many dictionaries, even having been challenged in its role as *princep* among dictionaries, its monumental binding seems to tell us that in it, amid changing usage, the linguistic canon is inscribed forever.

Despite appearances, this is not its philosophy. Far from being the monumental diachronic archive of the Castillian Spanish language, as its title and design suggests, the RAE's Dictionary proposes to register specific epochs and geographies of the living use of the language synchronically, such that each of its editions—twenty-two since the first, in 1780—more than constituting itself as the witness of Castillian Spanish for all times and places, sanctions, in each edition, the living use of one epoch, so avoiding a polychronic testification that disseminates meanings, feeding the heteroclite, and so weakening the contemporary intention and valence of each of its terms.[1] In this sense, whenever the *lengua viva* consults the edition that is in each case its contemporary, far from being decentered in out-of-date lexical ruins that only testify anachronistically, it will find in the Dictionary the mirror of its every day. The twenty-three editions would thus propose to us, its readers, a sequence of twenty-three synchronic stages of the language by way of the fetish that, in each edition, the map coincide with the terrain.[2]

Let us take as an example a word of particular interest here: the word *crítica*, which, as noted above, is a Latin ruin in the Spanish. In the first edition, of 1780,[3] which is almost contemporary with the French Revolution, the word *crítica* (critique) does not appear—suggesting that the "living Spanish" and the Dictionary's intention at the time were moving in a time different from that of the French Revolution.[4] The eighteenth edition, of 1956 (as well as the twenty-second, of 1992) remits *crítica* back to the Greek *kritike* and translates it, first, according to the "living usage" of the time, as *juicio* (judgment),[5] blocking the constellation of *krino* to which—somewhat like a splinter—*kritike* belongs. Similarly, and especially, the connection between *kritike* and *krisis* (which maintain an intense relation) is blocked, too. Jumping from one language to another, sheltering itself in the supposed referential equivalence of lexicons, *crítica* is then translated into the romantic ruin *juicio* (judgment—*juicium*).

In the same way that *juicio*, according to present *living use* (as inscribed in the online RAE Dictionary), is a *faculty of the soul that distinguishes between good and evil, the true and the false*—an *operation of the understanding* that consists in *comparing, attributing, predicting,* or a *mental state* such as *good sense, common sense, right judgment,* or its loss *(madness, delirium, rapture),* a *point of view,* a *perspective,* an *opinion,* etc.—critical activity is distributed according to a subjective principle as the action of a subject on an object, as an action that exists solely in relation to something other than itself: as theater, then, whose concise staging is the tribunal that is spatially arranged in stage and stall, judge and defendant, subject and object, not only within the juridical order *(sentence)* but in the medical order *(diagnosis)* and the theological order (the *final judgment*) that, secularized, will become the tribunal of history (the judgment of history).

As suggested above, the translation of critique as *juicio* (judgment)[6] produces a reduction that subtracts it from the apathy that is proper—or more proper—to the theoretical-contemplative register of those activities that are included under *krino,* activities that refer to a kind of discernment that separates, distinguishes, selects, analyzes, observes for differences, and in this sense does judge *(diakrino)* but does so from the contemplative vertigo that lets itself be carried away by whatever the matter at hand demands[7] and that, based on the meticulous obedience of the researcher, the arbiter *(krites),* the judge *(kriter),* the critic *(kritikos),* the tribunal *(arkhé kritike),* suggests criteria *(kriterion)* to contemplation *(theorein)* and the discernment of the infinite detail that is opened up by contemplation within the *krinein.* The translation of critique into judgment produces a reduction that attaches it to *pathos*—with an intentionality associated with salvation or condemnation, absolution or a moral—as well as to juridical and theological sentencing. Such a translation, insofar as it fetishizes the virtuality of critique within judgment's horizon, closes down the possibility of critique and justice—as the death of judgment, for example—as the *true state of exception,* which refuses to allow itself be reduced to an intention, a sentence, or a position.

If we inverted matters and questioned the Greek ruin that may be used as a translation of the Roman theological, moral, and juridical *judicium* and *judex,* then rather than arriving at *kritike, krino*—and the constellation of analytical and apathetic activities that are proper to theoretical-contemplative discernment that shatters against the fragmentation of things as they are dispersed under the dictate of their infinite detail—then we would arrive at the constellation of *diké* (justice, decision, arbitration[8]), *dikátho* (to judge, to sentence), *dikastés* (judge, jury), *dikaios* (just), *dikaíosis* (sentence, punishment), *diatheke* (testament), *ta díkaia* (things that are just, balanced, precise), *díken didónai* (pay the penalty).[9] In following *living Spanish*, and in translating *critique* (*crítica*) as judgment (*judicium*), the RAE Dictionary activates a terminological montage that superimposes the dramatic register of justice—that saves and condemns— onto the apathetic register of discernment (*cerno, kríno*). Such a montage hinders critique and the critic with a double legacy: on the one hand, with the theoretical-analytic-apathetic-contemplative discernment that is associated with *kríno*, and, on the other, with the pathetic sap of salvation and condemnation, crime and punishment, justice as the reparation of a broken harmony. With this assemblage, the critic is invested with the figure of the judge (*dikastés*) who saves or condemns as well as with the figure of analytic, apathetic, theoretical, de-dramatized intelligence—more proper to the constellation of *kríno*. The translation, the assemblage of *cerno* and *dike*, of *kríno* and *jus*, transforms both critique and the critic into hovering kestrels that contemplatively, melancholically examine their prey so as to awaken and pass pathetic sentences upon them. This assemblage provoked a number of aporia in enlightened modernity— among them, the need to autonomize the judgment of knowledge from moral judgment, theoretical reason from practical reason. Soon, the enlightenment *critique* that emerged as the proper name given to the processes of the secularization of the world was to find its dramatic epitome in the avant-gardist phrase: *to have done with the judgment of God.*[10]

The actual twenty-second, online version of the RAE Dictionary proposes an eloquent change in direction in the first use of the word "*critique*" (*crítica*) as compared to previous primary ones, a change that testifies to a shift in the understanding of its "ordinary living use" in the language (*lengua*). Rather than remitting critique (*kritike*) to judgment, it immediately remits it to crisis.[11] It thus incorporates a Greek reference that had not accompanied the word "critique" in previous versions. The actual online version of the RAE Dictionary displaces the reference to judgment to eighth place,[12] relegating the subjective activity of critique as a *faculty of the soul* and *use of the understanding*—relegating, too, its dramatic condition of a sentence, which saves and condemns—and upgrading the eminently performative stratum of the term "*crisis*" that comes from medical testimony. Critique now, both in the Dictionary and supposedly in living language, rather than the subjective faculty of emitting judgments, a faculty or tribunal applied to another thing separate from it, is performative crisis *qua* exceptional instance immanent to the development of *physical, historical, economic, spiritual* processes: "In our century," writes Koselleck, "there is virtually no area of life that has not been examined and interpreted through the concept with its inherent demand for decisions and choices."[13]

This is a displacement of *critique*, then, from its position as *faculty of the soul, use of the understanding,* and *subjective faculty of judgment* to the performative position of a crisis that takes place (rather than subjectively and without judgment) in the socio-historical interfaces of life's relations and *dispositifs* that preconfigure subjectivity, its conditions, as well as the possibilities of judgment.

If it is the case that subjectivity is constituted by a network of social relations, then a crisis of such relations will also be a crisis of what is deemed to be subjectivity—a question that motivates the investigation not into how subjectivity loses hold of the site of its autonomous principle of judgment but rather how it is that social relations prescribe subjectivity, its judgments, and decisions and how it is that these decisions and judgments are invaginated into the social relations that produce the judgment that also produces the social relations.

MARX'S CRITICAL TURN

By around 1843, Marx had outlined an idea of critique conceived as *the question of history* ("that is the question").[1] It was not a matter of critique reduced to judgments within the realm of a *philosophy of conscience* (as the capacity of a subjective faculty to judge) nor of critique as *the highest court of reason* or as a discursive operation. Rather, it was a matter of critique as a performative crisis of the *relations of production*, a crisis expressed—inasmuch as phenomena derived from these relations, into which they are also inscribed—in and as conscience, its faculties and judgments. For Marx, it was a question of critique as "the practical overthrow of the actual social relations . . . [by] revolution,"[2] which involves *hitting*[3] and *hand-to-hand fighting*,[4] a real breaking point that does not merely feed property relations but rather satisfies them by exceeding them, generating an overflow and transformation of their presupposition—a presupposition that they encounter "not under circumstances they themselves have chosen but under given and inherited circumstances[,] . . . the tradition of the dead generations weigh[ing] like a nightmare."[5]

Critical consciousness reels without foundation when it realizes that its transformative *pathos* does not constitute anything new and is rather old poison, the late wheeze of an older condition—a priori materials passed on through the archives as the stigma of belonging. It spins without flight, finally realizing that it is this infinite a priori material that reemerges as critical heart and head, prescribing "its" judgments, "its" distance, carried away by the fetish of constituting an autonomous, self-founding, immediate principle, the a priori material immanent to it alone, to its apparatus and technological interfaces, its historical and protohistorical weave, as well as to its anachronisms,[6] heterochronisms, polychronisms that, from far and wide, merge into a shared, monumentalized present and impose its inertia, preproducing and preunderstanding critique as one more instance in which immanence *performs*.[7] All attempts at transcendence or escape—the vertical gestures that affirm a *beyond*, the general sanctions that try to direct the course of things—belong to the surface of immanence like recorded voices on a magnetic tape. Speak they of God or of magnetic tape, they do not transcend the magnetism of the tape one bit. None of the voices is more than the others—"nothing is more" (*ou mallon*), as the skeptics say; none transcends the montage of tape and voices, although neither do they homogenize or dedifferentiate. With critique, understood performatively as *crisis* or as *a putting into crisis*, modernisms and avant-gardes measure their disruptive potential.

7

CRISIS AND AVANT-GARDE

No avant-gardist crisis responds to the transformative or conservative interests of a field (be it of consciousness, of art, of law, of science, or of the economy), however much this may be its starting platform. Nor does it start by representing a sector of the population or the interests of a minority, however marginalized it may be. It is the social relations, the shape of the world rather than its voices, its gestures, rumors, or discomfort, that the avant-garde (as an aesthetic rather than a historical category) proposes to abandon—without looking back. An avant-gardist crisis cannot confirm an already-past historical form in the proliferation of its linguistic experiments and vignettes that prattle on about its inhospitality and splutters a *novum* in the now-old relations of production. The Hegelian dialectic—according to which the truth of a process is revealed posthumously, with the setting of the sun, at the time of the concept—has no place here at all. The result as a presupposition has no room here, either. The new only erupts if it emerges outside of the presupposition in which it emerges. It is better, even, when it emerges without presupposition.

For the avant-garde, it is a question of performatively exceeding the form of the world, its relations of production, appropriation and expropriation, the historical interface that makes those voices possible, and whose conflict and multiplication confirm the world that nourishes its form. No given form should interfere with *new* matter. While the new is still pregnant with old relations, it remains a manifestation of what it itself intends to leave behind—remaining kidnapped inside a *corset machine* that does not let it be: "In the same way, the beginner who has learned a new language always retranslates it into his mother tongue: he can only be said to have appropriated the spirit of the new language and to be able to express himself in it freely when he can manipulate it without reference to the old, and when he forgets his original language while using the new one."[1]

The avant-garde does not propose the production of new vignettes within the same form, but rather the production of a new form whose vignettes are formally incompossible with the old form. If the avant-garde event were to take place, then the rhetorics of the debacle, the cut, of rupture, revolution, change, of the incursion into unknown territories would be interrupted because the subject itself, the mode of production of such proclamations, would become desubjectivized.

The avant-garde has "a changed consciousness of time" and "understands itself as invading unknown territory, exposing itself to the dangers of sudden, of shocking encounters";[2] "the avant-garde as a penetration into *terra incognita*,"[3] with the capacity to glimpse what lies outside the system,[4] would thus be a probe without distance, without vision, that says nothing about the place into which it is entering: a region of absolute strangeness.

Protesting against the given, the critique of the vale of tears, negativity, is just more tears in the vale. Avant-gardist evangelization is, too, *opium of the people*. What it points to as the future present, the past present, or present present is no more than an echo of the present arrangements.

The avant-garde manifesto—"a writing in which a sovereign, a party leader, a group of personalities . . . explain[s its] past behavior and defines the future objectives it seeks to attain[,] . . . making public a doctrine[,] . . . making public knowledge of a truth relative to a supposedly new and original praxis of life, which supports a proselytizing activity . . . presented so as to mobilize in favor of a transformative action"[5]—is the expression of the relations of production against which it turns. The future present in(to) which such a manifesto leans does not constitute an effective scission with the actuality in which it emerges because no people are ahead of their time; all people, in their day, "flourish inside [their] cranium[s]":[6] "It is not possible for any man, however revolutionary [he] may be, to differ from [his] epoch without confirming it."[7]

The avant-garde crisis has to happen, if it happens, outside of the language that proclaims it. In what language, then, would such a crisis speak? In one that changes the *language-form*. Whom might it thus speak to? Would it speak?

The avant-garde crisis is thus merely *consular*, mere *agitation*, if at the moment of its occurrence it feeds the language that it declares to be leaving behind, if the formal conditions of its composition do not interrupt the old form in which it matures. And when the rupture is such that *it does not feed the old form and speaks a new language as it forgets the previous language within it*, it would still feed the old form of sovereignty that establishes the exception, suspends the old form to found a new form. As a founding rupture, the avant-garde belongs to the schematics of sovereignty: *expropriation-appropriation/distribution/cultivation-promotion-naturalization*.[8] It belongs to political theology, to the attempts at secularizing it.

Avant-garde performance cannot propose objectives for itself that are possible. It cannot have objectives or only propose those that it cannot propose. Locutions such as "I interrupt history with a precociously lucid will! I live the actuality of my action with the clairvoyance of someone who knows they are inaugurating something new! Like a soothsayer-bird, I have penetrated into the labyrinths of the future and profited from the consequences of my actions! I can tell you the history of the first one hundred years of the new calendar, describe what is to come, what cannot but come, since necessity itself works within it! I am the gospel of the future! My hearing is tuned into the new music! There are no eyes or ears with which to be seen or heard! Do I even exist!"[9]—of what do they speak? Of a possibility? Of an impossibility? Of a power? Of powerlessness? Of power and powerlessness at the same time? Are these Nietzschean tropes avant-gardist statements—that is, negative in their affirmation? Foundational or sovereign in their affirmation? Or are they Deleuzian ones, postsovereign, post-avant-gardist, neither negative nor foundational, an affirmation, pure erosion, and becoming? (We will return to this.)

Of the new that overflows the given, one cannot speak, at least not in the way that one speaks. The new, if there is such a thing, is only expressed in the depotentializing of the ruling form. The new only speaks on making visible the language, the technology, the power (*potencia*) that speaks. When the invisible eyes that make the appearance of the visible possible begin to become visible themselves, other unsuspected eyes, impossible to catch sight of, are installed as a new invisibility—from which the now old and depotentiated eyes and their possible vistas may be glimpsed. We cannot delimit or situate the emergent power since it is, inversely, what situates and gathers us up from behind our backs. But we do become aware of it as we realize that we see the eyes with which we (once) saw. With frailty, the loose thread appears, the empty bottom, the bottomless bottom of the pot.

The vulgar understanding of time as a euchronic present seems to govern the avant-gardist crisis: it privileges the future as the sole vector, affirming a clean break with the past as a dead weight that has to be let go, a will to forgetfulness, negativity—affirmation as negation-foundation. The avant-garde's critique of the fetish is only possible thanks to another fetish: the fetish of a simple, substantive, significant rupture: "From now on, yes." The vanguard is activated from within an understanding of time reduced to the linearity of a before, a now and an after that do not contaminate each other: historicist metaphysics.

Musiaphobia, which epitomizes and condenses the avant-garde's battle against the past, empathizes, in its will to *novum puro*, with historicist museumography, the will to the pure past. Just as avant-gardism constitutes a foundationalism that posits a *novum* shorn of all anachronisms, historicism posits what has been as a datum, pure fact, cleansed of all anachronisms, while also positing exact knowledge of that fact in its absolute euchrony and empathy with it. It postulates "a neutral, dry intelligence, without history, capable of presenting any fact, from any epoch, truly,"[10] far from any untimely consideration. And if anachronism is inevitable, or the event is especially impossible to hold on to without arriving late, *post festum*, then the stronger is the demand to reduce it. The intrusion of one temporality into another is the dark beast of both the historicist[11] and the avant-gardist. Any interpolation means the death of either the historical fact or the *novum*, which should present themselves live, as present, in their own moment, without mediations. Avant-gardists and historicists promote a clean, euchronic break. They abhor polychronisms. Avant-gardist musiaphobia and historicist museumography meet in this understanding of time as a euchronic present.

We do not have words for the event; we only have words for the event. So we return over and over again to the same. The event is never contemporary to itself, nor is it homogeneous, nor is it present to itself. Not only is it the silent now of its own day but it is also the final effect of the robes, waves, traces in which it expresses and inscribes itself, in which it passes away as a before that posthumously reveals itself as rising very late in the day. In this sense, the event does not respond to the logic of presence; it never "is." The logic of the event is, thus, not the logic of the avant-garde.

At the core of the avant-garde—that is, of the "presentation of the unpresentable"—lies one of negative dialectic's aporia: that the unpresentable takes up its own word as of its own moment and instantiation, before all capture or containment, so escaping the objectivizing trap that brings the unrepresentable to a close in metaphoricity: "I speak, I lie," said Epimenides.

As an effect of the sign that presents it, the unpresentable passes away as unrepresentable, succumbs to the logic of the sign—that is, to the opposition between signifier and signified: the paradoxes of negativity that, on abandoning the binary terrain of simple opposition, only the supplement of the post-avant-garde or of late modernism (Carroll, Joyce, Duchamp) can weaken. As the presentation of the unpresentable, the avant-garde enters into a game with representation such that it sets its own goals outside of representation. And, as a game that is centered *outside of representation*, it responds to the *centered game* of the old Platonic cave. Paraphrasing Derrida: what we call the center of representation—which can be located both inside or outside of representation—can indifferently be referred to as either the origin (*archē*) or the end (*telos*) that activates negative movements in the form of a presence that it exceeds. All archaeology or eschatology (and the avant-garde is both) attempts to think the structure of representation on the basis of a presence that is both full and outside of the structure.[12] Thus the structure itself—this binarism—is the institution. In this sense, therefore, the avant-garde belongs to the institution; it is its left leg. As Derrida further suggests: if the history of the concept of structure is thought of as a series of substitutions or metaphorizations of the center (metaphorized successively as *eidos, arhke, telos, energeia, ousia*, essence, existence, substance, subject, *aletheia*, transcendental, conscience, God, man, life, etc.), and if the history of these metaphorizations is what is called the history of metaphysics as the history of the event of the naming of being, then the avant-garde partakes of such a history (with its names: life, the un[re]presentable, the surreal, double, etc.). Its matrix, the history to which the avant-garde belongs, is the determination of being, of the work, as presence. The "imperial grandeur" of the order of representation "makes it not just another" historical structure among others; "one cannot speak out against it except by being for it[;] . . . one can protest it only from within it." The revolution against representation is always limited to what is called, by a "department of *internal* affairs, a disturbance." In the end, only the fact of language resists being placed in parentheses. The greatest difficulty of the avant-gardist enterprise is both expressed and hidden in this simple question of elocution.[13]

Is a crisis in which absolutely nothing is reiterated—*that burns all previous referents in a great conflagration as the condition of a historical insemination*—possible,[14] as *a rupture that is productive, that founds history in the strong sense of the word, breaking with prehistory . . . liquidating the past in its sketching of the new?*[15] If this were the case, then the will to separation, foundation, break, the superlative negation of an epoch by another that affirms itself would be reiterated within it once again.

The avant-gardist will to the new (the *novum*)—*to efface the old canvas,*[16] to destroy the old city right up to the fields beyond its walls so as to found another[17]—negates by affirming, destroys by founding. It emerges as the shadow of affirmation and supplants it in the overcoming of a before and in the foundation of something new. It is, in other words, a case of negativity passing itself off as affirmation. In this sense, the avant-garde would be pre-Nietzschean.

CRITICAL ATTITUDE

Those Spanish speakers who have studied philosophy as part of their secondary education will remember Plato's *Allegory of the Cave*, until recently an obligatory text in the syllabus. In it, Plato provides a whole repertoire of locations (both near and far); of frontiers and thresholds, to-ings and fro-ings, ins and outs; of sources of light (and degrees of light and shade), its focusing and direction; of centers and peripheries; of captive and enclosed dispositions, fluent movements, sudden or slow changes in attitude, gradual variations and shifts in posture (of both heads and bodies); of investments in a *regard* that is pregnant with life-or-death consequences, in theologies of salvation or damnation as well as epistemic moralities of truth and falsity. Within this stage machinery of comings and goings, it was decisive that a center and a soul be established so as to tighten, order, hierarchize, and give meaning to movement and place. It was a question of the *orthótes*, the *correct direction of the gaze*, recognition of the *héteros tí*, of the beginning-principle (*arkhé*), of the prince who should be followed and obeyed.[1] Plato's text sets out a theater for the government of men and displays a permanent concern for the loose and the restrained, the heard and the unheard, according to an invariant. It is a theater that structurally reiterates that other theater—the classroom—however precarious it might be.

Something apparently analogous to Platonic *orthótes* also motivated Christian pastoral: "Each individual, whatever his age or status . . . had to be governed and had to let himself be governed[,] . . . directed towards his salvation . . . [in a] relationship of obedience . . . to the truth,"[2] as indicated in a writing, in a dogma, or by a pastor. In the pastoral, an "art of governing men"[3] was also set in train.

This question of government, of the prince and the principles of order, dominion and of the composition of things, of the *rules for the direction of bodies* and the consequent multiplication of the pedagogic, political, economic, and methodological arts that took place as of the sixteenth century,[4] cannot be disassociated from critique, the "critical attitude" that will be expressed in a more modern fashion in the question of "how not to be governed."[5]

This is a question that is constitutive of the principle of the modern prince, the sovereign, although not of the pastor, whose first equation can be summarized in the demand *not to be governed so as to govern*, not to be subject so as to be a subject—the demand to suspend the principle and the heteronomous prince, to empty heteronomous law, and in that void to sanction autonomous law, *the exception as rule's principle*. It is a demand, then, to erase the traditional heteronomy of the *I was*,[6] not so much as a function of the modern autonomy that is given in the *I am*[7] but rather of the *I decide, I am what I decide, I am the decision*—this latter phrase constituting the founding statement of the sovereign subject: *I am the exception* that founds what I am in every case. What am I in each case? The decision! The exception! The exception and the decision! The suspension and the foundation, the founding suspension.

SOVEREIGN CRITIQUE I

Insofar as it is exercised as an absolute beginning, it is demanded of sovereigns that they eliminate all presupposition. To begin is to be free of presupposition.

Sovereignty's demand is to suspend (*epokhé*) presupposition, heteronomous regulation. There is no prince or sovereign beginning-principle if it does not emerge from pure decision, without anterior motivation, force of habit, or histories. Otherwise, the sanctioned beginning is the product of a principle, a previous habit, rather than of pure decision. It is thus a question of suspending inheritance, of declaring—as far as it is concerned—a *state of exception*.

As the *art of government without being governed*, of *subjecting without being at the same time subject* (that is, of conditioning without condition), critique as a modern "critical attitude" was conceived in exemplarily fashion by Cartesian philosophy as *hyperbole* or the *evil genius* who decides on the beginning-principle without principle or beginning, without condition, on the beginning.

Since it is a question of principle (*principio*) and of the prince, of sovereign method and power, the principle that conducts and governs cannot but be sovereign. The rules *would be entirely theirs*, yet, in contrast, it *would be the result of nothing at all*. It is a condition of being the sovereign not only to decide on the principles (*principios*) but also to declare the suspension of the principles posed. The contrary would be to subordinate the decision to a rule that would itself subordinate sovereignty. If method is the rule, intentionality, teleology (and we are taking the Cartesian method as an instance in which method and intentionality are exemplarily identified) as sovereign judgment, then such intentionality demands the suspension of the prejudice—or prejudgment (*prejuicio*)—of the judgment, the erasure of the sovereign conditions of judgment. For the sovereignty of judgment must be exercised unconditionally to be such. Sovereign judgment will unconditionally sanction the condition—the law—lawlessly: the principle without principle. Similarly, the sovereign will be the possibility of being and of not being the law, of posing and deposing the law.

Before being a set of rules and procedures for attaining determined ends,[1] method involves a suspending machine—*methodical doubt*—that guarantees the sovereignty of the principles. As the suspension of prejudgment (or prejudice) that assures the sovereignty of the beginning-principle, methodical doubt, the quintessence of method, is staged in Descartes's first *Meditation* as an exhaustive series of exceptions (*epokhés*) that hyperbolically (*evil genius*) conclude by suspending the possibility itself of judgment and its conditions. It is not only a question of revoking the heteronomy of principles that enthrone the origin but of withdrawing from any that might alienate the *state of decision*. The modern subject, as the decision to subject itself and others—without, at the same time, itself being subject and captive in its own order and representations, that nonsubject(ed) subject—must forever produce and assure the conditions of its own sovereignty, decreeing the *state of exception*, the *state of decision*, as the only possible rule of sovereignty, the only way of deciding on the law without the law, like a god might produce worlds according to his whim, without any principles or motives that may oblige him to do so—and thus, in total indifference.[2]

For Descartes, the regime of production is governed from head to toe by the imagination, which is conceived as a power to compose landscapes of various kinds: physical and astrophysical, biological and anatomical, urban and peasant, including customs and manners of differing order and complexity; of portraits and more or less colorful anecdotal or abstract paintings; of illusions, memories, evocations with mixed overtones of mood, intensity, and passion; of echoes, specters, more or less plausible simulacra of dreams, reverie, daydreams, artifice, and so on.

And as its operation suggests, the *imagination* as a faculty that composes landscapes constitutes a finite power of infinite composition: It makes on the basis of what it does not make—on that which has been given to it. It requires material(s) and principles of composition. Rather than displaying an interest in a varied universe of compositions, Descartes is concerned with the order of the elements, the *table of principles* and the *elements of the world* on the basis of which compositions are composed. He is concerned not only with the possibility, the power of composition that resides in the principles and elements but also in composition and the possibility of power. Whosoever governs the principles of the composition of worlds not only governs the worlds but also possibility, the power of these worlds.

It is a matter, then, first, of suspending the universe of compositions in order to deduce from them the elements and mechanisms on the basis of which they are composed—elements and mechanisms that without themselves being composed constitute the basis of composition—the principles and materials on the basis of which the imagination composes, principles and materials that condition the imagination as the constructive possibility of worlds. Once the principles and materials are cleared away from the imagination in an analytic that moves from the composed to the uncomposed in the composed, what hits one in the eye, so to speak, is the scenario of imagination's conditions—conditions that are not, in principle, the product of the imagination but rather, on the contrary, its previous law, its *a priori* limit, the prescription on the basis of which it is *free* from producing as many compositions (infinite, probably) as it would like but subject always to the principles that contain and govern it (without itself being able to govern them).

On this level, the possibility of the imagination lacks sovereignty. It does

not consist or lie in its own constituent power. As with automata, it is only constituent on the basis of constituted principles. Its power is consular rather than
sovereign.

The principles that condition it are the *principles of the understanding*. As
we have said, in order to constitute the conditions of the imagination such principles cannot be imagined or composed by it. Rather, it imagines and composes
according to such principles. Thus, it becomes a question of the imagination-less
conditions of the imagination, the imageless conditions of the image. The understanding both opens and limits the possibility of the imagination, without, it
seems, the imagination being able to suspend the understanding that contains it
and makes it possible. The understanding stands tall as the sovereign principle
of the imagination.

The imagination finds its limits in the understanding. And the understanding?
Is it sovereign with regard to its own categories and principles? Can it declare
the exceptional character of its principles? Is the understanding the constituent
power of the principles that constitute it?

This, I believe, is the turbulence on which the question of the sovereignty
of the beginning-principle (*principio*), the prince, the subject—as the nonsub-
jected subject of subjection—must be focused.

10

HYPERBOLE

The question concerning the sovereignty of the principles of the understanding in the Cartesian text initiates the hyperbolic turbulence of sovereignty, of
the possibility of a compositional principle or of an imagination that, over and
above the understanding or over and above principles, would be that which
without principle decides on the principles, an imagination that without rule,
without motive, without preoccupation, without condition, and with total indifference, as exceptionality and pure *fiat*—unconditioned—could create, among
other things, the principles and conditions of the understanding as the limits
of a nonsovereign imagination that is subject to another sovereignty. This tur-

bulence refers to the theological question of God as a poetic genius or miracle that without principles or rule gives or takes the rule, as it does to the question of the gift, of the economy, of the sovereignty of donation, not as a rule but as a position that is not mediated by the law.

Hyperbolic turbulence also appears in the constellation of tensions that the text itself sets out in the relation between finite understanding, infinite will, and imagination, as a genius that donates the law without the law, and without the law takes away the law. This constellation of tensions that counterbalance each other come together in the suspension of judgment, of the principle of judgment, in the principle of composition's declaration of the *state of exception*—the *state of exception* of prejudgment as a *plain* (*pleine*) without judgment for the position of sovereign principle and judgment.

The hyperbolic question concerning the sovereignty of the understanding installs the suspension of judgment in the text as a *state of exception* within the regime of production of the understanding but installs it only momentarily, for an instant in the skeptical and contemplative counterbalancing of tensions— a constellated instant, that is—which in its clashes or encounters initiates the interruption. They initiate the instance of exception, however, only to close it again in the very same instant, in the conatus of the position that (without principles, criteria, motives—with only the conatus of the decision) will sovereignly found the rule, the order—the imageless concept that will regulate the image as the sovereign dictatorship of analytic geometry. The suspension of the law, the home, the city, representation, the world initiates—for an instant at least—the lawless thing, the homeless thing, the cityless thing, the world-less thing, which as a sovereign thing decides—without law, without home, city, or world—on the law, the home, the city, and the world.

For Descartes, it is a question of an executive opening of the *exception* so that it may then be efficiently closed in sovereign representation. Cartesian sovereignty, its *state of exception* or extreme hyperbole, functions as a resource for extreme decision. It suspends representation so as to found regimes of representation. It suspends the law so as to conserve or to found regimes of law. It suspends the *I am* in the *I am not* so as to sovereignly reaffirm *again*—from the *I was*—the *I am*, but as *I decide* and as the ego's decision.[1] It suspends history, the past, memory—including their transmission—in order to found it, but now as discourse on method, a discourse that *progresses infinitely, half way between nothingness and God*, an infinite progress that is no more than the exceptional progress of the rule—that is, the *state of exception* as the condition of the progress of the law, of empire, of the principle (principio), the organism, the sovereign machine, the machineless decision within the immanence of the decision-less machine.

The thematization of the heteronomy—its placement at a distance and "objectification"—finds its possible summary in the idea that automata are not to be praised because they carry out this or that movement but rather because of their creator,[2] since everything depends on him and he depends on nothing.[3] There is no government—only inertia—without decision, if, that is, it does not come from pure decision—without law, motive, or previous history. The opposite would be to submit decision to a previous decision,[4] the immediate to an anterior mediation. Anteriority, mediation, inheritance, the archive must, therefore, be suspended: *demolish the inhabited home,*[5] erase (*effacer*) *the painted canvas,*[6] initiate the *exception, level the city of Paris*[7] or the ancient city,[8] or create a blank canvas[9] on which the new law, the city, the sovereign decision can be cleanly traced. It is not only constitutive of the power of the sovereign to decide on the beginning-principle but also to suspend it, to declare its own *state of decision.* In this way, the principle depends—that is, hangs on— the decision—it is the decision—just *like the laws of a kingdom depend on a king*[10] or like the way in which the *laws of nature depend on God*[11] although God, the King, the decision, do not depend on the laws of nature—*being able to change them at will.*[12] The sovereign decision involves posing and deposing the law at the same time. It constitutes the critical, atopical instant of (de)position, the moment without law of the law, the agile subjection of subjected agility, the moment of (un)conditionality that, theologically, is ascribed to the miracle and, secularly, to method, to the *discourse on method,* its quintessence—methodical doubt, extreme hyperbole (the *evil genius*) and extreme decision[13]—as the originary prosthesis or *tekhné* of sovereignty. It is in this sense that *methodical doubt,* hyperbole, crisis, exception, the *state of decision* is to the secular sovereign what the miracle is to the saint.[14]

Methodical doubt is the lawless hyperbole that posits the law—the conditionless reduction (*epokhé*) of the condition—without beginning-principle of the principal. Decision and sovereignty become simultaneously the possibility of the being and nonbeing of the law and of the suspension of the law, the possibility of posing and deposing the law at the same time. They govern without letting themselves be governed, not even by their own government. This is what the *critical attitude* is made of, *metaphysically*: the instant, the critical point, the vacillation of the decision as modern rule, which in its hyperbole introjects exception and the unconditionality of the decision—sovereignty's *outlaw* character—so as to *position the law* of sovereignty as modern law, which puts sovereignty to work as the sovereignty of its position.[15]

The sovereign who decides and posits himself (as well as everyone else) without being captured by his own decisions and positions must permanently guarantee (immunize) the unconditionality of his sovereignty, the exceptionality of his decision and position, in the decisions and decrees in which it is arranged. It must persevere at a distance, indifferent, apathetic with regard to every *need to*: intensions, interests, motives, and inclinations. It must keep prejudices and clauses, heritage and archives, implied habits, including those of its own set of decisions and exceptions at bay: the only way of not pathetically bowing to the law, of remaining sovereign, decisive, exceptionally *outside the law inside the law*, producing, conserving, and destroying worlds without principle that may oblige it, in total sovereignty.[16]

11

SOVEREIGN CRITIQUE II

In his book *Dictatorship*, Carl Schmitt distinguishes between the *commissary* and the *sovereign* forms of dictatorship. The former, designed within the universe of Roman dictatorships before Sulla and Caesar, is characterized by acting in an exception that is provided by the law of the republic in order to conserve and safeguard the law. In this case, the dictator is named by the senate to carry out specific tasks, such as to eliminate a dangerous situation, to make war, to repress an internal rebellion, or to celebrate a popular assembly. Sovereign dictatorship, however, exercises dictatorship by suspending the law of the republic. According to Schmitt, Caesar embodies the historical model of the sovereign dictator: "Appointed dictator . . . initially for one year only[,] the mandate was then prolonged and finally extended to his lifetime."[1]

The difference between both dictatorships is more empirical than structural. When safeguarding the law, the dictator has, with the authority of the senate, the prerogative of breaking the law so as to preserve it. The *sovereign dictator*, however, derogates the constitution so as to found another constitution, making an exception of its principal—the rule under which one exists.

The critic, too—a certain kind of critic—works, like the police, as does a com-
missar, violating rules, cannons, or constitutions so as to preserve them or to
sovereignly found new rules.[2] The parallel between dictatorship and critique,
and among dictatorship and modernisms, modernizations, avant-gardes, and
progressivisms, passes through the relation that these maintain with exception,
conservation and the (re)foundation of (the) rule—that is, with sovereign verisimilitude. The limit of this verisimilitude is constituted by the *true state of exception*. As noted, this does not conserve or found rules, the law, frameworks
of containment insofar as it is the *true state of exception*. Critique in this sense
rather subtracts itself from the sovereign paradigm.

In his *Dictionnaire historique et critique* (1702), Pierre Bayle portrays critique as a *true state of exception*. Indeed, he tackles it in relation to the limit, the
critical line, the crisis point, the *pit*. On "this side" of the limit, critique lies within
the law, the church, the state—within some order or cannon. "That side" of the
limit is within another law, another church, another state. On this side or that
side of the limit, critique works in a consular fashion, commissarially, preunderstood by a regime that governs it (without being criticized by it). Similarly, Bayle
locates critique *on* the limit, neither on this side nor that side, neither inside
nor outside the churches, in the vacillating, suspensive, uninclined, but rather
contemplative *interregnum* as an instance of unconditionality and constituted
only by an impulse of unconditionality. According to Bayle, this impulse received
the names of *reason* and *theory*. Critique, reason, and theory do not, therefore,
constitute orders of knowledge but rather a kind of *a true state of exception* or
suspension of knowledge, as the suspension of its condition. Only in this sense
does critique embody *free thought*, the *republic of letters*: "Cette république est
un état extrêmement libre. On n'y reconnaît que l'empire de la vérité et de la
raison, et, sous leurs auspices, on fait la guerre innocemment à qui que ce soit.
Les amis s'y doivent tenir en garde contre leurs amis, les pères contre leurs en-
fants. . . . 'Non hospes ab hospite tutus/non socer à genero.' Chacun y est tout
ensemble souverain et justiciable de chacun."[3]

Rather than negating determinate positions or chapels and affirming others,
the *republic of letters* presented itself as the unworking of every position that
enabled their recognition, location, and desubstantialization. It was this contemplative unworking, according to Koselleck, that created the space for the
principle of the *transcendental*, as that which lies beyond (*meta*) all empirical
positions. On invoking the suprapartisan transcendentality of reason and theory,
and considering the state as just one more position among others, the *republic
of letters* situated critique above politics and the state, affirming as exclusively its

own the reason that emerges—literarily—outside of established doctrines, public dogma, potentializing a flow of thought and commentary that runs wild of state directives and "legal" discussion. Protected within literary "privilege" (*fuero*), the unconditioned drift of critique, of a thought that grows and breaks through barriers, rules, and contracts, the *republic of letters* exercised critique exoterically, in the public order, to become, according to Voltaire, the tenth muse, the muse of muses that would banish worldly foolishness.

Critique would thus become a systematic distancing from whatever the conditions may be, so as to begin, in each case, from its own. In this sense, its exercise could not be carried through without permanently dissolving itself, like an undercurrent that systematically washes away the ground under its feet. "In these circumstances there was nothing left for the critic but to see progress as the temporal structure appropriate to this way of life. Progress became the *modus vivendi* of criticism."[4] And while that *modus* remains, its *state of exception*—rather than insisting on the limit as the unconditioned instance—becomes the structural means of modernization(s), allowing itself to be contained within the verisimilar of the sovereignty, the exception that it founds, of the exception as the rule of existence or life.

12

THE EPOCH OF CRITIQUE

"Our age is the genuine age of *criticism*, to which everything must submit,"[1] writes Kant around 1781. A century and a half later, Benjamin writes that only "fools lament the decay of criticism. For its day is long past."[2]

What delimits the *epoch of critique*, the epoch inaugurated by the *Critique of Pure Reason*, Kant's critical philosophy? The *epoch of critique* separates itself from *dogmatism*, that long epoch of many epochs and multiple schools whose *natural disposition* Kant referred to as "metaphysical."[3]

Before even the arbitrary universalization of beliefs, values, actions, points of view, and particular judgments, dogmatism consists in the inadvertent setting in motion of the presuppositions, conditions, and limits of such judgments, convictions, and values as well as the ways in which such presuppositions, conditions, and limits preconstitute the object on which these are applied and that they, in part, determine. Dogmatism lies not so much in the intransigent affirmation of an opinion or doctrine as it does in the unsuspecting application of unforeseen conditions, which is why it often also circulates as a liberal or flexible disposition. One can be flexible and tolerant with regard to discourses and at the same time unsuspecting with respect to the form, the grammar, the syntax into which they flow and that make them possible. Dogmatism refers less to a relation with the figurative content of judgments, doctrines, and representations than to the prediscursive form that makes them possible and rules over them, silently disciplining them, obliging them to say and figure in certain unsuspecting ways when they are supposed to be exercised in freedom. Critique as the critique of dogmatism does not consist for Kant, therefore, in a figurative, empirical critique of books, doctrines, chapels, opinions, or systems[4] but rather in the critique of its frame, its enabling condition. And it is the thematizing and revealing of the frame, and the frame of the frame, that is critique's concern,[5] the *a priori* condition of possibility of doctrines, books, systems, and judgments, whatever they may be—the *a priori* condition that predetermines and threatens judgments, doctrines, and books, restricting them to utter their thematic contents under athematic inferences, permitting and warning them, inadvertently, to enunciate in a determined manner: affirming, negating, or undetermining in a categorical, hypothetical, or disjunctive way (problematically, affirmatively, or apodictically), establishing relations of inheritance, causality, reciprocity, predetermining the use of subjects, copulas, and predicates—in the masculine, feminine, or neutral, and thus, before affirming or negating at all, setting unexpected conditions that compel, imperceptibly preestablishing their form, mode, and style.[6]

In their invariance, such conditions make credos and opinions of the most varied kinds possible, the endless disputes between followers of heterogeneous schools, the questions that could not possibly but be posed but, similarly, not be resolved, either—because such conditions predispose them, nourishing their stances and pretensions to universality, their conflicts and polemics (polemics without end, while their stances remain inadvertent as regards the presuppositions that induce them). The invariant *a priori* encourages what is expressed and what lives in such credos, positions, and counterpositions, because "nothing is so firmly believed as whatever we know least about."[7] Thus, the true source of dogmatism is the result of an athematic, inertial use of the form in whatever the circumstances may be—a form, moreover, whose inadvertent use instructs as to what it is applied to. The most efficient and violent dogmatism takes place alongside the most inadvertent and innocent form that, as lulling host, welcomes its guest, which, in part, it has produced itself. It is in this way, for example, that the combatants fighting each other, weaving a human network of antagonistic heraldry and flags, feeds—without knowing it—*the style of the canvas on which they are painted*[8] or the mode of production that the relations of exchange have come to arrange as war. Any figuration that pays no attention to the clauses in which it is figured is dogmatic, incautious. A minor, says Kant, being ignorant of her conditions and limits, lacks the autonomy, with regard to those conditions and limits, with which to decide, or not, her arrangements with them. In this way, the minor replaces a sovereign relation, with its own limits, with a heteronomous one with books, doctrines, and quacks.[9]

It is this athematic condition, the tympanum, that—in each and every case—critique must thematize so as to inaugurate a coming of age, nondogmatism, the limitlessness that sovereignly permits the assumption of limits, but no longer under the predominance of the Cartesian instrumental emphasis of *not letting oneself be governed so as to govern*, of *initiating the exception so as to become the rule*, but rather with the speculative emphasis of making the condition visible and the condition of the condition, without the foundational closure that appropriates, distributes and feeds. Critique, in its Kantian interface, returns on itself in an epic that advances like a Chinese oarsman, making its clauses visible, putting before his eyes what lies behind him.

13

CRITIQUE WITHIN THE FRAME, CRITIQUE OF THE FRAME

"It will, however, of course, be understood that we only ascribe universal education to one who in his own individual person is thus critical in all or nearly all branches of knowledge, and not to one who has a like ability merely in some special subject."[1] Aristotle's phrase underlines an aspect that stands out in the traditional understanding of critique: it does not prosper among those who carry out research within a specific field of knowing-and-doing, which mainly encourages a critique of the "eaves" of the tympanum that shelter it and so subordinates itself to the fundamental terms of its polytechnics, feeding them. Critique will thus only take place when the limits, the conditions, the laws of the field are thematized,[2] transforming said law from being the "subject" of knowledge-practice into the position, now, of examined object. The performance that interrupts the field's condition initiates the exception with respect to promoted, established, cultivated knowledges. Not only is critique located in the exception, but it also reveals instituted knowledge as an exception become rule or cannon.

As suggested above, critique as the initiator of the *state of exception* has, in turn, two or three declensions. The first is commissary exception, which suspends order so as to preserve it—like the police officer or the *consular dictator* who breaks the law so as to protect it. Second is the exception that suspends the field so as to found a new one, appropriating, distributing, and fomenting it as does the *sovereign dictator*. In this case, critique activates a process of double estrangement. On the one hand, little by little, familiar life becomes distant, strange: although not without twists, it is deemed faulty and thus to be gradually abandoned and replaced with a new unfamiliarity that, little by little, not without twists, becomes a new familiar, a "new" plane on which to move undisturbed and that leaves the previous one behind like it would a frightening memory. This hybrid process of defamiliarization is thus hegemonically inscribed into everyday language, which conserves the same names to refer to changing entities: state, right, university, art, war, experience, critique (we could extend the list here to include the complete lexicon).

The third understands critique as an interruption that neither conserves nor founds another order, being interested rather in systematically thematizing the condition, the limit, and the limit of the limit. This, as we have noted, reaches its first apogee with Kant. In *The Conflict of the Faculties* (1798), the space of critique is constituted by the *faculty of philosophy*, a *lower faculty*, for Kant, because it lacks executive, determining, bureaucratic power. Motivated solely by the possibility of unlocking the condition and the condition of the condition, it also lacks a founding principle. The *lower faculty* does not formulate, nor is it established within a code; it does not found or conserve representations or grammars. It only thematizes or expounds on them, taps on its tympanum, bent always toward deposing closure as a visualization that exceeds all tessitura. As a *minor faculty*, critique must reflect the technical position of knowledges and principles. In doing so, it gathers and suspends them, not according to positive criteria, but according to a substraction (*epokhé*), an indefinite unworking. Critique, or the *lower faculty*, constitutes the vortex that interrogates the techno-institutional division of knowledge and labor, a vortex that, whenever grammars constitute its concern above all, turns out to be unsubsumable to a grammar.

It is in this sense that the *epoch of critique* depends on the *lower faculty* (and that, with regard to the determining, bureaucratic, *higher faculties*,[3] it performs a task of the highest order).

Rather than a disciplinary field, critique, the *lower faculty*, refers to a performance that—without discipline—ventures into the conditions of the disciplines. This operation of defounding does not itself belong to any disciplinary field and can emerge in any order of knowledge. (As I will propose below, the *lower faculty* reaches its highest point in what Benjamin calls *the real state of exception*,[4] an exception that neither conserves nor founds representations, and that preserves the very moment of legibility in its most hesitant breath, the moment that detonates its interruption.)

Heidegger proposes an analogous operation with regard to the work of art— as if the question of the work of art were to *clear away* all preunderstanding: he writes that when artists "[sculpt] a head, it seems as if they are just reconfiguring visible surfaces; but in truth they are reconfiguring what is really invisible, that is: the way in which that head looks at the world, the way in which it dwells in the openness of space and attends to it. . . . The artist makes a figure of the invisible . . . and in each case . . . lets what had once remained unseen become so."[5] What would thus concern the sculptor of a head, as an artist, in the process of sculpting is to thematize the preunderstanding at work in each case of sculpture, making a theme of the preunderstanding implicit in all understanding, beginning with the understanding of the sculptor herself and her process.

If *poiesis* means to "give birth," "deliver," "remove," exhibit, reveal, then critique would be a kind of *poiesis* that brings preunderstanding to light. The *poetic*, productive, creative moment of critique—precisely because it does not sluggishly adhere to a preunderstood framework but rather is exercised against the grain of the inertia of any frame, thematizing it—supposes an *effort*, a force that is more than—surplus—inertia. That surplus movement, within and against the grain of movement, would be the *creative*, critical *conatus*, that which is proper to what is called (according to the above quotation) "art."

14

MANET: THE KANT OF PAINTING

According to Greenberg, it was Kant who brought this interruptive gesture to an exemplary moment of concretion: "'Because he was the first,'" he writes, "'to criticize the means itself of criticism' . . . Kant did not see philosophy as adding to our knowledge so much as answering the question of how knowledge was possible."[1] Kant interrogates the condition of possibility not only of this or that knowledge but of the frame of all possible knowledge, of the preunderstanding that is in play in the notion of possibility itself. Critique in painting would consequentially consist not in painting something that would add painting to the already painted by painting, but rather in interrogating in painting how the painting that is possible is possible—without thereby merely nourishing painting but rather interrupting it by revealing its condition as the painting exercises that condition. The person who repeated the Kantian critical operation in painting, according to Greenberg, is Manet.[2]

- Manet was the first in Western art to cause the return of the condition on whose constructive (architectonic) erasure the science of painting was built as an autonomous, specific field. That specific condition or event is the *canvas object*, the autonomous field, the athematic and a-pictorial graveyard—as the zero degree of painting—on whose immunity the science of painting—its history and scientific community—took place. The *canvas object*, the condition of painting, will not become painting's object until Manet. Until Manet, writes Foucault, whom we are paraphrasing here, the appearance of painting, the universe of its questions, experiments, propositions was established on the basis of the canvas's presence, but only by omission and absent from the construction that it supports. With Manet, what should not return in painting and with painting—if the latter were to be preserved through painting (which could only be the case by maintaining its founding repression in place: the canvas)—returns.

  With Manet, the neutral vertical and horizontal spatiality of the canvas that the tradition erased by constructing a fallen pyramid remerges. *Music in the Tuileries* privileges the strong lines and vertical axes that are represented by some trees. The spectator or painter looks at the scene slightly from above, such that very little of what is behind them can be seen. The depth preserved is sufficient to suggest the extenuation of depth. The characters in the foreground, through a frieze effect, hide what is happening in the background. In *Masked Ball at the Opera,* the background is blocked. There is only depth enough to signal the disappearance of depth. *The Execution of Emperor Maximilian* also blocks out depth with a thick wall. The distance between the border of the painting and the background is, again, minimal, hardly sufficient to signal its disappearance; its characters, again, project themselves forward, as in a relief. The violent closure of space leaves all the characters balancing on a step. There is no distance between the executioners and the victims. The canons of the rifles practically touch the chests of the executed. For this reason, distance cannot be perceived, is not offered to be seen, but is rather indicated through the sign of it reduction. In *A Bar at the Folies-Bergère,* there is no longer any depth. Instead, we find parcels of volume and surfaces. The goal of Manet's figuration is the purely spatial properties of the rectangle. What he undoes in these small rectangles are the principles of both traditional pictorial perception as well as those of everyday perception. Manet brings us into a pictorial space in which conventional perception is blocked because of the function of the plane—the horizontals and verticals. What are in play in *The Port of Bordeaux* are the horizontal and vertical axes of the rectangle. In the upper left center of the canvas, a set made exclusively of lines is unfolded that are cut into right angles to form a board—the representation of the geometry of the canvas itself, like Mondrian's series of variations on the tree (painted between 1910 and 1914). We thus see Mondrian born from Manet.[3]

Greenberg demands of critique that it thematize the founding concept, the only procedure that engenders significant crises: a demand to drum the tympanum in which the dense division of functions within a given frame unsuspectingly unfold. Without such a drumming of the tympanum, critique feeds the founding concept and would be no more than a commissary critique, inscribed within the invisible limits that govern and produce the visible.

At its highest level—as the interrogation of decisions, of the fundamental frames, the final categories—critique's object, before anything else, is not only the condition of knowledges but also its own condition, the frame within which it itself operates against the grain and in which it preunderstands its own performance. Its attention is concentrated, too, on not merely feeding this frame without defounding it, touching its limit so as to make the principle of its own functioning tremble, initiating its own exception with regard to itself.

Malevich affirmed that the process of reduction (*epokhé*), the suspension of forms, of the frames, must be taken to its hyperbolic extremes so as to thematize the finally irreducible, that which cannot be suspended: the extraspatial, extratemporal, and extrahistorical. This irreducible is inscribed into the *Black Square*, the epitome of Russian modernism. "The *Black Square* is, so to speak, a transcendental painting—the result of the pictorial reduction of all possible concrete content. . . . It is a sign for the pure form[,] . . . nothing[,] . . . the pure potentiality of all possible existence that revealed itself beyond any given form."[4]

15

HEIDEGGER'S DEMAND

In *After the End of Art*, Danto similarly suggests conceiving of critique by alluding to the third paragraph of Heidegger's *Being and Time*. Heidegger precipitates the demands for critique and crisis in the following terms: "The totality of entities can, in accordance with its various domains, become a field for laying bare and delimiting certain definite areas of subject-matter. These areas, on their part (for instance, history, Nature, space, life, *Dasein*, language, and the like), can serve as objects which corresponding scientific investigations may take as their respective themes. Scientific research accomplishes, roughly and *naively*, the demarcation and initial fixing of the areas of subject-matter."[1]

What does Heidegger mean by "*naively*"? Something similar to what Kant called *dogmatic*.[2] The naivety of positive scientific research—and we are paraphrasing Heidegger's paragraph here—gravitates around the fact that its effective scrutiny of a field of objects that are generically determined by a *basic concept* neglects—precisely because it is concerned with what is expressly put before it as an object of research—what is imposed on it behind its back as an unrecognized preconcept. The more thematized the positive object becomes, the more athematic becomes the preconcept into which the positive research is inscribed: *it sees what is illuminated but does not notice the beam of light*; it sees what is visible without seeing the regime of visibility. The positive research proceeds a-critically, naively, dogmatically, with respect to the preconcept. And while the more significant the empirically determining advances are, the more naïve and dogmatic, consular and administrative they will end up becoming with respect to the inferred preconcept under which they operate. On working within a comprehensive seam that is itself unresearched, such advances would not have a sovereign, *revolutionary* character, writes Heidegger, but an incidental one. *The real movement of the sciences* is the product of *how far it is capable of a crisis in its basic concepts.* In these crises, not only would the basic concept vacillate, but the relation of the positive research with the things that they empirically investigate would, too, as would the entities comprehended within the frame of the basic concept—including the researchers' positions, the financial funding of the research, the value of the results themselves.[3] Everywhere today, the various disciplines reveal a tendency to put their basic concepts into crisis.[4]

In the passages that he quotes from Heidegger's paragraph, Danto blocks the appearance of the text's effective demands on critique. In his text, Heidegger makes it clear that putting the basic concept into crisis remains inadvertent if it does not interrogate *the preunderstanding* or *the meaning of being* that in each case dominates the basic concept in question. The standard of the field of research is measured not only by its ability to thematize the basic concept but, above all, to thematize *the preunderstanding of being* that dominates the basic concept, to put said *preunderstanding* and its history into crisis. But the possibility of experiencing crisis in this last sense is no longer called "critique" or "crisis" as such. The Heideggerian name for it is "destruction" (*destruktion*), whose repercussions, insofar as they are inscribed within *the technical interpretation of thought*, is to make the limits of critique and of crisis resound. (We shall return to this expression.)

The highest point of critique, therefore, does not consist in thematizing the basic concepts but rather in a questioning what *goes behind* the basic concepts, their crises, and their displacements, an interrogation that thematizes and unworks the preunderstanding of being that such fields presuppose. If each of these fields carries out its performance on the eaves of a basic category, then it would be the *category of category* that is common to them all that still remains to be questioned. The destruction of the *category of category*, which is thus placed into abyss *from behind* the categorial and its historical-evental positionings—abandoning the categorial itself as a context of thought—would thus be more originary than critique.[5]

Without an elucidation of the *category of category*, which, as a technology of ends, determines the preunderstanding that operates as the foundation of the diversity of fields of research, *critique* would remain imprisoned within the categorial-ontological preunderstanding that can be found, to paraphrase Heidegger, written on our own history's birth certificate, the birth certificate, that is, of the present age, which comes to us (if not beyond us) from the Hellenic age. This is what first determines the fundamental and most intimate characteristics of our Euro-Western history (*Geschichte*), the ontological dispositif that establishes why the West and Europe are—in their historical course—philosophical in an originary sense—configuring a tradition that is, and will remain, unique. This is why, in each case, the way in which the question "What is?" is posed (What is this, our age? What is the present? What is art? What is philosophy? What is being?) athematically emplots the imperial dominant of categorial preunderstanding— be it under the material aspect of words, be it under the question of a hermeneutics of meaning.[6]

The Heideggerian text attempts to situate itself behind the imperial-categorial *dispositif* and to destroy the condition of the history of metaphysics itself, overflowing the frame, the cave, ontological containment—that is, a determinate understanding of being and time as *presence*, which preunderstands and imperially rules common understanding in its different languages (and which were called languages and natural languages by philosophy itself), sending them on their way, along the path of philosophy.

According to it, Westerners would make their history governed in advance by a de facto preunderstood frame of reference that has been unelected by them but that, as *a priori* material, has been bequeathed to them—*a priori* preunderstood material in which they find themselves and that preconstitutes them. As Marx notes, this frame or field *weighs on the brains of the living*. And when the living dedicate themselves to criticizing or revolutioninzing their present, to understanding and to understanding themselves, to transforming and to transforming themselves, they do so framed by this a priori *material* that precedes them, that they reiterate, and that courses through the constellation of the most diffused, common, and everyday words and feelings associated, above all, with the infinitive *to be*. The epoch and the history of epochs is thus, before anything else, the trace of an originary *dispositif* in which the epochal interfaces are outlined— philosophers all, therefore, and categorial, from the most unsuspecting and unaware to the most critical and habituated: shaken by this preunderstanding (while its imperium has not been destroyed, thematized, unmasked, unworked) from behind their own backs.

Heidegger will call that *understanding* that does not comprehend the framework of its understanding—that comprehends only on the basis of the lack of understanding of the preunderstanding that feeds it—the *technical interpreta-*

tion of thought: an interpretation that unfolds from an athematic forgetfulness that irrigates the spheres of understanding-and-doing, a forgetfulness that, as the condition of possibility of the technical interpretation of thought, cannot be processed by it without said interpretation, in all its historical effectiveness and prepotency, not being exposed from another power or potency subtracted from it—and that could only be discerned obliquely in the event of its destruction.[7] The *technical interpretation of thought* would be what is initiated within a constitutive forgetting that makes tradition, that maps the community of the West as a technical, metaphysical community. The attempts to bring down its closure, its frame, the series of philosophical texts (inscribed within it as works of thought, of art, literary or political), having done no more in each case but to reiterate, translate, the very same closure.

"Critique" would achieve its *highest point*, according to Heidegger, when it presents itself as having suspended this long tradition of *philosophical texts* that has attempted such a critique—a long tradition that is put together by Heidegger from the highest of points (or *acme*): the destruction, the *clearing*, the *explanation of ontology*.

The most critical of questions would then be: What is philosophy? What is the founding regime governing Western knowledge-and-doing, including questioning and the questioning of questioning? This question demands overcoming (destroying) the trace of the text of philosophy and the performance of said text at its limit. This most critical of questions would thus challenge the closure that the philosophical text has traced—including its own questioning, a kind of "epoch of epochs," an epoch of epochs that should be put at a distance—a distance that does not mean a mere rupture or simple negation but a transformation of what has been transmitted in that trace.

In the paragraphs that he cites from the third paragraph of *Being and Time*, Danto thus blocks the effective demand that the text sets out for critique. Nevertheless, he turns to another, even more crucial demand for critique: "What makes Heidegger a 'modernist' philosopher is that he takes the ancient question of Being, and, rather than confront it head on, he asks what kind of being it is for whom that question arises, so that in effect his inquiry is about itself,"[8] so that rather than considering it immediately from the point of view of its own tradition, he asks about the conditions of possibility of the question itself—that is, of the *thing*, and the structures of the *thing* that make the question itself possible—putting the *destruction* of the *preunderstanding of being* to work, thematizing its regime *through* the entity that asks the question and in which the regime of preunderstanding is embodied. The destruction of ontology thus demands,

before everything else, critique: the destruction of the entity in which said destruction is both possible and becomes necessary.[9]

16

CRITIQUE AND FIGURE

We would like to inquire into the "form" of philosophy, or more precisely, to place it in doubt; for, what if, in the end,
philosophy were nothing but literature? We know how insistent philosophy—metaphysics—has generally been in
defining itself by contrast to what we call literature. We also know, particularly since Nietzsche, to what extent the
battle against metaphysics has approached or even identified itself with a specifically literary effort. We should like
to ask, then, whether what philosophy has maintained since its "beginning" as a dream, a desire for a *pure saying*
(a speech, a discourse which is purely transparent to what its signs ought to signify unmediatedly, i.e. truth, being,
the absolute, etc.), has not always been compromised by the very practice of writing itself, that is, by the necessary
passing through a text. Therefore, we might also ask whether philosophy has not always been obliged to use modes
of exposition . . . which are outside its domain and which it usually has no power to control or even reflect upon. In
other words, we would have to question this more or less veiled and silent obsession with *the text*, which is perhaps
one of the deepest obsessions of metaphysics, but which nevertheless reveals one of its most primal limitations.

> —Lacoue-Labarthe, "The Fable (Literature and Philosophy)," trans. by Silverman, H. J., Research in
> Phenomenology, 15, 1985, pp. 43–44

The turn toward the material multiplicity of the text as terminological immanence characterizes an important aspect of contemporary philosophy—as the
moment of its de-differentiation from literature. Jacques Derrida is the philosopher who with great tenacity opened up philosophical hermeneutics to its non-
hermeneutical limit, to the spectacular immanence of its terminology, exposing
it to its (own) crisis. "There is not Logos, there are only hieroglyphs. . . . Everywhere Proust contrasts the world of signs and symptoms"—including encounters, events, aggressiveness, depression—"with the world of attributes, the world
of pathos with the world of logos," against essences. "Philosophy has not at all
undergone similar revolutions or experiments as those produced in science,
painting, sculpture, music, or literature."[1] The status of philosophical terminology has thus been transformed while towing philosophical discourse itself behind it, changing its history into traces.[2] There is no thought except under the
duress of signs. Intentional thought is the effect of machines, of the clashing of

involuntary forces (Benjamin). Discourse *awakens* to its terminology by opening itself up to the virtuality of a language that, in the immanence of its testimony, has no centering function.

Consideration of the terminological dimension blocks the referential univocity sustained by frames and final categories. It revokes the totalization and fetishization of terminological multiplicity through a common preunderstanding or transcendental. And it locates the activity of critique within this multiplicity and virtuality as a performance that is immanent to the installation and staging of figures and the weave of its fibers—its thresholds of tension and irritation. It suppresses the pit and returns critical distance into the immanence—without distance—of a plane of tactility. In each and every case, critical activity now coexists as just one more text in a relation of friction within the same intertextual frame. On this plane, judgment in the name of a higher instance is naïve, while immanent evaluation becomes damning: a matter of affect, of an "I love or I hate" rather than an "I judge."[3] The possibility of critical impact, its validity on this plane, is no longer related to a drumming on the limit—the final frame that operated as first principle thanks to its invisibility—and making it visible. Its power is ventured rather in the staging and performative arrangement of materialities.

Critique speaks: I can only take risky but necessary flight with any possibility of success if, rather than wearing the waxed wings of meaning, I take strength from the destructive construction of montage as the surprising exhibition of a facticity that is not directed to any result whatsoever, without having to "*say*" anything. Merely show. I shall purloin no valuables, appropriate no ingenious formulations. But the rags, the refuse—these I will not inventory but allow, in the only possible way, to come into their own: by making use of them,"[4] undoing articulations and setting them on edge, breaking barriers and stabilizations, reintroducing discontinuities, infinitely delaying territorializations, removing the death masks of common understanding, states of representation.

With Benjamin, critique assumed the performativity of *collage*, the art of putting together (as in montage) images as the concrete expressions, in each and every case, of historical transitoriness, choosing, assembling the extremes of an idea concretely produced in the crossing of the images themselves, "refrain(ing) from any deductive abstraction, any prognostication, and, within certain bounds, even any judgement."[5] The coimplication of the arranged elements, each cutting across the others—but especially the coimplication of their limits, of their *(in) betweenness*, their mutual interruption—disrupts contracts, the juridical, political, aesthetic, and disciplinary dialectics that the universalizing understanding of language guarantees.

Montage, installation, dissolves theater: it never represents another,[6] and it never fulfils either the metaphoric or metonymic function of communicating transcendent meanings or objects. The immediate medium of its figure expresses no more than the figure itself in its singular virtuality. The boundaries of its expression and testimony are coextensive with its tracing. This, its figure, is its testimony—by itself and for itself. But this "itself" has to be taken *cum grano salis*, because if the figure is exempt in its origins of anything, it is of self-sameness, in each of its elements. Every element or component is testimony to itself, not, however, as in a sum game, thanks to which the rumor of its singularity is progressively led to a complete synthesis, to a result. This is because a figure is constitutively slippery: its polychronicity and supplementary tensions can never be synthesized, since each figure is constituted in the intervals that engender discontinuity. It is no more and no less than its materials. Its content is, therefore, its *form*, and vice versa, undecidedly, and in that sense, it coincides with its *thing*. But the thing with which it coincides is always another thing. It testifies to its distribution not as a homogeneous or synthetic moment but rather as a plethoric, heterological one.

The figure is thus not constituted thanks to a dialectic that culminates in it, as the end of a process. Nor is it a spontaneous effect or "intended to describe the process by which an existent came into being, but rather to describe that which emerges from the process of becoming[,] . . . an eddy in the stream of becoming, and [which] in its current . . . swallows the material involved in the process of genesis."[7] In each case, it always gives testimony to more than it testifies to.

17

THOUGHT AND FIGURE

Confronted either with a book or with images in a gallery, readers may feel as if such signs will survive them. They already have on coming before them. Viewers feel that they are the weaker pole in this relation, just passersby, grieving shadows. Before an image, "we must modestly recognize . . . that it" constitutes "the element of duration,"[1] and that often it possesses more testimony and thought (in multiple directions), more future (although fewer recollections and testimonies) than the witness who looks at it. It testifies and thinks before, during, and after the witness. The thought of an image "is the essence of all that is transmissible from its beginning, ranging from its substantive duration to its testimony to the history which it has experienced. . . . An ancient statue of Venus, for example, stood on a different traditional context with the Greeks, who made it an object of veneration, than with the clerics of the Middle Ages, who viewed it as an ominous idol."[2] The image is the *medium* of thought.[3] "Medium" here does not mean that thought is obliged to use modes of exposition that are improper to it or incontrollable by it. It means rather that the image, the figure, is the proper dimension of the thought, that there is no thought except within, and from, the opacity of the figure.

Before the intentionality of meaning, the totalizing univocity of genus and species, before judgment and argument, thought is the virtuality that is immanent to the terminological figure. Terminology is the figure as thought.[4] Its perimeter, its limits, are (un)defined according to the figuration of its components. To think of a bird does not consist in identifying its genus or species but rather in floating in a singular virtuality of poses, colors, and sounds, a heterogenesis that thought incessantly roams in, a roving over made up of n number of components and variations, passing and returning over them like an old story without ever producing a totality (Deleuze). Thought as figure occurs in the immanent overflight of a finite number of heterogeneous components at infinite speed.

It does not follow from this that the intentionality of judgment, the univocity of the concept, constitutes the "nothing" of thought, its absolute emptiness (vacuum). It does follow, however, that teleology, argument, the univocity of the concept, the intentionality of judgment, genus, species, constitute, in each and every case, a barrier to thought, the death mask that falls on the testimony of its figure, of its terminological flesh, containing it so as to found univocities, the rules and pathways (*orthótes*) of thought, like phallic mothers who already at the moment of delivery idealize their children, blocking their multiplicity.

The solitude as well as the singularity of the figure refer, like the Benjaminian (or Deleuzian) monad, to a populace of virtual currents in becoming, never to one direction of meaning, an *orthótes*, an organism, a stabilizing center. The terminological flesh is the plexus of thought in becoming that makes for virtuality— not structure, nor representation or intention.

No intention is a figure, although every intention becomes with(in) it, immanently, within its multiplicity. No intentionality transcends the figure in order to totalize it. Figures slide in multiple directions, strata, rhythms, with and without a *timerose*, with and without heterochronic simultaneities.

The figurative term always bears witness to something more than what it gives testimony to: not a totalization as with the verb "to be" (the "IS") or the Universal, but rather an overflight of the elements or a melancholic sinking into the details that are enumerated according to the conjunctive logic of the *and . . . and . . . and . . .* , always accompanied by a *furthermore*, a *together with which. . . .*[5] It is in the materiality of the singular term, and nowhere else, where thought is disjunctively traced. Thought constitutes such immanence, constituting itself without subjectivity within the figure, without *ipseity*, performatively. As in allegory, in Benjamin's terms, "there is not the faintest glimmer of any spiritualization of the physical,"[6] unless we consider the virtuality immanent to the physical "spiritual."[7]

It is not that thought does not think when it defines. But it does block the term, the figure, under the general mediation of a signified, a judgment, an argument. The term becomes a thought according to the movements, tremors, the testimony of its figure in its encounters with another, without freezing into anything specific. Its dry report, *like the corpse that reiterates the same sign*, always invites perplexity, *surprise*, and *reflection*.[8] One can return to it many times, an indefinite number of times, as if it mutated into an indefinite number of intentions without any of them becoming definitely fixed. Although the figure does not change (nothing enters it, nothing leaves), its aspect (*eidos*) is always other, as in *The Book of Sand* (J. L. Borges), like a bible that *always says something else according to the ways in which different epochs look at it*. To establish the signified of a *term* with respect to the social structure of the time in which it emerged consists in describing, on the basis of the history of its effects, its ability to provide both remote and foreign epochs access to its own genesis: "The past has left images of itself . . . comparable to those which are imprinted by light on a photosensitive plate. The future alone possesses developers active enough to scan such surfaces perfectly. Many pages in Marivaux or Rousseau contain a mysterious meaning which the first readers of these texts could not fully have deciphered."[9]

18

THE LEVELING OF THE PIT

The word "theater" (from the Greek *theatron*) speaks of a voyeuristic, perspectival doubling, a sacrilege in which cultish immanence, without (internal) distance with regard to itself, exceeds itself, alienating itself from *itself*, opening within such estrangement a significant difference that tears apart the sacred immanence of ritual to display it as spectacle, point of view—a division of labor between action and its spectating. This is the moment, the instant, in which cult value, in the zero degree of its circulation, becomes exhibition—that is, takes place as *exhibition value*—too. The emergence of a repetition, of the event's *double*, of its translation into another mediation in which the latter, precipitated outside of itself, returns to itself to constitute it as a first time in the spectator's second time, as vacillation with itself, reflexivity, a conflict between stage and stalls—a theater that can erupt in victims themselves when they turn to look at their executioner or at themselves, or at the scene of sacrifice in which they are playing a part, splitting themselves in two, actor and spectator (before they are split),[1] thus giving origin to the difference between stage and stalls, to the representation of the event, to the event as representation.

Within the order of theater, what was referred to as critique was traditionally lodged outside of the stage, on the other side of the pit that puts the stalls at a distance, situating itself far from the spectacle, on the periphery of the stage. Structurally, the pit signaled the autonomy of the staging, of the actors and the lights; it also signaled the margin, the stalls, the dark, immobile, barely whispering silence. The pit makes possible not only the autonomy of spheres but also the travel of things from one side of it to another, a compensated exchange between places that the pit itself has made possible. Freud described this porous, fragmentary, and discontinuous wall between stalls and stage, conscious and unconscious, as a reef rich with charges and countercharges: a catwalk of cross-dressings and disguises, euphemisms and veils, across which—as if in a trance—costumes are always moving, even if only slightly, and both compromising and not compromising the trancelike crossing—and not crossing—of the reef. This frontier made the stage-stalls commonplace possible; it also made possible the dialectic of invasion of the one side by the other: from the timid incursions of the actor into the stalls, the sometimes captive, sometimes disenchanted exclamations of the anonymous public, the unaccommodating noises, even the totalitarian assault by the stalls on the stage (the totalitarian politicization of the stage), or the inverse assault by the stage on the stalls (as the aestheticization of the stalls, or total choreography).

If the most original critical behavior is characterized by distance, and if distance is the constitutive passion and condition of the possibility of critique[2], the *opening*, the plane on which we find ourselves, is no longer that of theatrical critical distance, that of *the age of critique*: "For its day is long past. Criticism is a matter of correct distancing. It was at home in a world where perspectives and prospects counted and where it was still possible to take a standpoint."[3] It is "the abyss," insists Benjamin "which separates the players from the audience as it does the dead from the living, the abyss whose silence in a play heightens the sublimity, whose resonance in an opera heightens the intoxication—this abyss, of all elements of the theater the one that bears the most indelible traces of its ritual origin, has steadily decreased in significance. The stage is still raised, but it no longer rises from an unfathomable depth; it has become a dais."[4]

When Benjamin writes that "mankind now is an object of contemplation for itself [that] can experience its own destruction as an aesthetic pleasure,"[5] he reiterates the unilaterally exhibitionary condition of experience under the Industrial Revolution's serial matrix—of which the avant-gardes and fascism would be partial expressions, posthumous precursors.

Fascism and avant-garde are proper names that designate attempts to erase the pit, distance, the commonplace, representation, the theater of the bourgeois autonomy of spheres and the transferential conflict between them. Fascism, as the inversion of the avant-garde will to politically storm the stage, stages a total spectacle—as an expanded stage that aestheticizes the city—in a ritual in which the masses meld, without distance, into the relations of property and auratic expropriation.[6]

But more original than the avant-gardes, whose critique of the theater and representation would be effective figuratively, morally,[7] quixotically—rather than technically[8]—would be the *mass matrix of mechanical reproduction* (the Industrial Revolution), metonymized in photography and film, which would consume the performative closure of the pit. In the serial matrix of the expanded industrial machine, "the urge grows stronger to get hold of an object at very close range." To suppress the aura, the unapproachable distance, "to bring things closer" by way of serial production, renouncing the singularity of each datum by accepting its reproduction is a desire of the masses, constitutes the mark of a perception whose "sense of the . . . equality of things" has increased to such a degree that it asphyxiates the unrepeatable.[9]

19

THE CLASH OF FILM AND THEATER

Many are the passages in "The Work of Art in the Age of Mechanical Reproduction" in which the industrial matrix demands to be read—perhaps in a Heideggerian vein—as the moment of consummated metatechnics that, in their planetary
unfolding, *monopolize the totality of historical existence*, subsuming under it,
like a factual transcendental, every other mode of production, dissolving the idealized presence of the aura—unique and unrepeatable—in the massive presence
of serial commodities that cannot be dispelled, satisfying the masses "at very
close range" and substituting the scarcity of the singular manufactured product with the undeniable proximity, the massive presence of the serial commodity. Beginning with one's own postproduced subjectivity, now fashioned on the
basis of stereotypified "experiences"—a subjectivitythat all encounter *ready-to-
wear*: "One comes along, one finds a life all prepared, one only has to put it on."[1]
Since it circulates, I made it mine!

In the serial matrix of the expanded industrial machine, "the urge grows
stronger to get hold of an object at very close range by way of its likeness, its
reproduction."[2] Polytechnic design is now a condition of what is proper (to one).

If spectators in the theatrical matrix retreat contemplatively into themselves
before the work—concentrating on it while being absorbed in its perspectival
ideality, so deeply submerged in its aura as to disappear into its distanced interior, far from its materialities (just like in the story told about the Chinese
painter who, on contemplating his finished painting, was lost in it to the point
of disappearing) under the polytechnical matrix of the image—then the masses
are pressed close without distance and converted into becoming part of the
design—that is, a unit, a stereotypical industrial pose. The cinematographic *instrument of ballistics*[3] does not allow for contemplation and suppresses the
theatron and point of view within a continuous tactility, introducing *profound
changes in the perceptive apparatus* on a grand scale.[4] This is in contrast to the
canvas that *invites the spectator to contemplation*[5] and before which we can
abandon ourselves to the flow of the association of ideas. Before the film screen
the fascinated eye is subsumed in the *movement image* without noticing the
metamorphosis that it suffers: "*Before the movie frame . . . no sooner [have] his
eyes grasped a scene than it is already changed. It cannot be arrested.*"[6] While
painting "demands concentration,"[7] film, publicity, disperses, uproots all interi-

ority and auratic distance from the eye, placing it into the flow-without-distance of total circulation and mobilization. In the cinema, "I can no longer think what I want to think. My thoughts have been replaced by the moving images."[8] The ego cogito, like an internal thunderbolt (Descartes) that brings order to the world, is now a magneto-phonic cliché, as told in industrial *toy stories*—with "the turning of a crank."[9]

Just as painting is avant-gardistically invaded by the exterior objects and materialities that, rather than represent, now *present*, or as painting is externalized so much as to become objectual art, installation, performance, so subjectivity is also led from the economy of the closed room of an autonomous consciousness to an economy of the "filling station."[10] More and more works, consciousnesses, are born pregnant with(in) a *ready-made* relationality, with(in) *postproduction* as a presupposition. One thing is to penetrate subjectivity as a principle that reunites infinitely with the ideality of its always-distant aura. Another is that now polytechnic exteriority enfolds and fetishizes subjectivity—and so fetishized, it circulates massively, like "water, gas, electricity."[11] The material *a priori* of the industrial matrix is now the effective *plane* on which *consciousness*—with its dreamlike *memories*—circulates as if it were a byproduct.[12]

From the eighth to the tenth fragment of "The Work of Art in the Age of Mechanical Reproduction," Benjamin sets out in constellatory fashion the clash between the theater and film, focusing on the case of the actor in the multiplicity of direct, collateral, and virtual consequences that this clash implies: "'The film actor . . . feels as if in exile—exiled not only from the stage but also from himself. With a vague sense of discomfort he feels inexplicable emptiness: his body loses its corporeality[;] it evaporates, deprived of reality, life, voice, and the noises caused by his moving about' . . . for the first time—and this is the effect of the film—man has to operate with his whole living person, yet forgoing its aura . . . 'in order to be changed into a mute image, flickering [for] an instant on screen. . . . The projector will play with his shadow before the public.'" On the film set, the metonymy of the panoptic disciplinary city, the actor, the author, the everyday singular subject becomes an accessory to the mass matrix. On the (panoptic) set, his performance gradually "is by no means all of a piece; it is composed of many separate performances . . . that split the actor's work into a series of mountable episodes. . . . 'The greatest effects [are] almost always obtained by 'acting' as little as possible,'" while "lighting and its installation require the presentation of an event that, on the screen, unfolds as a rapid and unified scene in a sequence of separate shootings that may take hours at the studio[,] not to mention more obvious montage. . . . The feeling of strangeness that overcomes the actor before the camera . . . is basically of the same kind as the estrangement felt before one's own image in the mirror," a mirror that is now "transportable. And where is it transported? Before the public. Never for a moment does the screen actor cease to be conscious of this fact. While facing the camera, he knows that, ultimately, he will face the public, the consumers who constitute the market. This market, where he offers not only his labor [Thayer adds the word "power" here in the Spanish original—Trans.] but also *his whole self, his heart and soul*, is beyond his reach. During the shooting, he has as little contact with it as any article made in the factory."[13] For the everyday subject of mass society, the image that the mirror reflects back is an inquiry into wage survival. Before the mirrors are anticipated, as in tests on the film set, the demands of arranging their ignorance into the cosmetics, characters, and protocols of circulation. The mirror, like no one else, knows which protocols the living being will adopt during the day, which are their weakest flanks, the unhappinesses covered over (and hidden) with makeup. Circulation has become the mercury of the mirror that, elevated to everyday editor, examines the *backgrounds, handicaps* and the damage that the mirror image reflects with regard to what each and everyone needs and desires to be *qua* mass subjectivity. This mirror is arranged as a panopticon, a camera—not so much as a center of surveillance but as an architecture of the eye that the living automatically aims at themselves, to watch the (un)making-up of the body and, where necessary, disciplining it.

"Today the most real, the mercantile gaze *into the heart of things* is the advertisement," writes Benjamin. Advertising abolishes the breathing space or margin that theater demands, "and all but hits us between the eyes with things as a car, growing to gigantic proportions, careens at us out of a film screen. And just as film does not present furniture and façades in completed forms for critical inspection, their insistent, jerky nearness alone being sensational, the genuine advertisement hurtles things at us with the tempo of a good film. Thereby 'matter-of-factness' is finally dispatched . . . and in [the] face of the huge images across the walls of houses, where toothpaste and cosmetics lie handy for giants . . . just as people whom nothing moves or touches any longer are taught to cry again by films."[14] Industrial subjectivity learns to cry.

20

CRITIQUE'S LOSS OF AURA

In the first part of the *Communist Manifesto*, Marx and Engels celebrate the revolutionary character of the industrial matrix that, as the trigger of *capitalism in its specific sense*, "has resolved personal worth into exchange value . . . for exploitation, veiled by religious and political illusions, it has substituted naked, shameless, direct, brutal exploitation[,] . . . stripped of its halo every occupation hitherto honoured and looked up to with reverent awe. It has converted the physician, the lawyer, the priest, the poet, the man of science, into its paid wage labourers."[1] Baudelaire also celebrates the defetishization of moral values that the predominance of the auratic makes worse: "Friend you know my terror of horses and carriages. A few minutes ago, hastily crossing the boulevard, jumping over mud, through that chaos where death comes galloping from all directions at once, my halo, jarred, slid off my head into the muck on the asphalt. I hadn't the courage to retrieve it. It seemed less annoying to lose my badge than to get my bones broken. And then, I told myself, sometimes misfortune has its good side. Now I can stroll about incognito, do mean things, launch into debauches, like ordinary mortals. So here I am, just like you, as you see."[2]

"What, in the end, makes advertisements"—the commodified gaze—"so superior to criticism? Not what the moving red neon light says—but the fiery pool reflecting it in the asphalt."[3] Not the aura of the luminous sign, but the aestheticization, the auratization of a mirage, the broken-down aura of the serial commodity.

The serial matrix returns the Kantian *use value* of critique to the expanded circulation of *exchange value* in process, with respect to which its *use value*— its *aura*—would be no more than an aestheticizing accessory: the *use value of value*, the *use value of capital*. The *aura* is assembled as an accessory in a planetary "cooperation" that adds more and more functions (of activity as well as of time) that are directly governed by capital, making of every specificity and quality of work and its objects mere functions of the *process of the valorization of capital* as value in process. "Some work better with their hands, others with their heads, one as a manager, engineer, technologist, etc., the other as overseer, the third as manual labourer or even drudge. . . . Here it is quite immaterial [what is] the job of a particular worker, who is merely a limb of this aggregate worker"—that is, of abstract labor, the *use value of value*, in the process of the self-valorization of capital.[4] Critique and the critic, too, sunk in the asphalt of expanded circulation, enliven the process of abstract valorization with their fire.

The fictional de-aurization of critical activity and revolution carried out by Marx in the sixth, unpublished chapter of *Capital*,[5] consists in making visible the *use value* "critique," or the *use value* "revolution," as *use values of capital*, as the immanent *reflux* of capital. From here, it would follow that "insofar as the theorist wins, therefore, by constructing an increasingly closed and terrifying machine, to that very degree he loses, since the critical capacity of his work is thereby paralysed, and the impulses of negation and revolt, not to speak of social transformation, are increasingly perceived as vain and trivial in the face of the model itself."[6]

21

CRITIQUE AND MASS

Critique's "day is long past," writes Benjamin in 1923.[1] And writing about film in 1936, he notes that it "put[s] the public in the position of the critic";[2] in other words, critique has become more present than ever as a mass phenomenon. There is no contradiction between these statements. Their apparent discordance is the result of a parallax illusory effect—that is, the effect of the mode of production within which each attains its perspective. The first is inscribed within the theatrical order between stalls and stage, "an exterior with respect to an interior"[3] in which "the periphery conquers the center (the first destiny of critique as it overthrows and takes power), or the center assigns it a place, subordinating it to the periphery and using it according to its own dynamics,"[4] according to a dialectic of places, "at home in a world where perspectives and prospects counted and where it was still possible to take a standpoint."[5] Such critique, that of a theatrical *mode of production*, is incompossible with the industrial-cinematographic *mode of production* in which the dialectic of places, perspective, the pit, critical distance have been erased into a new immanence that makes the stage/stalls, *cult value/exhibition value, use value/exchange value* differend insignificant. That critique is more present than ever as a mass phenomenon thus refers to conditions in which critique's possibility is governed no longer by the categories or functions that the theatrical interface presupposes—distance, points of view, prospects, autonomous places, transference, dialectics—but rather by a technology without distance or pit that is governed by a *tactility* of *the very close range that cannot be put at a distance*[6] in which every distance creates a *fold*,[7] a technology that demands the elaboration of a category of *critique*—and in general, of all categories—according to the arrangements and order of this new interface, which is not characterized above all by responding to a general principle but rather is exercised as a constellation of interfaces of coexisting *modes of production* without a general mediation that gathers and contains them.

That critique as a mass phenomenon has become more present than ever does not suggest, however, the absolute extenuation of the theatrical technology of critique. It only indicates that the latter coexists with the industrial-cinematographic within an actuality in which technologies clash, producing, in their relation, effects of domination and collateral drift.[8]

Benjamin writes that the "mechanical reproduction of art changes the reaction of the masses toward art [in a way that] is characterized by the direct, intimate fusion of visual and emotional enjoyment with the orientation of the expert. . . . Everybody who witnesses its accomplishments is somewhat of an expert. . . . Its approach is that of testing."[9] Here, he is not suggesting that the "epoch of critique," the event of *The Critique of Pure Reason,* has become a mass, universal epoch or that the age of the Enlightenment is realized in the plenitude of the figure of the mass critic. What he is suggesting is that the epoch or the mode of production of critique as a question concerning the condition, and the condition of the condition, clashes and finds its limit in another epoch or technology that asks other questions of critique—a technology in which the Kantian demand only takes place as the aestheticization of a postcritical, postauratic serial rather than a singular, purely exhibitionary gesture that stereotypically reiterates the question of the condition, a stereotype that synthetically assembles the Kantian technology of critique with the exhibition technology of industrial experts, experts who consume and reiterate opinions fabricated polytechnically for them by the cultural machines that have made the critics, and their critiques, as opinionated subjectivity (the subjectivity of experts who, nevertheless, exercise critical judgments as if they were their own—fetishized as they are within an *aestheticized autonomous I* who enjoys standard fare and reproduces the stereotype under the illusion of criticizing it).

The eclipse of the pit, of theater, the asphyxiation of distance, of the theatrical condition of critique as critical distance produced by mechanical reproducibility, is not, however, according to Benjamin, absolute. In effect, in "The Work of Art in the Age of Mechanical Reproduction," Benjamin outlines the condition of the Industrial Revolution's mode of production hesitantly. On the one hand, the text sets it out as a tendency *toward subsuming the totality of historical existence*, in which nothing might be experienced as an exception to its rule. On the other, there are a number of passages in the text that suggest that *mechanical reproduction* constitutes an interface—as invasive and expansive as it may be—that does not subsume the totality of modes of production that it itself imitates, serially and with which it establishes relations or clashes. This thus reduces the *totalizing* range of *mechanical reproduction* and now passes from constituting an absolute closure, an all-subsuming and withering transcendental *factum*, to constitute a relative closure, a fragment in an *opening* without totality, an opening without totality that enters into relation with other modes of production, fragmented in their turn, interrupting thus the nihilist principle of homogeneity and totality.

Along this route, which is the one that we are following here, the mode of production of advanced exhibition and display coexists and circulates as a piece within an actuality, or *mosaic opening*,[10] without totality, in which other *modes of production* that are both irreducible to each other and unrepeatable (unproducible) of each other cohabit: singular in this sense, although not pure, insofar as they affect each other, quote and interrupt—supplementing—each other. In this opening, the mechanical reproductive mode of production does not constitute the totality of a historical present, a homogeneous planetary *nomos*. And however hegemonic it may be, it floats as a fragment in a constellated actuality without a generalizable present, without totality or identity.

It is in such a tense interface of coexisting and clashing heterochronic technologies that Benjamin will liberate a nonjudicative, a nontheatrical, nonfounding, and nonmodernizing performance of critique—a purely performative critique, as an interruptive montage of materialities that frees an *instance of legibility* or an *awakening*; an awakening or instance of legibility whose possibility lies in the tension and conflict between existing modes of production, technologies, and heterochronisms in which one would no longer be captured by the endogenous effect of any one of the modes of production or technologies but rather be suspended in the *between* of modes of production, in the interregnum of the double gaze of a Janus face that suspends the stability and identity of a point of view. The proper or most proper name of that interval of legibility or awakening is *destruction*, which is also close to Benjamin's notion of justice as citation, untimeliness, vacillation, imbalance, an opening to the infinite virtuality of the singular. "Awakening" does not mean to pass from the condition of being asleep to one of wakefulness, from the lethargy of dreams to everyday routine, for example—which would be equivalent to passing from one technology, from one homogeneous present, to another. Awakening involves remaining hesitant on the frontier between both technologies, without becoming alienated in either, while similarly without remaining outside of either, as if in an autonomous *third space*. Awakening is not to be found in dream technology or in the technology of wakefulness, nor in that *third space* that is autonomous from both and that considers the former as that from which it differs. Awakening perseveres in the undecidable, unsteady zone in between the first, second, and third without their synthesis or mere addition. Nor is it a simple residue, an undecidable zone that (re)launches each of the terms onto each other, destabilizing their homogeneity, identity, their property (and self-sameness)—a *Hamlet-like* zone of virtuality and *immanence*, of vacillation and topological indecision, of systematic destruction of identity, simplicity, homogeneity, property, an *eddy in the stream of becoming*[11] that has the citation or the dialectical image as the primordial scene of its critical performativity: Benjaminian destruction.

- On extracting a fragment inscribed within one context of intentionality and rearranging it within another, the citation enhances its destructive power with respect to the series of compossibility in which it had been placed. It shatters the original intentionality, the intentionality of the new place that receives it and into which it is rearranged, as well as the supposed intentionality of the quoted that is fragmented itself. The power of citation resides in the destruction of what is proper to the contexts of both its starting point and of its end point. Quotations, like translations, make what is taken to be one's own suffer.[12] It unworks self-sameness, negating and preserving the original context, that of its destiny, as well as that of the displaced fragment itself. It makes the latter appear as that (with)in which it *had not been written*, as if *its ink had magical powers*—as in a *book of sand*. A citation is both the *passion and the death* of the Same. Quotations, says Benjamin, "are like wayside robbers who leap out armed and relieve the stroller of his conviction," of their beliefs and judgments.[13] They host the other within the same. Benjamin ironizes the bourgeois understanding of the quotation as the metonymy of an original. He ironizes the referential illusion with which the avant-garde *collage* uses citation as representation. He also ironizes the prejudice that there is a host text supporting the arrival of a parasite from an original text, such that the host text strangles the guest in its hospitality, homogenizing it as an element servicing its totality. The destructive power of the quotation interrupts the dialectic that digests the guest in its totality (*qua* hospitality). It makes identity, position, hierarchy, and the subordination of guest to host tremble. In the encounter of both, the host is also parasitical of the guest that it lodges; it is parasitical according to the hostility and hospitality with which the "guests" lodge the host that lodges them. There is simply no guest that is not also a host, nor simply a host that is not a guest. They interrupt each other. There is no original, copy, host, or guest that is not at the same time respectively copy, original, guest, and host. There is no way in which the host does not change and is not changed by the guest; there is no way in which the guest does not change and is not changed by the host. As Michel Serres insists, the parasite is an insidious infection that takes by giving.[14] There are no hosts or guests that are not invaginated within the intertext that they constitute. The quotation is a plethora of vacillations that we cannot appropriate: a paralysis that trembles. In its tension with the regime of bourgeois representation and hospitality, this vibration is what Benjamin calls the purely destructive and interruptive *dialectical image*. The quotation, its clash, constitutes the primordial scene of Benjaminian thought, of the destructive or interruptive character of Benjaminian thought—namely, the citation that, without founding or conserving representation, puts into question the supposed solidity and identity of being as present to itself, as a clean(sed) commodity. The quotation belongs to a regime of immanence, not to that of the act or of self-presence. For Benjamin, it is the supplementary clash of these historical-technological constellations that are relaunched on each other, altering their self-sameness, that constitutes the *performatics of awakening* as the interruption of homogeneous time, the instance of quotation or of montage, of the clash, the instance of that suspending construction, a purely destructive moment that never becomes rule. In this sense, the pragmatics of the dialectical image looks to "make a place," to "clear," to open up "paths everywhere," "even to erase the situation in which it finds itself," to disrupt "all understanding," "all cover," as well as what "lasts" or is "fixed." Like "Focillon's *acme*," the dialectical image weakly oscillates in its elements.[15]

22

NIHIL AND PHILOSOPHY

As upsetting and as liberating as it may have been, the Nietzschean phrase *"God is dead"* is not primarily related to the end of the Western monotheistic God who for so long a time framed—as trace and familiarity, center and meaning, communion and judgment—the pain of history. What was liberating was not so much the announcement of the end of the living God's hold or care, his justice (*judicia*), and the beginning of a pain without God but rather of the decontaining lucidity of there really having "never been a God" who was never a frame, never universal or a totality (or ever *difference, differend*, the division of labor between action and meaning, action and totality)—and who was also not derived from fragmentary, immanent conditions of survival. "Nihilism is in no way some kind of viewpoint 'put forward' by somebody, nor is it an arbitrary historical 'given,' among many others, that can be historically documented. Nihilism is rather that event of long duration in which the truth of being as a whole is essentially transformed and driven toward an end that such truth has determined."[1]

Accordingly, the long Western trace of the living God, preindustrially allegorized as the crucified God and as the frameless trace that is initiated by the phrase *"God is dead"*—a phrase subsequently translated into the photograph of the earth taken from the moon (that defetishized the earthly paradise as an island floating in the void and circulated on the cover of *Life* magazine)[2]—were both inscribed as the threads of an event forever without God, salvation, or condemnation, except as a trivial immanent performance, the *will to power*, as *pure affirmation* of life, of a small number of ephemeral animals existing in tormented conditions "in some remote corner of the universe[,] . . . hanging in dreams . . . upon the back of a tiger."[3] Engels had written something similar, although his statement is articulated more as a negation than an affirmation: "The essence of the state, as that of religion," he writes, "is mankind's fear of itself."[4] No affirmation or negation can either save or condemn us within the fragmentary immanence of the multiplicity as *justice*.

In the phrase *"God is dead,"* "God" means God, but it also means "everything that, in rapid succession, has sought to take his place—the ideal, consciousness, reason, the certainty of progress, the happiness of the masses, culture: everything that, not without value, nonetheless has no value of its own[,] . . . no thing of value other than through the meaning, in the end suspended, that man gives to it."[5] To this list of God's prostheses, one might add *genus*, the *concept*, the *universal*, the *general mediation*.

The homogenizing gesture, the "equalization of the unequal" within a general principle,[6] constitutes the homogenizing plasma of the *nihil*.[7] And philosophy would be this plasma, the universal, the unifying logic that tends to subsume multiplicities within a common order, within *the successively without limit—or measure—of the ever-same and indifferent*.[8] The "equalization of the unequal" would constitute the characteristic gesture of what is generally called philosophy, a gesture that consists in the reduction (*epokhé*) of the multiplicity within the fetish of a one and self-same thing. If Thales became the epitome of philosophy, it was not because of his labor as a physiocrat, the empiricist investigator of the plural. What was extraordinary about Thales, and what immortalized him among Westerners of the earth and made of his nickname a dead man's signature that circulates infinitely more that its bearer did, was the invention of nihilism, universality, the general mediation that subsumes singularities into the fetish of the transcendental, transforming multiplicity into the manifestation (*physis*) of the same principle (*arkhé*): "For an artist, for example, who while standing by a waterfall and seeing in the watery masses that leap toward him the playfully created models of men, animals, masks, plants, rocks, nymphs, griffins—the whole typology, in fact, of sculpture—might well find the proposition, 'all is water,' a true one."[9]

Thales (or whatever was his name) was the first to see the forest (the concept) *through* the singular trees that had prevented him from seeing it. He invented the universal, the *nihil*. From then on, this technology set a pattern: the forest (the concept) has blocked the multiple (without genus), singularity *minus* representation.

Marx translated Thales's water into *capital* or *self-valorizing value*, an automatic process without a subject that, adopting infinite appearances, produces and reproduces. Yet Marx's *water* responds no longer to a transcendental, homogeneous principle but rather to the immanent becoming of the Industrial Revolution, metonymized in the Jenny.

23

JENNY

Marx figures the *expanded circulation of capital* as it spread around the planet in the becoming of the *spinning Jenny*—a complex machine-tool[1] and the epitome of the Industrial Revolution—whose performance is explained in *Capital*[2] and the *Grundrisse*.[3]

What is the power of the Jenny (beyond having the same name as Marx's wife), such that he granted it the status of an event, an event that reveals itself posthumously as the trace of the Industrial Revolution, the trace of which only today, postindustrially, has entered our field of visibility? What does the Jenny consist of, and what is the figure of its becoming?

The complex machine-tool is a mechanism that executes functions that are analogous to those carried out by artisanal labor power that uses similar tools,[4] except that the number of terminals (working organs) that artisanal labor power can manipulate at any one time is limited by the particular power and auratic skill of the specific manufacturing labor power involved. The Jenny, which at first spun with twelve, eighteen, and even with one hundred spindles at a time, broke out of the limits imposed by the working body-machine of fixed, endogenous, specialized terminals of the artisanal mode of production, liberating them—quantitatively at first but then qualitatively, too—for use by the vertiginous agency of a machine-body of nonspecific, abstract, an-organic, polytechnic, transdisciplinary labor that was arranged according to a protean becoming, a regime of the unlimited virtualization of its usefulness.

As a mechanical body, the Jenny had already been dreamed of in the seventeenth century by Descartes in his *Treatise on Man*, but which might best be referred to as a *Treatise on Artificial Man*.[5] Here, Descartes investigated the medical possibility of an immortal body-machine through the transplant of parts and theorized the possibility of a body-machine mathesis of infinite composition, decomposition, and recomposition not only of its parts and mechanics but, above all, of its elements and principles, a sovereign machine, an evil-genius-machine unconnected, in the first instance, to art "because art requires a habitual exercise and disposition of the body that obstructs many arts being learned and exercised at one time, by one man, since the hands themselves cannot adapt to cultivating the fields and strumming the zither, or with various different tasks with such ease as with one alone, such that their excellent exercise demands that their dedication be an exclusive one."⁶ A sovereign machine detached from the principles of art, too, from the compositional principles and elements of all arts in general.⁷

Again: the activity liberated by the incontinence of the Jenny will erode those contracts in which skill is confined to a feudal interface. With the *spinning* Jenny, the virtuality of the productive forces will be freed into ever more unspecific, polytechnic proliferation, according to this becoming of terminals in constant transformation. Such productive virtuality—until then subject to the social relations of manufacture and conditioned and disciplined by the artisanal *use value of manual labor*—will enter into contact with the whirlwind, the *evil genius* of the Jenny, which will assemble artisanal habits into other relations of production open to *exchange value* without limits—a limitlessness without teleology in which all the *specialized use value* of labor will become the *abstract use value* of labor, the *use value of value*. Feudal relations, bodies, tastes, and their uses are thus swiftly rearranged as accessories within a new "cooperation" of increasingly unspecific *machines* that, under the direct command of the virtuality of exchange value, add more and more functions to the bodies and working organs to become *abstract labor, use value of value*.⁸

With the Jenny, however, the abstract becoming of hand and labor—of *use value*—will necessarily be at the same time compatible with maximum specialization and the containment of the body at work terminals (including the specific, disciplined movement of labor)—always, that is, as the labor of capital, the specific *use value of value* conceived as the fetishization or aestheticization of *exchange value in process*.

Just as many tools constitute the organs of a machine-tool, many *machine-tools* constitute the organs of a collective motor. A machine-tool such as the Jenny simultaneously operates many and diverse—potentially infinite—tools. A *collective motor* operates many—potentially infinite—machine-tools. The *combined machine* of many, potentially infinite machine-tools, gradually constitutes a simultaneous, heterochronic becoming that is composed of various kinds of machines and groups of machines. The more perfect is this becoming, the less segmented and more continuous and fluid, the more abstract, its general movement (and that of its parts).

Workers and their tools will be redistributed within the immanence of the Jenny more or less suddenly, assembled at first inside a mechanical monster whose body will fill up entire sheds and whose demoniacal power—hidden by the solemnly rhythmic movement of its gigantic members—will explode into the fevered and vertiginous mad dance of its innumerable middle and terminal organs. Soon, the Jenny will proliferate within networks of combined machines (many of which will be machines to produce machines) and networks of networks that will configure a polytechnical and polychronic surface of *abstract cooperation*. This is the way in which mechanical spinning became mechanical weaving and, with bleaching, printing, and dry cleaning, also revolutionized chemo-mechanics. Similarly, the revolution in spinning was extended by the cotton gin, the machine that separated cotton fiber from the seed, leading to a revolution in agriculture that, in its turn, unblocked the conditions of social production, catapulting into circulation masses of capital and workers, armies of the unemployed, and lumpen (*lumpfen*[9]) at various levels—or agencies—of the production process. The Jenny rapidly became world trade, integrated into networks of steam riverboats and ocean liners, railways, and telegraphs—the febrile acceleration of mass production on a grand scale.[10] The world market will thus assemble histories and literatures on a planetary scale to include eventually everyday chores and belongings, lifeworlds at every scale.

With the maturity of the Jenny, the *specifically capitalist* mode of production makes itself present: an abstract invagination of lifeworlds. It is this invagination that becomes the real agency of skill, virtuality, the becoming-abstract of production in which undefined fetishizations of abstract labor participate, as useful labor, and that together cooperate to constitute the abstract machine of value in process.[11]

Nature, Marx writes, does not build automatic spinning machines, nor locomotives, nor railways, nor electric telegraphs.[12] These are the products of the power of fantasy in the becoming of manual skill—of the hand as skill and virtual becoming, of skill and virtuality in the becoming of the hand.

It had been imagined that it was the natural hand that at first led to the creation of the Jenny as an interface and that, in a second moment, the interface so created developed into an expanded field with no limits whatsoever—and whose unlimited character included, as one of its possibilities, the "so-called natural hand" that now floats as just one more terminal or working organ among all of the Jenny's possibilities, its immanence and abstract multiplicity.[13]

If, beginning with this metamorphosis, the Jenny seemed then to advance through disciplinary steps—jumping from the milieu of one technical division of labor to another, from one phase to another, according to stages or technical states—then it soon began to behave in a baroque fashion—like herpes or streams—that, as in inverted parentheses [ )( ], grew through the middle (undermining its banks, its bed, wearing away contracts, containments, exceeding them, exceeding itself, creating new drifts and clearings without coming to a final stop or identifying with any of them): an abstract flow trampling on structures of recognition, releasing possibilities without ever pausing in a beginning, middle, or end—a becoming without plot (beginning-middle-end) or teleology—in turbulent topos.

If the spread of the Jenny is set out both representationally and pedagogically—and sometimes, in Marx's text, as a discontinuous *via crucis* according to stages and couplings—then its becoming will abandon such discrete syntax for a continuous flow without connections or seasons. In much the same way in which a meteorite only perseveres while it cleaves the atmosphere, and exchange value while it grows and valorizes itself without freezing into any specific quantity, the Jenny dies if it stops eroding, eroding itself and stabilizing, if it stops changing and changing itself, if it establishes itself—even for a moment—into an identity. In contrast to Aristotle's *ananke stenai* (the necessity to stop), the Jenny and *exchange value* plunge themselves into a becoming without beginning, middle, or end, occurring only as an excess or *surplus*. And it is not a matter of an *excess of* . . . this or that, growing by way of an overcoming of a previous state but rather of *pure excess*—and never an *excess of* . . . —without place (*topos*), without presence: *excess minus presence*, immanence plus virtuality.

If technically for Marx *lumpfen* refers to what proliferates as a "remainder," as a nonsubsumable virtuality in the clash and becoming of heterochronic machines, then the *lumpfen* or *lumperic* might best figure as the name of this virtuality that, immanent to machines, belongs to none but rather grows between them, eroding them, without being subsumed by any machine, class, or subjectivity whatsoever. In this sense, the Jenny *is* lumperic.

- According to Marx's text, in the transformational becoming of the Jenny, as in the *process of the expanded valorization of capital*, there is less *becoming* than *process*. If we privilege process over becoming, then the abstraction of the Jenny, its polytechnics, becomes the factic transcendental subsumption of singularities, a homogenous *nihil*—the equalization of the unequal—rather than the immanent erosion and disassembling of transcendentals as pure becoming without point of departure or arrival—an abstract becoming that refuses to *metaphorize*, that lacks stages, like a flow without course, or frame or border, without recognition, and in the midst of the immanent proliferation of multiple singularities. This, *grosso modo*, suggests a differend between the Deleuze there is in Marx and the Marx there is in Deleuze.

24

THE EPOCH OF NIHILISM. *NIHIL* AS EPOCH.

Contemporary nihilism as technology—as the epoch of the consummation of the nihilism of many epochs—is, in well-known texts by Heidegger,[1] pathetically exposed to its precursors, its trajectory, and limit as the homogenization of multiple tendencies and efforts into the rigid uniformity and identity of an end-time (*endzeit*). The homogenizing tone of the Heideggerian analysis of nihilism—the fundamental axis around which this planetary uniformity takes place, that transcendental factum of which he speaks—is of a kind of thought that is characterized by calculation, representation, and a planned dominion that organizes, regulates, and subjugates everything.[2] It concerns the question of technology as the essential configuration of what is, and this question embraces all aspects of being. The expression "technology" does not designate isolated dimensions of mechanical equipment and production by machines. Rather, it has a privileged position of power, implicating the vectors of administration, autonomization, bureaucratization, communication, functionalization, information, and securing and should be understood in such an essential manner as coming under the heading of "completed metaphysics."[3] The Heideggerian exposition traces the nihilism latent in the entire history of the West, a nihilism that is fulfilled in accomplished modernity and that finally sketches a possible nihilization of nihilism.[4] In "Concerning 'The Line,'" which was written in celebration of Ernst Jünger's sixtieth birthday and which, according to Blanchot, adopts *the form of a treatise on nihilism*,[5] Heidegger writes as follows: "The movement of nihilism has become more manifest in its planetary, all-corroding, many-faced irresistibleness. No one with any insight will still deny today that nihilism is in the most varied and most hidden forms of 'the normal state' of man. . . . The best evidences of this are the exclusively reactive attempts against nihilism, which, instead of entering into a discussion of its essence, strive for the restoration of what has been. They seek salvation in flight . . . from a glimpse at the worthiness of questioning. . . . The same flight is also urgent where apparently all metaphysics ["nihilism" in the Spanish-language version—Trans.] is abandoned. . . . The totality of the 'human component realities' ["human existence" in the Spanish-language version—Trans.] can only cross over the line when they step out of the zone of complete nihilism. . . . Nihilism is fulfilled when it has seized all the component realities and appears everywhere, where nothing can assert itself any longer as an exception, in so far as it has become a normal state."[6]

From the homogenizing perspective of Heideggerian nihilism—what Nietz-sche had in his day announced as the future global war—political tendencies and worldviews necessarily clash, and their struggle is real in an immediate sense. In the last instance, however, such conflict will still constitute the perspectives that feed nihilism's leveling design, the homogeneous background of the present age:

> The struggle between those who are in power and those who want to come to power [is that] on every side there is the struggle for power. Everywhere power itself is what is determinative. Through this struggle for power, the being of power is posited in the being of its unconditional dominance by both sides. . . . This struggle is in the service of power. . . . Power, however, overpowers various kinds of humanity in such a way that it expropriates from man the possibility of ever escaping from the oblivion of Being on such paths. This struggle is of necessity planetary and as such undecidable in its being because it has nothing to decide, since it remains excluded from all differentiation, from the difference (of Being from beings). . . . Instead, it develops the completely equipped plan and certainty of all plans whatsoever in every area. In the encompassment (circle) of areas, the particular realms of human equipment necessarily become "sectors"; the "sector" of poetry [and] the "sector" of culture are also only the areas, guaranteed according to plan, of actual "leadership" along with others. . . . The way in which artificial insemination is handled corresponds with stark consistency [with] the way in which literature is handled in the sector of "culture." . . . The need for human material underlies the same regulation of preparing for ordered mobilization as the need for entertaining books and poems, for whose production the poet is no more important than the bookbinder's apprentice, who helps bind the poems for the printer by, for example, bringing the covers for binding from the storage room.[7] . . . Nor does the uniformity of the course of history of our present age consist in a supplementary assimilation of older political systems to the latest ones. Uniformity is not the consequences, but the ground of the warlike disputes of individual intendants of the decisive leadership. . . . [Uniformity] also conditions everywhere in advance of all national differences the uniformity of leadership, for which all forms of government are only one form of leadership among others.[8]

Within such a framework, the critiques of nihilism that take the form of avant-gardist proclamations of actions and gestures against it, the affirmation of an antagonistic will that would overcome nihilism, crossing its "line"—sovereign, foundational, or consular critical gestures—merely feed the technologies of its equipment. Such gestures and actions would unsuspectingly have nihilism as their own presupposition and so nourish it. An unsuspecting critique of nihilism fails to realize that it—critique—will only become possible once it understands that the long-extolled theatrical technology of critique—presented as transcendent, separate, and autonomous from what it criticizes—is the most tenacious enemy of critique. Nothing critical comes into view with the reaffirmation of negativity, the mainspring of nihilism. Neither progressive critique nor even the theoretical will of critique stand a *chance* against nihilism. This is because they come from it and adhere to it as another of its folds, feeding its technology. Any activity that presents itself in terms of overcoming, of discursive autonomy from nihilism, or of a restauration of a presumed reality beyond its horizon suspends the possibility of critique. Rather, it is nihilism's *chance* that is activated when its enemies do so in terms of expiry, overcoming, and the foundation of horizons of meaning and presence, or even in the name of mobilization—or when the unsuspecting understand the term consummation as the absolute end of representation. The unsuspecting critic's use of an avant-gardist language of producing significant breaks with nihilism embraces nihilism as it confronts it.

Alternatively, and at a distance from avant-gardist opponents, the erosion, the nihilization of the *nihil*—of the transcendental, the factic universal, the uniforming design that the word *teckné* adopts in Heidegger's text as a *planetary realm*—contained in the Deleuzian notions of *desire, becoming, movement, creation, thought* are well known.[9] These notions are never associated by Deleuze with negativity or with any contestation: not with *frenetic voluntarisms*, or *positional disagreements in a cultural field lived as an entrenched battle field* with a *vibrant force of opposition*, or *utopian excess*. The movement of *desire* is blocked, frozen, and nihilized (that is, universalized and transcendentalized) when its *positivity* and *affirmative* character are critically understood as negativity, reactive opposition, as utopian or as arborescent foundation. Desire is equally blocked when it is teleologically illuminated according to the pragmatic needs of action.

Insofar as critique is conceived as the *critique of . . .* , in antagonism with, announcing, sentencing, or establishing distances, it becomes an enunciation that affirms negating, subordinating affirmation to negation, and deploying negativity as its principle of movement. Critique and *critique of . . .* are nothing without what they criticize, and vice versa—hence the rule of the negative, unable *affirmatively* to move thought. The negative, as a position that affirms itself *against*, blocks desire, fixing it to an end. The affirmation most proper to desire does not exist at a *distance from . . .* or *in pursuit of . . .* , submerged in a negative or teleological order, it withers as representation. Its affirmation, its occurrence, lacks position and presence. It erupts through the middle, stratifying the coexistence of planes. As becoming, desire has no point of departure or of arrival; in all its turbulence, it erodes without founding topologies, immanently: neither before nor after, nor first or second, nor constituent or constituted, nor interior or exterior, freeing possibilities everywhere.

Deleuzian affirmation never requires a nihilization of nihilism in its critique of the predominance of a factual transcendental or of the metatechnics of capital as value in process (from which, after the death of God, as Heidegger suggests in his interview with *Der Spiegel*, "only a God can save us").[10]

The Deleuzian-Nietzschean version of nihilism refuses capture by the factual transcendentals of metatechnics, absolute telemarketing, all-consuming value in process. Instead, it debilitates and de-auratizes the universal satellite that leaves nowhere in the shade. The instance of readability provided by the Nietzschean exposition of *active nihilism* (that erodes transcendence, the universal, the transcendental) that Deleuze offers does not lead into the immanence of a leveling planetary *factum* of technology's making, an all-involving general site that dominates everything but rather into the fragmented immanence of the *multiple singular* in which no universal or transcendental has a place, except as the empirical fetishes or spells (both great and small) that are proper to the containing designs and drifts of the *Aristotelian cinematographer*—with her snapshots of genus and species, cause and effect, substance and accident—a cinematographer who, like another piece of a *patchwork*, folds into the immanence of the multiple.

The patchwork has no center. It is made up of blocks and contiguous assemblages that do not weave either melodies or harmonies. In its *piece-by-piece*, potentially infinite addition of cloth in all directions, without warp, the patchwork constitutes a collection of autarkic bits whose assemblage can be carried out in infinite ways. In the very making of the patchwork, aleatory workgroups—such as the *quilting party*—are constituted. "If we follow the history of the quilt over a short migration sequence (the settlers who left Europe for the New World), we see that there is a shift from a formula dominated by embroidery (so-called 'plain' quilts) to a patchwork formula. . . . The first settlers of the seventeenth century brought with them plain quilts, embroidered and striated. . . . But toward the end of the century patchwork technique was developed more and more, at first due to the scarcity of textiles (leftover fabric, pieces salvaged from used clothes, remnants taken form the 'scrap bag'), and later due to the popularity of Indian chintz. It is as though a smooth space emanated, sprang from a striated space. . . . Patchwork, in conformity with migration, whose degree of affinity with nomadism it shares, is not only named after trajectories, but . . . becomes inseparable from speed or movement in an open space."[11] Patchwork, like felt and silicon memory, are smooth, inorganic spaces—a mosaic—without a center. It suggests open rhythmic values that do not return on themselves, crazy patchwork especially, which fits together pieces of variable colors, sizes, and shapes that play with fabric, the striation marking the autonomous or autarkic patches.

25

THE EXHAUSTED AGE

How to criticize the nihil—this age of ages, including that of critique—without feeding its pluripotent interface, without its becoming just one more fold within its immanence? How to dodge it without the feint being reappropriated beforehand as one more input into its polytechnics? How to question it if the interrogation owes itself to and presupposes what is questioned? How to activate the critique of the nihil if its exercise is carried out with materials and technologies that will, on intercepting it, also continue it? Has resistance—opposing and confronting the nihil—not been one of the most available of its resources?

Critique as the critique *relative to* . . . is nothing without what it criticizes. Critique *relative to* . . . is always in need, lacking what it criticizes: the utterance, the book, the work, the mode of production and understanding of an epoch, etc.—all doubtful—customary—discursive unities. Structurally constituted as the *critique of* . . . , referring to some other, to a presupposition, its starting point is thus always reactive, its affirmation and positivity belonging thus to the domain of the negative.

If critique is constituted in relation to an object, it will remain internal, from the very start, to a logic of recognition, of genus and species, and thus of the *nihil*. Alternatively, without a genus that subsumes and objectivizes multiplicity under general mediations, without the equalization of the unequal, without universals or transcendentals, without framework, could there ever be critique or crisis? What, then, would it be a critique of . . . ? Can there be critique without subject matter or object, without its being a *critique of* . . . ?

The "age" is stuttering to an end. The supposition that there are periods, regularities, *basic concepts* that can be constituted as historical unities is exhausted. The understanding of a determinate multiplicity or of *a priori* immanent material populated by singularities, materialities, technologies, heterochronic modes of production—some obsolete in relation to others—as an epoch or homogeneous present, as a rich synthetic totality of what *is* today, a today (a uniform, general, portmanteau time that nihilizes multiplicity in *each and every case*), no longer holds. This means that phrases such as "Constant revolutionizing of production, uninterrupted disturbance of all social conditions, everlasting uncertainty and agitation distinguish the bourgeois epoch from all earlier ones," or "The ideas of the ruling class are in every epoch the ruling ideas" (Marx and Engels), or "Every period mentally constructs its own universe . . . out of . . . everything that distinguishes it from preceding periods,"[1] or even "the present age," "the Christian Age," "the age of the Industrial Revolution," "the Age of the Enlightenment," "the Cold War period," "the age of consummated nihilism," "the age of mechanical reproduction"—all such phrases no longer work. The power of one of the great fetishes of modern philosophy, which not only constitutes itself as an epoch but also as an age that reflects upon its own actuality as a particular present,[2] has been lost—if such an age ever really existed.

Mechanical reproduction as a mode of production is often nihilized in the form of a metatechnics—*the age of mechanical reproduction*, metonymized into photography and film—making it a transcendental facticity that eats away at and subsumes, unifies, and homogenizes everything in an uncontainable and multiform planetary unfolding, which is all-present, and in relation to which all critique would be empty and thus integrated into its multiformity as just one more of its commodities. Such nihilization of mechanical reproduction can also be carried out *à la Marx*: as a process of the *real subsumption* of all auratic value within the matrix of mass seriality, establishing thus a parallel between the becoming of the Jenny or *complex machine-tool* and the becoming of the *photographic-cinematographic machine* whose deployment would subsume any other mode of production, leveling it.

Benjamin shielded himself from the *nihil* that is contained within the totalitarian matrix of mechanical reproduction as a mode of production that tends, as a reflection of its power, toward total mobilization. He did so by embracing mechanical reproduction's totalitarian serial matrix, not as a planetary metatechnology of the epochal consummation of the ages of Western history but rather as a *singular* mode of production that coexists and clashes with other modes of production and temporalities within a polychronic milieu.

In "The Work of Art in the Age of Mechanical Reproduction," which sets out the clash of epochs or modes of production (that of painting with photography and of theater with cinema), Benjamin stages the *destruction* of transcendentalism and universality, of the transcendental *age* conceived as a continuity. The technology he uses for this is heterochronic montage.

The clash as such—without for the moment considering the technologies involved in each case—refers to a performative construction that was dear to Benjamin, and not only Benjamin. It is a question of *collage*, of citation, which Benjamin also refers to as *constellation* and *mosaic*. On staging the clash between theater and painting with cinema and photography,[3] Benjamin understands time not as a succession of historical interfaces but rather as the coexistence of technologies and polychronic montage. In this sense, in "The Work of Art" essay, he presents not a passing from one epoch to another of one present to another, but the interruption, multidirectional turbulence and vacillations that are experienced by the understanding in said clash of the ways in which each of the technologies involved unravel. What Benjamin wants to expose is the clash itself—and the moment of the clash—in that *between* of modes of production conceived as antagonistic heterochronic singularities (heterochronic also in their relation to themselves within the clash). For Benjamin, it is the clash of these historico-technological constellations—which in supplementary fashion return onto each other, altering their self-sameness—that constitutes the *performatics of awakening* interrupting homogeneous time and the dialectical continuum. Here, in this crossing or clash of technologies or heterotemporalities, is where the *lumpfen*, the nonauratic, nonpresentist, nonidentical singular belonging to no homogeneous series emerges. And it emerges as the "genuinely singular," which is to say as "genuinely political." In "Convolute S" of *The Arcades Project*, Benjamin writes as follows: "Politics recognizes in every actual constellation the genuinely unique—what will never recur." And in "Convolute N": "It is the inherent tendency of dialectical experience to dissipate the semblance of eternal sameness, and even of repetition, in history. Authentic political experience is absolutely free of this semblance."[4]

Benjamin also refers to this clash with the terms *moment of readability, destruction,* and, most strongly, "justice" as it is linked to *citation*.[5]

Mechanical reproduction as a mode of production is thus set out in Benjamin's text *as* and *within* vacillation. And this is where we are balanced. On the one hand, the text suggests that mechanical reproduction as a mass totalitarian matrix and homogenizing principle is constituted as a general age that subsumes the totality of modes of production, imposing itself as a universe outside whose rules nothing might be experienced. On the other, there are a number of passages in the text whose tension within it suggests that mechanical reproduction is a *mode of production*—as invasive and expansive as it may be—that does not subsume the modes of production that it serially imitates, with which it clashes or *interrupts*. In this way, it redistributes the epochal, nihilistic character of mechanical reproduction that, from suggesting itself as transcenden-tal, becomes a fragment clashing with another, an ungeneralizable heterological actuality—mechanical reproduction as a mode of production that, on clashing with others, dissolves and interrupts the endogenous and exogenous principle of homogeneity so as to produce in that clash a *third* that enters into the play of frictions in order to break down both presence and identity. The stance of mechanical reproduction (or of any other historicist totalization) toward a total and homogeneous present appears, in the text, as a nihilistic-fascist *chance* or *opportunity*. In contrast, the understanding of mechanical reproduction as a col-liding fragment within a heteroclite actuality activates its destructive *possibility*. Benjamin's politics of exposition in the text works with both sides of the vacilla-tion. The advanced form of exhibition as a mode of production thus circulates as a piece of an actual mosaic in which it coexists with other modes of produc-tion, each one irreducible to the others. Among them is the auratic mode of production of painting and theater, unrepeatable anachronisms, singular, and so unsubstitutable for one another but which also—insofar as they cite, erode, and intervene in each other within their temporal strata, reciprocally supplementing their constitution—are not pure.

THE COEXISTENCE OF TECHNOLOGIES: MARX

In his 1873 Postface to the second edition of *Capital*, Marx presents an archi-pelago of singular times, a montage of anachronisms, of clashing modes of pro-duction that, citing one another, become unstable as to their own identity, ar-ranged in a vacillation of influences and contagions, mutual interruptions, and infections that make any presupposition of a present, a common transcendental that contains them all, unviable. This is the case for the self-complacency of each with respect to its specific present, and as regards their endogenous categories of self-understanding. Marx writes:

Political economy remains a foreign science in Germany, up to this very moment. . . .
The living soil from which political economy springs was absent. It had to be im-

ported from England and France as a ready-made article; its German professors always remained pupils. The theoretical expression of an alien reality turned in their hands into a collection of dogmas[,] . . . the uneasy awareness that they had to master an area in fact entirely foreign to them. . . . Since 1848 capitalist production has developed rapidly in Germany. . . . But fate is still unpropitious to our professional economists. At the time when they were able to deal with political economy in an unprejudiced way, modern economic conditions were absent from the reality of Germany. And as soon as these conditions did come into existence, it was under circumstances that no longer permitted their impartial investigation. . . . Let us take England. Its classical political economy belongs to a period in which class struggle was as yet undeveloped. Its last great representative, Ricardo, ultimately (and consciously) made the antagonism of class interests . . . the starting point of his investigations. . . . But with this contribution the bourgeois science of economics had reached the limits beyond which it could not pass. . . . The succeeding period, from 1820 to 1830, was notable in England for the lively scientific activity which took place in the field of political economy. It was the period of both the vulgarizing and the extending of Ricardo's theory, and of the contest of that theory with the old school. Splendid tournaments were held. What was achieved at that time is little known on the European Continent. . . . The unprejudiced character of this polemic . . . is explained by the circumstances of the time. . . . The literature of political economy in England at this time calls to mind the economic "storm and stress period" which in France followed the death of Dr Quesnay, but only as an Indian summer reminds us of spring. With the year 1830 there came the crisis which was to be decisive. . . . In England and France the bourgeoisie had conquered political power. From that time on, the class struggle took on more and more explicit and threatening forms, both in practice and in theory. It sounded the knell of scientific bourgeois economics. It was thenceforth no longer a question of whether this or that theorem was true, but whether it was useful to capital or harmful, expedient or inexpedient, in accordance with police regulations or contrary to them. In place of disinterested inquirers there stepped hired prize-fighters. . . . The Continental revolution of 1848 also had its reaction in England. Men who still claimed some scientific standing and aspired to be something more than mere sophists and sycophants of the ruling classes tried to harmonize the political economy of capital with the claims, no longer to be ignored, of the proletariat. . . . In Germany, therefore, the capitalist mode of production came to its maturity after its antagonistic character had already been revealed, with much sound and fury, by the historical struggles which took place in France and England. Moreover, the German proletariat had in the meantime already attained a far clearer theoretical awareness than the German bourgeoisie. Thus, at the very moment when a bourgeois science of political economy at last seemed possible in Germany, it had in reality again become impossible. . . . Just as in the classical period of bourgeois economics, so also in the period of its decline, the Germans remained mere pupils, imitators and followers, petty retailers and hawkers in the service of the great

foreign wholesale concerns. . . . Nearly thirty years ago . . . when I was working at the
first volume of *Capital*, the ill-humoured, arrogant and mediocre epigones who now
talk large in educated German circles began to take pleasure in treating Hegel . . . as a
"dead dog." I therefore openly avowed myself the pupil of that mighty thinker. . . . The
mystification which the dialectic suffers in Hegel's hands by no means prevents him
from being the first to present its general forms of motion in a comprehensive and conscious manner. . . . In its rational form it [the dialectic] is a scandal and an abomination
to the bourgeoisie and its doctrinaire spokesmen, because it includes in its positive understanding of what exists a simultaneous recognition of its . . . inevitable destruction;
because it regards every historically developed form as being in a fluid state, in motion,
and therefore grasps its transient character as well; and because it does not let itself be
impressed by anything, being in its very essence critical and revolutionary.[1]

27

REFERENTIAL ILLUSION

The plane of actuality as the coexistence of modes of production, technologies,
heterochronisms, and the weave of its fibers must not be confused with the *illusion* that such coexistence produces when a technology, a mode of production, imitates and represents other modes of production in its own medium.
Thus cinema, although a specific technology, produces the illusion of subsuming
pre- or a-cinematic technologies and temporalities into its own plane of immanence. It is not that Shakespeare, Rembrandt, Beethoven, all the myths and leg-
ends, the heroes and founders of religions, including each of their technological
singularities, rushed, as suggested by Abel Gance, to be resurrected on screen.[1] In
cinema, photography, digital publicity, photomontage, electronic mixing (and,
more generally, in the operation of *citation*)—all materially realized within the
same mode of production—there is no clash of modes of production but rather
the endogamy of the same medium's homogeneous productivity. The clash or
anachronism is here nothing more than the reiteration of the same technology
under the fetish of presenting another. When photography represents painting
photographically, it does not clash with painting; it only exhibits itself, representing itself and its power to produce images. When cinema represents painting,
the oral tale, Greek mythology, the expanding Roman Empire, the extermination

of the Native Americans in the United States, when it propagates the culturalist integration of exemplary lives in Hollywood superproductions, it only tautologically represents its own power to fabricate cinematographic images and stories. The only revival or resurrection is that of cinema and its possibility. When Pixar digitally produces an analogical Pinocchio, there is no clash between the analogical technology of the image, the digital technology of Pixar, and the Italian literature of Collodi. It only endogenously presents its own medium in the illusion of presenting an artisanal manufacturing framework within that of industrial cinematography. Painting is only about painting. Cinema about cinema. It is the same for digital images. In the digital circulation of the image of a disappeared person, the latter is not represented. And if we aestheticize the image with the aura of the disappeared—that is, when spectators allow themselves to be produced in the illusion of confronting their *sacred cloak*—then another level of their disappearance, as appearance, is exhumed in digital circulation.

Pure media simply do not exist. When *truth begins as two*,[2] there can be no *pure media*. There is no pure cinema or figuration, except as referential illusion, the foundational *will to* of a specific mode of production (in the sense of Dziga Vertov's "Kino-Eye" manifesto).[3] Where there is a medium, there are already media, just as where there is color there are always colors. Each medium constitutes itself referentially, as in the *Bororo* myth,[4] a *patchwork* or citation of many media, a translation that always says and does in a medium what in another cannot be said or done.

Not only the age but also the mode of production is exhausted. Perhaps there never was either an age or a mode of production, except as the illusion or myth of a singular technology whose framework of understanding endogenously organizes a multiplicity, nihilizing it under a common principle or a general mediation.

28

CRITIQUE AND INSTALLATION

The breach in which the question concerning the possibility of critique is now posed can no longer simply count on the dogma of an "age," on mediation, the mode of production, or on a generalized present that, deployed as a frame of

reference and containment or as *property relations*, encourages *forces* of interrogation to drum against its limits, thereby thematizing it. A general framework,
the closure in which the multiplicity of fragments—it's *there*—might be surprised
by an *epokhé* that places it *outside of itself*—outside of its *there*—is thus lacking.
Such a *there* is now exhausted. And the opening or breach is disseminated within
the coexistence of anachronisms in what Ernst Bloch called the "nonsynchronic-
ity of the synchronous,"[1] as if we had jumped from *the forest (concept) that
does not see the trees (the singularities)* to *the trees (singularities) that*—like
objects in an *installation*—*refuse nihilization in the forest (the concept)*. (The
fragments or elements of an *installation* are preinscribed within a totality that
arranges them like bodily organs or parts of a landscape or composition. In this
sense, the singularity does not allow itself to be framed or organized. The [fram-
ing] framework is in each case the result of the friction of one fragment against
another. The drumming of limits or of the tympani thus takes place where fragments cross. In an installation, the frame is the supposed frame that emerges
from the clash of fragments without a world.)

Because of the fragmentary effect of the opening, reductions (*epokhés*) of a
general or significant kind (thanks to which something like an "age" might become the thematic object of interrogation) become impossible. Thus conceived,
the question of totality is inscribed as just one more fragment of the patchwork,
one of many tensions and echoes that refuse to be instituted as a privileged site
and/or perspective. With the totalizing gesture that poses the question of the
limit, it is thus the fragmentary opening that is confirmed, for it only then to be
retracted.

The temptation to confuse this opening with a transcendental is always present, resisting the coexistence of anachronisms without an *underlying oneness*.[2]
The opening comes neither before nor after its folds, and it redistributes transcendental gestures within the immanence of the patchwork. In this opening,
which is no longer a horizon but another of its folds, a critique that drums on
the tympanum is no longer possible. There, where there are tympani everywhere
and openings nowhere, there is no longer a tympanum to drum.

In such an aperture, in which the opening is a fold and not a frame, all attempts to criticize know that critique is no more (*ou mallon*), as the skeptics
say; it no longer fulfills transcendental, epochal, historical tasks—although it
can undo, unblock, affirmatively grow by way of the thick and the thin as well
as overfly and survey incompletely, at an indefinite speed, but in step with the
overflown and surveyed (that is, the installation of the case).

This *waning*, however, is relative. It does not proclaim the absolute waning of
an *epoch* or a transcendental facticity but rather its redistribution and retraction

from the dignity of a *general framework* to that of a frameless fold-in-becoming without a *there* or an underlying oneness that contains it. The dissolution of the frame is thus relative to its insistence within the unframeable fragmentary constellations that are organized under common mediations, fragmentary constellations that are fragmentary and not totally lacking in the oneness that singularizes them—although no longer so under the logic of genre and species or of categories that equalize the unequal but rather under a monadic performance of the figure in which a finite fold of infinite distribution and proof is set, in which the category is deployed not as a container or a portmanteau but rather as an element: the monad includes what includes it, just like the aleph, being "one of the points in space that contains all points," including the line and the infinite alephs that include it (multiplying it),[3] not synthetically or organically but, more like Benjamin's *judgment day*, as a citation coexisting lacunae-like *à la ordre du jour.*[4] Such constellations do not float as beings in a world but as fragments in an installation, vacillating between its outside and inside, including of "themselves," as signs in *The Book of Sand.*[5]

The change in the frame's distribution causes havoc that is analogous to that suffered by a museum or a cemetery that has been robbed not of its works or cadavers or tombs or coffins but of the *angles and the frames of its assembly*[6] and, with them, of their *there.*

The interruptive power of actuality has no frame. Everyday frames of understanding or warps of containment and representation that nihilize singularity constitute further elements that are traced within multiplicity without frame, without nihil. Opening without containment constitutes a provocation for any privileged site or "hide" (as the term is used by hunters) that pretends to install itself as a metaprinciple of organization, a metaplace or center of performative hierarchization of cannons, as a general containing *nihil.*

Actuality's opening is predisposed toward exchange without containment, without decision, without a politics that establishes a *nomos of the earth.* In such an opening, all transformation (un)folds as a procedure within multiplicity. There is no containment in a patchwork made of pieces that are assembled contiguously with no other hierarchy than togetherness. The *piece by piece* summing of fabrics of various kinds is potentially infinite and in all directions. The space that the patchwork singularly proposes in each fold is unlike that of a fabric made up and "contained" by the warp of its threads.[7] There is no warp in the patchwork. It thus has no public friends or enemies, center or periphery. There is no *there* in the patchwork, but openings like graves in a *land unblessed.* Each element is outside, inside, or on the limit, in the *middle* or *in between*, in the *erosion* of channels: topical virtuality. What we call *actual opening* makes of both the epic and lyrical aspects of questions—such as: *What is an epoch? What is art? What is to be done? What is the world like? How is this world, which indeed is possible, possible?*—small or medium, sustainable or unsustainable enterprises, immanent to the multiplicity of anachronisms, of what is obsolete with respect to others. What does critique mean in a multiplicity without a *there*, without a transcendental, in a fragmentary plane of distributions without a general frame?

"The paradigm of the contemporary is that of the collage as defined by Max Ernst. . . . Ernst said that collage is 'the meeting of two distant realities on a plane foreign to them both.'"[8] What limits Ernst's view is that there is no longer a (transcendental) plane on which distant realities can meet. That plane is now just another splinter that "meets" others on a plane of multiplicities, a plane that is also a splinter: it is a question of the encounter between planes without a plane of encounter. There is simply no longer a plane on which distinct realities are inscribed. There is simply no nihil. Collage, actuality as collage—and this is the question with which to bid farewell to the question concerning critique—is the encounter of realities that are far from each other, that are, at the same time, far from themselves and that, dislocated from self-sameness and from themselves, thus find themselves—that is, are distributed without a surface of encounter.

The notion of *actuality*, of *opening*, does not refer to a beyond (*meta*) or substrate (*upokeimenon*) behind (*adela*) the elements or to a general mediation whose unlimited welcoming of the mapped multiplicity contains it (*katekhon*). Actuality does not transcend its elements at all. Without being ruled by any one in particular, it unfolds according to *in situ disturbances and disorder* (*taraxias*).

The monster created by Mary Shelley's Frankenstein may serve as a diagram here. Its body is not anterior to the pieces from which it is made, nor is it an *a posteriori* synthesis. Frankenstein's monster is disseminated in the multiplicity of polychronic grafts that activate it. Its desire for family, totality, and representation is part of this dissemination, of this flesh that, in each of its fragments, unworks the totality as well as the totality of the fragment. Such multiplicity should not be understood as a multiplicity composed of pieces coming from original bodies but rather a multiplicity whose fragments came from bodies conceived, like Frankenstein's monster itself, as *collage*, in which *citation* or *translation* are its primordial scene: "an extraordinary montage of heterogeneous times making anachronisms,"[9] polychronisms, assemblages in which each element defers its self-sameness in a simultaneous, reciprocal, and variable double and triple link with the providing assemblage that makes it, the displacement of the voyage, the assemblage of the new settlement—infected already with the multiple differ-ences of time without being located in any one. Citation, *collage*, belongs to the regime of *immanence* that puts into question the supposed solidity and identity of being as a substantive presence.

- How does montage differ from a conventional epistemological construc-tion? What authorizes Benjamin to vindicate [for example] "the constructiv-ist principle" of montage, rejecting the "construction of history," comparing them with the "military orders that torment and confine life to the bar-racks"? What montage constructs is intercut, [vacillating] *movement*, the complex sequence of the polyrhythmic time found in each object.[10]

Movement is never a present; it never *is*. It occurs and only occurs as immanence and vacillation.

The plane of *actuality*, the opening, is not a present, not even a time. It constitutes a polychronic constellation of heterochronisms in which any present becomes untimely: a mosaic, a kaleidoscope of deferred times, reciprocally out of joint and obsolescent. Like constellations, which cannot be thought as being before, after, or even simultaneous with the particles or stars that make them, actuality *does not precede, does not succeed nor preside over*[11] the archives that populate it, and is constituted within the plethora of times (far from each other as well as from themselves) that coincide activating archives, opening up passages, clearings, and that disaggregate—all without a center, fragments ar-ranged according to a set of accelerations that, on clashing or brushing against each other, juxtaposing and crossing its archives, interrupt each other so as to produce times that are quicker than presence, absence, or synthesis, exceed-ing all resolved orders of representation and testimony. In each case, actuality appears in the plots, the crossings, and interruptions of chronotopes, always exceeding their particular dialectics. Its horizon of phenomena—diverse and dispersed in type and technology—is polymorphous, polyamorphous, and (dis) continuous. Actuality is characterized by its eclecticism, a vacillation of the limit. Its multiplicity modulated *in situ* according to strict protocols, none of which is elevated to general mediation or permanent principle that regulates its folds in movement.

What we have said about the *mosaic of actuality* must be repeated of each and every interface: They do not constitute synthetic unities centered on the technology of a presence-to-itself but finite figures of indefinite spectrality, het-erolinear folds lacking a stable design. They are rather *seismic*, following uneven heterogeneous directions, according to variations in speed, drift, and direction.

The accumulation of singular operating *dispositifs* sets a multilateral (un)veri-similar actuality in place as folds in which the fragments and their relation with each other become undecidably obsolescent and/or useful among themselves.

As we have suggested, it is not a matter of actuality that is conceived as a general site but as a multiplicity that projects itself from each interface or monad as singular and a place where thinking and acting have become convergent, immanent activities with regard to each other. From this cumulus of apparatuses—and their activation of undefined "nows" without present—actuality can be remapped as a distribution that, amid the clashes of materials and fibers, flashes with lightning.

For this reason, we do not know, cannot know, what actuality is. We rather know what it *is not*, that it happens or becomes, and that we can only know it categorially, that is nihilistically: the categories with which we nihilize their multiplicity inside generalizing statements constitute further singularities through which multiplicity traces its performance. What we say or what we write—the interrogative lyric posed in questions such as "What is its nature?," "How are we disposed in its regard?," "What can we expect from the continuation of such an arrangement?"—joins its chorus, the power (*potencia*) of cooperation without a center, without organization into a *transcompossibility*.

This is an actuality without a mode, which reveals that every present is untimely, "like the library of San Marco convent, that place of anachronism par excellence: thoughts [inks, grafisms] of all ages—nineteen centuries at least, from Plato to Saint Antoninus—gathered on the same shelves"[12] (where the shelf is a fold, one more book of time). We could not name this *plane of coexistence* in a way that does not belong to this plane as an *intertwining of its fibers within an essential impurity*.[13] Naming, whatever it may be, is immanent to the vestiges and belongs to the scrambled nontranscendentalizing remains.

The *doctrine of the eternal return* proposes the idea of an infinite time and space in which a limited number of elements are combined. Once these combinations, which will always cover one part of the infinite, are complete, they will repeat endlessly.[14] Such repetition transforms the unrepeatable singular into a kind of serial module of infinite iterability, a photograph or protohistorical industrial design.[15] The doctrine's understanding of time and space as homogeneous portmanteau continents[16] able to contain infinitely revolving finite elements, once more repeats the categorial nihil of a general time (of containment). But if we understand time, space, *actuality* no longer as a portmanteau or a continent, not as a general form in which multiplicity is included as in a *physical sack*,[17] but as the distribution in each case of multiple singularities and the tensions between them, then space, time, *actuality* will no longer be shared continents but will become in each and every case singular and fragmentary. If temporality is in each case distributed *in situ*, in "the ruffle on a dress, for example,"[18] then it will be conjugated according to its materials and the weave of its fibers—the technologies of each case. Universal transcendent time will become a montage of anachronisms that are immanent to the fiber of things, its interruptions—so that experience no longer depends on the thread of spirit or absolute time (Didi-Huberman) but on the frayed wicks of related images in which multiplicity unfolds. It is no longer in the name of the eternal presence of the idea or the universal but of surviving singulars that the latter become immanent to the distribution of the fragmentary. It is no longer the universal that realizes itself in the singular but the singular that, without totality or universality, fabricates an *understanding* that is proportionate to the extension to which it is applied according to the measure of its elemental distributions and conjunctions.

Actuality is not presented by circumscribing elements within a general mediation so as to capture its predictability inside a frame. Rather, it is presented according to the singularity of every fragment in its becoming *in situ*, avoiding general principles of articulation that block the testimony of its materials in the clashes of time, avoiding at the same time sinking into a heterogeneous *continuum*—and, thus, in blocking the *continuum*, encouraging the multiple testimonies. Objects considered in their singularity according to their details and gradations constitute constellations of anachronisms and testifications that unfold their performative content, which only the violence of genre might reduce to representations or a testimony. How then might critique or crisis work here? What might critique here mean?

CRITIQUE AS THE UNWORKING OF THEATER

In "The Author as Producer," Benjamin sets out the demand, the *artistic* or *political coefficient*, that Brecht made of *author-actors*, of critics, not only to feed with their performance the contracts, distributions, and territories that, in each case, make their circulation possible through fascination, but also to interrupt the inertia of such fascination as far as it is possible.[1] To nourish these illusions *in situ* without such interruption represents "a highly disputable activity"[2]—even more so if the materials, vignettes, and moods enhancing this fascination present themselves as revolutionary in nature.

In memorable pages from his essays, letters, and memorabilia,[3] Poe suggested writing a poem conceived as an absolute commodity, "defining beforehand the points of sensibility upon which the poem most surely must act"[4] so as to absolutely fascinate. To cast a spell, fascination, is what any commodity tautologically seeks—rather than to awaken or to establish a distance. The author, the director, the actor, and the modern poet would surely wish to exercise the power of reverie in which the spectators in the salon embody their hopes "in order to satisfy them passionately."[5] It is this fascination that repels Brecht. What he seeks is total disillusion, the degree zero of fascination, constructing a clairvoyant spectator who sees herself as well as the theater (which preconditions their seeing without seeing, to see blindly in a determined way). "The spectacle of those fascinated people who listen but do not hear, who stare but see nothing, sleepwalkers immersed together in a dream that stirs them, deprived of judgement, bewitched and fundamentally insensible"[6]—it is this catastrophe of everyday understanding, of the self-complacent state of a nearly fossilized thought, that Brecht wants to interrupt through a pedagogy of *awakening*. In the preamble to The *Exception and the Rule*, he writes:

Examine carefully the behavior of these people;
Find it surprising though not unusual
Inexplicable though normal. . . .
Consider even the most insignificant, seemingly simple
Action with distrust. Ask yourselves whether it is necessary
Especially if it is usual. We ask you expressly to discover
That what happens all the time is not natural.
For to say that something is natural
In such times of confusion
Of ordained disorder, of systematic arbitrariness
Of inhuman humanity is to
Regard it as unchangeable.[7]

As in Plato's "Allegory of the Cave," for Brecht it is a question of liberating the spectators, unfettering their heads and changing the direction of their gaze (*orthótes*), destroying the immediate, prereflexive relation that is established in the theater between actors and spectators, who are stuck to one another like the hypnotist and hypnotized: *an abject contiguity that silently reiterates real rela-tions*, as happens in passionate sentimental relationships, in which passivity is at its blindest. Brecht will concentrate his efforts in creating a gap between the different elements that make up the theater, between the author and the story, the acting and the event, the actor and the character, but above all—its major gap—between the actor and the audience, between the two halves of the theater. In the critical language of the day, Brecht called this the alienation and distancing effects (*verfremdungseffek*).[8]

The task of the author, the director, and actor, of the curator, of the writer in any field consists of activating a performance that at the same time as it feeds the technologies and contracts that constitute it beforehand and that make it pos-sible, also interrupts these technologies and contracts as far as possible by way of themselves. Critical performance may be structurally defined as an unwork-ing of the fascination and spell—an unworking of the hypnosis that the habits induced by the contracts and technologies that make the work possible and that the work automatically includes: an unworking that should not establish or stabi-lize new contracts and technologies—new naturalizations or fascinations, spells, illusions, commodities—that refound the theater.

Like the unworking of the theater in the theater, the performance of critique must also activate itself, in each case, in any zone in which polytechnics are at play, by making the prevailing contracts, distributions, and habits visible, through them in the closest of proximities, as it unravels, within them, generating in and with them an awakening that is internal to the pregiven distributions, partitions, contracts, and technologies, their tactility, without founding limits or topologies.

In Benjamin's view, epic theater "proceeds by fits and starts, in a manner comparable to the images on a film strip. Its basic form is that of the forceful impact on one another of separate, sharply distinct situations in the play. . . . As a result, intervals occur which tend to destroy illusion,"[9] interrupting the repre-sentation, letting in clearings and perspectives that allow for what *should not be seen* so that what is seen may be seen. This montage of clashes is what Brecht calls *estrangement or distancing*. To estrange and to distance involves showing the situation of seeing, seeing that one "is seeing," seeing that such "seeing" and what is "seen" is the effect of a set of habit-forming technologies that dominate and naturalize the image, the sign as a homogeneous representation. *Estrange-ment* disarticulates habit, breaking down its support and machinery as well as its preconstructed intentionality. It defamiliarizes the spectator with the famil-iarity in which they slumber, "familiarizing" it with its familiarity as it distances it—showing it also to be the effect of a montage. Distancing reveals the lacunary character of every representation, opening up its disjunctions and hyperbola, making the fetish *uncanny*, what Freud called *unhomely* (*unheimlich*) and Benjamin *dialectics at a standstill*. The evidential or *primary illusion* is revealed to be a fetish by *secondary evidence*, the evidence of the evidence that unworks the self-evident. The secondary evidence is not, however, "the truth" of the first, nor a truth at all but the opening of a virtuality, thanks to which the enchanting power of the *natural state* is broken down: a broken-down power that now must simultaneously work upon the opening of virtuality as the virtuality of this virtuality.

"In each sign sleeps that monster: a stereotype," writes Roland Barthes,[10] dualisms, dichotomies, binary divisions: masculine/feminine, singular/plural, nominal/verbal, particular/universal.[11] Politically, a language, continues Barthes, "a speech-system is defined less by what it permits us to say than by what it compels us to say. . . . Language—the performance of a language system—is neither reactionary nor progressive; it is quite simply fascist, for fascism does not prevent speech, it compels speech. . . . If we call freedom not only the capacity to escape power but also and especially the capacity to subjugate no one, then freedom can only exist outside language. Unfortunately, human language has no exterior: there is no exit. We can get out of it only at the price of the impossible: by mystical singularity, as described by Kierkegaard when he defines Abraham's sacrifice . . . or again by the Nietzschean 'yes to life[,]' . . . a kind of exultant shock administered to the servility of speech. . . . But for us, who are neither knights of faith nor supermen, the only remaining alternative is . . . to cheat speech."[12] This trick—which allows for listening to language in language, power in power, spatializing it, making it stutter in a nonfounding exception(ality)—is what may be called critique. Barthes calls it literature, as *the splendor of a permanent revolution* whose power stages language instead of just using it, speaking of interdiction while working within it[13]—that is, as in Benjamin's suggestion, feeding while interrupting it.[14] Proust had already experienced this when the writer, on creating a new language *amid* a given language, eroded the density of the grammatical and syntactical contracts, unworking the dense layer of intentionality that banalizes it, making it crackle once more. "When another language is created within language, it is language in its entirety that tends toward an 'asyntactic,' 'agrammatical' limit, or that communicates within its own outside."[15] This limit is not simply outside of language—just like history is not outside of the present and is "made up of visions and auditions that are not of language, but which language alone makes possible." Such visions and auditions constitute *erosions* that critique, as an excess, traces as it slips away.

30

DESTRUCTION

It is in "One-Way Street" and the *Arcades Project,* understood as performances rather than discourses, as well as in other of Benjamin's crucial essays on destruction[1] that we can find a diagram of critical performance, of Benjaminian destruction,[2] and that, far from all transcendental conditionality, stresses *in situ* singularity, the *in each and every case.*

It is in the performance of the *installation,* of *montage*—in their performative coimplication and rigorous weave of their fibers, technologies, temporal strata, each in tension with the others—but above all in the coimplication of each of their limits and excesses, a coimplication that relaunches interruptions and destabilizations, the unworking of one fragment by another, disturbing their homogeneity, their totality, and their position in topical turbulence and the systematic desistence from identity and what is considered proper (to one)[3] where specific contracts, juridical dialectics, aesthetics, polytechnic interfaces that are distributed, shared, and arranged as a priori material—not of a theater in general but in each case of a singular *there* without general frame—must be *awakened* and thereby put into a *minor* or *pure crisis.*[4] It is in this performative tactility that releases virtualities *in situ* where the tensions between technological strata of performance will destroy the installations, distributions, and terminologies that, in each case, are arranged as blockages and specific apparatuses of mediation, work, containment, and capitalization. Destructive performance is nothing outside of the specific case of the installation in question. In this sense, its singular (ir)relevancies are undecidable outside of its occurrence. This is because its affirmation decides nothing, in each instance opening up "clearings," "disjunctions," "pathways," "awakenings," "instances of legibility," "making space" from its world-less *there,* filtering, "uncovering," making for the "death of intention," disrupting "all understanding" as well as what "lasts" or is "fixed." Destructive montage "oscillates weakly," "does not bow" or found, sustaining the vacillation, the melancholy performance of indecision[5] that, "in the figure of its vacillating immobility, in the slight imperceptible tremor, lives."[6]

The apocalypse speaks: but haven't we always been part of a performance without totality or frame, always inside an installation, a heap of elements in tension, whose disposition as interrupted dialectic orders nothing? That is, are we not part of an actuality that brings together and juxtaposes anachronisms and modes of production, within an immanent, flowing multiplicity—of a kaleidoscope without present, in which strata and modes of production *extract and retract* and are (un)sociable, (un)working, (non)simultaneous, (non)successive blocks of singularity? Have we not always been in the moment of the *final judgment* or at the end of judgment, in *justice*, in Benjamin's sense, that without coinciding with any fragment, any judgment, any intentionality, any position, any *epokhé*, or interruption, excludes none? Because if it is the case that no one fragment is justice or the figure of justice (which is, in its turn, itself a fragment within this figure), then none is bereft of justice, of its figure, which is active not according to the logics of containment, prohibition, foundation, or stabilization, of totality or synthesis—although vacillating with it in the performance of interruption, of the *citation à la ordre du jour*, of awakening, of translation. What did critique mean here, in justice *without a there*, or a general framework or theater? What might critical performance be in an unworked plane of actuality that is composed of multiple anachronisms?

If, as has been suggested, *lumpen* refers to the "lumperical" that always proliferates as a "remainder," as unsubsumable virtuality within the clash of heterochronic *modes of production*, then the *pure lumpen*,[7] the *lumperical*, might figure as the name of that virtuality, for that moment of legibility that, immanent to the clash of modes of production, belongs to none but rather erodes away *between* them all.

31

SOVEREIGN EXCEPTION, DESTRUCTIVE EXCEPTION

As noted above, Benjamin's "Theses on the Philosophy of History" refers to a regime of sovereign representation as "the 'state of emergency' in which we live . . . [that] is the rule."[1] By this, he means that the paradigm of sovereignty is constituted teleologically from exception, as the means toward an end: the foundation and conservation of representational regimes.[2] And in this sense, as a *commissary-sovereign state of exception*, it is functional to a policing critique and a politics whose prerogative is to put the regimes of representation into

crisis—to suspend so as to conserve, found, or refound them. This is a prerogative that subsumes the *destructive character* of the exception within a dialectical
concentration of the rule, making of the spectrality of destruction (the hyperbole of the *evil genius*) a function of the system of representation, of its trace
as progress.[3]

For Benjamin, the "'state of emergency' . . . [as] rule" is equivalent to "progress . . . as a historical norm."[4] The synthetic assembly of exception and progress, the dialectic between violence and progress, violence and foundation,
violence and representation, constitutes for Benjamin the "storm" of modern
sovereignty, the "catastrophe [of history] which keeps piling wreckage upon
wreckage,"[5] a catastrophe made into a *philosophy of history*, a philosophy of
progress and rationalist theodicy that legitimizes each infamy as a necessary
stage in the unfolding of freedom[6] but, most of all, as it is transformed into everyday life, a *natural state* and document of culture.

In the *philosophy of history*—which, like every philosophy of progress, is a
philosophy of victory[7]—what we are presented with first, writes Hegel in passages from both *The Philosophy of History* and *Elements of the Philosophy of
Right*, is "a vast picture of changes and transactions . . . [in which] we behold
human action and suffering [as] predominant. . . . Actions of men proceed from
their needs, their passions, their character and talents. . . . The miseries that
have overwhelmed the noblest of nations and polities, and the finest examples
of private virtue . . . [form] a picture of most fearful aspect. . . . The slaughter-
bench at which the happiness of peoples, the wisdom of States, and the virtue of
individuals have been victimized" in a way that "forms a picture of [a] most fearful aspect, and excites emotions of the profoundest and most hopeless sadness,
counterbalanced by no consolatory result."[8] It is not easy to discover the positive
aspect carried inside pain in the "course of history" because "it may be the case
that the individual is treated unjustly. This does not, however, concern universal
history at all, which individuals serve as the means for its progression. . . . To find
the bad in all places is the maximum sign of superficiality[,] . . . the illusion that
history is a mad and senseless chain of events,"[9] and thus obliterating the finality
that governs them: the "course of universal history," the "realization of Spirit,"
of "the State" and "of Freedom" is the philosophy of history's principle concern.
States, peoples, and individuals are the unconscious instruments and means of a
transition to a higher "stage" that is prepared for by spirit through them. "Justice
and virtue, wrongdoing, violence (*Gewalt*), and vice, talents and their expression in deeds, the small passions and the great, guilt and innocence, the splendor of individual and national life, independence, fortune and misfortune of

states and individuals—all of these have their determinate significance and value in the sphere of conscious actuality, in which judgement and justice—albeit imperfect justice—are meted out to them. World history falls outside these points of view."[10] "It is easier," writes Hegel, "to discover a deficiency . . . in Providence, than to see their real import and value. For in this merely negative fault-finding a proud position is taken—one which overlooks the object without having entered into it."[11] The Calvary of the spirit rises above the *small perspectives* that make it possible, internalizing them (*Er-Innerung*) in the final judgment of the concept, the contemplation of universal history realized under the changing spectacle of its events. "For the History of the World is nothing but the development of the Idea of Freedom. But Objective Freedom—the laws of real Freedom—demand the subjugation of the mere contingent Will. . . . Philosophy concerns itself only with the glory of the Idea mirroring itself in the History of the World. Philosophy escapes from the weary strife of passions that agitate the surface of society into the calm region of contemplation."[12] The never-univocal lacunary appearances, matted simultaneously with the partially remembered and forgotten, with the (in)voluntary memories and immemorial zones constitute variable apparitions: "opinion, endeavor, caprice," writes Hegel,[13] rudimentary glimpses in a process whose results the universal panorama of absolute recollection (knowledge)[14] will *overcome* and leave behind, reappropriating them, purged of their *small* perspectives, their shadow, their *minor* singularity, and whose terse testimony— which it remembers and knows without lacunae[15] (standing tall and victorious above the lacunary)—might be stated as follows: all was once (érase); all was (érase): *erase it all.*[16]

So that such testimony can take place, it is, in Hegel's terms, necessary to assure that the sequence that subsumes the singular is constituted in a continuum without fissures. This continuum is the negativity whose general *telos*, although its effective principle, is however not available to the lacunary. A minimal fissure interrupting—subtracting from—the continuum of negativity would allow picturing said continuum and its promise (*absolute knowledge*) as a lacuna among lacunae, the *most arrogant of all,*[17] as well as the most portentous construction without more (or less) basis than euphemism—that is, the complicit forgetting of the laborious workshop of writing: "Only by forgetting . . . [the] sum of human relations which have been poetically and rhetorically intensified, transferred and embellished . . . [do] they seem to a people to be fixed, canonical and binding . . . truths."[18] To present itself as philosophy, as history, *philosophy writes, erasing that it writes.*[19]

Toward the end of the *Phenomenology of Spirit*, absolute recollection translates the condition of possibility of mere recollections and recognitions into its condition of impossibility—placing them in an impracticable situation.[20] Absolute recollection as unconditioned sarcophagus contains singularity, but absolute recollection is essentially purged of itself within the univocity of the concept. Through its own performance, mediation imposes its good offices to subsume singularity within the system, dispossessing it of its inorganic bagginess, evacuating its occurrence in the name of a finality that transcends it—a system that, like a death mask, "positively" universalizes (nihilizes) the singular event blocking the work of the negative. Absolute recollection is only possible within the calcification of singular archives,[21] which it contains in a monumentalism that is more akin to a cenotaph than to the arch of triumph,[22] or to the arch of triumph as cenotaph.

Each element or perspective that is touched by the process is enrolled as a primary resource. This is because they entirely depend on the task that they have been assigned, without any sense of finality—the arch of triumph, the greatest of constructions, of domes (everyday life, peace, promotion)—but cleansed of singularity, of the *primitive accumulation* of the absolute cathedral in which they are to be universalized. With no more guarantee than its own movement, spirit as primary life only affirms its own immunity. It arrogates to itself both the right and the control over everything it undertakes, be it unmeasurable, large or small, refusing to be intimidated by however difficult the task. No passion or value is too large for it. The abundant paranoid talent that it possesses justifies convincingly anything (the means to an end): it institutes as freedom what happens as barbarism, as justice, a long line of crimes, and as a self-satisfied everyday life, the agonies of war and plunder. Prohibited all retreat, it must convince whatever it confronts—it dies if not victorious. The pain of history is the clamor that accompanies its continuous growth. No one can survive it so as to bear witness, for only it bears witness to and for them. The witness only emerges for the first time in its testimony: they are born disappearing into the result. Since the "truth" of the beginning is only revealed at the end, the beginning and its development take place posthumously, when they have stopped happening—or, they have already done so, before happening, because only what already exists has attained existence.

- "It can be said of the teleological activity that in it the end is the beginning, the consequent the ground, the effect the cause, that it is a becoming of what has become, that in it only what already exists comes into existence, and so forth." Therefore, violence . . . is nothing but the illusion of an opacity that is posited so only to then be made transparent. The realised end governs the moves of the subjective end, of the means and of the object, from the final point of the process, using them as pieces on a chessboard to carry out its own strategy to the end. Violence is nothing but the optical illusion of one who observes from a limited point of view . . . , of one who looks at the finite without understanding that the unity of the process is completely permeated by the Notion. The subject of this view from the exterior, which grasps the violence of the finite without penetrating the complete rationality into which it is inserted, is the faculty of the Understanding, which holds the finite firmly in place without grasping the vital relationship with the infinite.[23]

If the process of writing the rule is not recovered, as it happens, in the very rule that the writing produces, then how could the rule (that results) pause to consider the point of view that in the result would only exist purged of itself? Violence, the *midwife of history*, as suffered in immediate experience, writes Hegel, is an optical illusion or the incidental perspective of that which has not attained the point of view of world history. It is not violence that acts, but its ends—the *state of exception* as the rule's means, of *progress as historical norm*.[24] However criminal the acts that the immediate perspective of the *philosophy of history* proposes, they will become part of a movement that finds its meaning in its totality[25]—a meaning that internalizes the apparent barbarism of the occurrence in which God's knowledge and justice (theodicy) are involved, the undefeated advance of the concept as supreme judge of the event.[26] In *The Philosophy of History*, Hegel refers to this disquiet of history and to the way in which it uses the instincts, passions, desires, and actions of individuals to realize its universal destiny—leaving them behind like "empty shells"—as *the cunning of reason*.[27] This being the case, in the result, in the Hegelian final judgment, these shells do not only appear in its court in their nonrecoverability, in their always already lost particular occurrence, but will do so as something that has never existed—such that their loss and mourning become phantasmatic, damaged right from the start: the disappearance of what never was.

But if history is traveled on foot, as Benjamin suggests, at the event level, without climbing up into the airy heights of the concept, then the modest chronicle of everyday life would not allow itself to be dissolved into the arborescent heart of a philosophy of history or a generalizing representation. For the pedestrian, each step constitutes an inflection that opens perspectives at a variety of levels and in a number of directions simultaneously and whose occurrence does not disappear into the frame of a posthumous revelation. At the moment of presenting its pathway, the traveler will only posit broken totalities that interrupt the unitary story of a group representation. At ground level, the teleological shoots of progress are distributed—its center shattered, as in Pascal's sphere—all over, such that we are witness to the scattering of fragments scattered every-where—with totality nowhere to be found. If history is traveled on foot, with-out flying over the *vales that resound with misery*,[28] then the blind passions, the crime, and oppression—including the moments of good among them—will not appear as incidental lapses that are justified by modernizing tendencies but rather as a *collage*, which nihilizing violence reduces to progress and moderniz-ing intentionality. At the ground level, it is not clear how what is called progress can be separated from violence, nor how it can become its adversary: violence is the midwife of progress. Nothing can be done about violence if it is confronted in *the name of progress as historical norm*—and how progress might come to a halt remains similarly invisible. We never stop progressing, at least according to the military and the *mass-media* philosophy of modernization,[29] which demand an understanding of it that is not astonished by the embrace of violence and pro-gress (that is, by modernization's kiss).[30]

If, for a certain Marx, "revolutions are the locomotor of world history,"[31] then it is nevertheless important to elaborate an idea of revolution that corresponds to the "gesture made by the humanity that rides in the train to pull the break,"[32] an idea of revolution to which Benjamin alludes in terms such as *real state of emergency, awakening, pure violence,*[33] *and destruction*, among others[34] that, like these, must not be flattened into equivalents.

In the third thesis of "Theses on the Philosophy of History," Benjamin creates a tension between the chronicler's judgment day and that of Hegel's theodicy. The *final judgment* of Hegelian absolute recollection aspires to the monumen-tal fluidity of the *continuum*, while the chronicler's is expressed rather in the fragmentation of montage as a *citation à l'ordre du jour* that destroys the monu-mentality of the testimony contained within fragmentary witnessing, destroys the equalization of the unequal that revokes the lacunary moments and affects in which experience, points of view, clearings, and minor becomings—which do not become representations—are sustained, retaining the kind of primary character that brushes against the constitutional grain. It *puts an end to judg-ment*, to the *justice of God* as totality, universality, transcendence—with God as judgment and work. The chronicler's final judgment immerses itself in a justice without trial, without contention or prohibitions. No intentional aim or phrase is excluded from justice, while at the same time no phrase represents justice or destruction. The justice of the chronicler—the only thing we cannot talk about—is all that we can talk about. We only talk of or in it, without anything that we say representing justice. No act, no judgment is excluded from justice, but justice itself is not a judgment; rather, as suggested by the third thesis of "Theses on the Philosophy of History," justice is the interruption of judgment or its end, the rendezvous and citation *à l'ordre du jour* of many, endless judgments in their inter-interruption.

If "the modern concept of sovereignty amounts to a supreme executive power on the part of the Prince" to decide on the law above the law,[35] then the corresponding Benjaminian understanding of it is to make "the most important function of the prince to avert" the *state of exception* from being a *state of decision*.[36] In Benjamin's words, the prince, "who is responsible for making the decision to proclaim the state of emergency, reveals, at the first opportunity, that he is almost incapable of making a decision."[37] A *real state of emergency* is thus revealed, as sovereign without sovereignty, without decision—a prince of weak judgment whose heritage, which he hosts, wavers in the archive, no longer as a resolute archon but as just one more guest. The real prince, the real state of emergency, is not the principle of decision but of haste, a *waterfall* of indecision, which does not necessarily indicate a lack of responsibility on the prince's part, but rather that a change in the constellation of responsibility has been produced. Responsibility has now become allegorical, vacillation,[38] a weak messianic (in)decision.

This ability or power of indecision, this eclecticism or melancholy of decision, is what characterizes the real prince: destruction as the "real state of emergency," whose conatus is frozen in the moment of judgment, in the immanence of its feint without conatus, as what might be called—following Benjamin's thoughts in *The Origin of German Tragic Drama*—the "delirium of contemplation."[39] If sovereignty, as classically deployed, involved intentionality, rupture, incision, judgment, sovereign concept, here sovereignty rather adopts, in destruction, the courage of a pause, the paralysis of decision that keeps the exception without decision in suspense—a purely destructive sovereignty that neither installs nor conserves right, opening a supplementary fold between "exception and the rule," "exception and judgment" that no conatus can fulfill. The melancholizing of sovereignty by the real prince and principle (as with Hamlet)—in contrast to the Cartesian prince—suspended in the delirium of counterbalancing possibilities, does not opt for one with the intention of subsuming the others. The real prince, the real state of emergency, Hamlet, Segismundo, simultaneously opts for all in a vertiginous constellation of times (divergent, convergent, parallel, and simultaneous intentions), multiplying outcomes that become the points of departure for further bifurcations that cross, cut across, tangentially approach, ignore, greet each other, to include many possibilities. The real state of emergency reviews its infinite oscillation with the "dignity of *sosiego* (tranquility)."[40] Its tense *ataraxia* is the effect of the essentially untranquil tranquility of a sovereignty without judgment.

"In all fictions, each time a man meets diverse alternatives, he chooses one and eliminates the others; in the work of the virtually impossible-to-disentangle Ts'ui Pen, the character chooses—simultaneously—all of them." As in Benjamin's *Arcades Project*, in which decision becomes infinite, Ts'ui Pen "creates, thereby, 'several futures,' several times, which themselves proliferate and fork. . . . Ts'ui Pen . . . unlike Newton and Schopenhauer . . . did not believe in a uniform and absolute time; he believed in an infinite series of times, a growing, dizzying, web of divergent, convergent, and parallel times. That fabric of times that approach one another, fork, are snipped off, or are simply unknown for centuries, contain all possibilities."[41]

- Benjamin wrote that "everything one is thinking at a specific moment in time must at all costs be incorporated into the project then at hand," by which he did not intend to endow subjectivism with a pretension to knowledge that he did not recognize but, in every actual association of ideas, to count on a temporal thickness of images built (in the sense of montage) into one another,[42] and so to interrupt all intentionality and depth. "If there is a dream that has never left me," says Derrida, "it is of writing something in the form of a diary . . . an exhaustive chronicle. . . . How to write fast enough to keep everything that happens in my head? I have revisited some of my notebooks and diaries, but each time abandoned them, finally giving up, so that now I don't keep a diary. But it's the regret of my life, because what I would have liked to write is just that: a 'total' diary,"[43] "to put the film together suddenly, all at once, suggests Vertov, not in the sense of a gesture bespeaking superior dominance . . . but rather as the assertion of an infinite circulation of elements defined only by their power of interchange."[44]

"Criticism is not modest. . . . It is inordinate; it brings the absolute into its game. Always and at every moment it says something final, even the briefest note. . . . It [is] the last to arrive . . . [and] speaks last."[45] But this coming and going of the last word prevents its coming to a halt as a final word or judgment. For the fact that every intention may be followed by another, that every judgment may be followed by another, and another, critique prepares the death of judgment and of intention. The critic, the absolute affirmation or negation of the discussant, confirms once more the and, and, and . . . , the conjunctivitis of the rhizome of intentions—which, in all its modesty, it joins (a rhizome that itself lacks any generalizing intentionality).

Rather than the patient work of putting prejudice at a distance—the dense layer of voluntary and involuntary mediations, the heteronomies that preemplot judgment—so that once free to clearly and definitely affirm and sustain it in its self-founding decision, destruction provides a platform for the dense layer of prejudices that make up the heteroclite sediment of the "what has been," of each thing, or partial thing's (including the subject's) potential of citation and testification—with or without intentions, making a dense layer of prejudices and the involuntary that, in their citational clashes with each other or with whatever the actuality at hand, interrupt judgment so as to disseminate it and render synthesis impossible.

More than a will to secure the knowledge that method, qua *discourse on method*, made possible, destruction consists in the vindication of the rights of that heteroclite layer of testimony that suspends general intention, the sovereignty of method, the self-sameness of the work, not so as to found another kind of judgment but rather to open the way to what Benjamin calls "the final judgment" as the dissemination of "citations *à l'ordre du jour*": citations-rendezvous that in their tense constellations, crossings, assemblages, and clashes systematically interrupt judgment, suspend synthesis—the dialectic—so as to produce a *surplus* of memory that would not take place without the crossing.

Understood constructively as montage, the crossing as a nonfounding, *pure interruption*, the *real state of emergency* that is only destructive, is de-auratized of its theological content *qua* miracle, mystical ecstasy, sacred act.[46]

THE ABSOLUTE DROUGHT OF CRITIQUE

As we have noted above, in his "Theses on the Philosophy of History" (1940), Benjamin refers to modern representational or juridical sovereignty as one in which *the state of emergency in which we live is the rule*. The paradigm of modern sovereignty is constituted structurally on the basis of the *state of excep-*

tion as the *means to* an end, for the foundation and conservation of regimes of representation.

In Benjamin's earlier essay "Critique of Violence" (1921), violence is, before anything else, representational sovereignty declaring the *state of exception*, be it to found or to conserve regimes of representation. If, in this sense, one could derive a maxim from Benjamin's essay, it might say: the more the foundation, the more the representation, the more the violence, and the more the *catastrophe* insofar as it involves the becoming regular, everyday, and familiar with violence. *Absolute knowledge* and *recollection* would be, in this sense, *absolute violence*, the *absolute catastrophe*, absolute regularity—the absolute drought of critique, of destruction.

According to this maxim, all that presents itself as means for the foundation and the conservation of the founded will fall on the side of violence (the police). Precisely for this reason—and this would be the terminological vacillation into which the coherence of the text is fastened—purely destructive violence, which does not found or conserve but only interrupts regimes of representation—such violence, the Hamlet-like violence of indecision—falls outside of *sovereign violence*, as if the text were say to us: the more the destruction, the less the violence. Violence is not on the side of destruction but of right itself,[1] of regularity, security, familiarity, "peace," the promotion of productivity progress promises.

The "Critique of Violence" is not a critique that from the autonomy of the law (be it natural or positive) is exercised with respect to all those violent attempts against it. The critique of violence is a critique of sovereign right itself, a critique of the violent opening initiation in which it consists—a critique of the violence of which the subject, judgment, and sovereign power are made. And if "the critical exercise is considered to have judgment as its condition of possibility, then the critique of violence as the critique of judgment will inevitably also be a critique of critique,"[2] but not a critique of critique and crisis and nothing more, "in general," but rather a critique of a critique that has been reduced to sovereignty's framework, the framework of judgment.[3]

The sense in which *representation* and *violence* embrace in Benjamin's "Critique of Violence"—just like destruction and nonviolence—also makes itself evident in his fragments about the concept of history. Violence here is, mainly, the dialectic that puts *exception* to work for the triumphal cortege of representation, establishing a *continuum* between violation and progress. The *state of exception as rule* is, for Benjamin, the equivalent of *progress as a historical norm*, of progress as historical violence. The synthetic ensemble of *exception* and rule decants violence into progress, the *document of barbarism*, the *horror* of sovereign exception, into heritage or the cultural booty of the victors. The catastrophe toward which the *angel* turns is not only the *pile of debris that grows skyward* but also the dialectical transmutation of this debris into progress and representation. That dialectic is the *storm* that the angel of history looks at, astonished, as it witnesses the barbarism that is contained in the arch of triumph's testimony, the arch of triumph that makes up the everyday.

33

SOREL: SOVEREIGN CRITIQUE

In his *Reflections on Violence* (1908), Georges Sorel presents himself not just as a thinker of violence but as a violent thinker. That he may be a violent thinker does not, however, obviously lead to the conclusion that in *Reflections* he produces an apology for violence,[1] for war,[2] for the *proletarian general strike*[3] as undifferentiated within a single revolutionary conatus that would destroy the relations of property and expropriation of the historical scene in which his text unfolds. Nor does it underline Sorel's well-known evangelization of the violent strike, upheld as the *illegitimate means of pursuing just ends*, nor his intention to confront *legitimate but unjust regulation*: the means of an employer's domination become general law, which the state embodies and the police defend. Sorel is a violent thinker not because he adheres to the different kinds of *de facto* violence that the workers' strike poses against *de jure* violence but because the technology through which his *Reflections* think feeds the violence that it aspires to interrupt—thus joining it. This technology may be schematized as follows: *just ends might be attained through illegitimate means.* Sorel repeats the schema *to break the (unjust) law so as to install a (just) law, to cancel* the law that rules so as to *sanction* the law that would rule, *to suspend the way of the world so as to found a world in another* way.[4] In this way, he equates the justice and violence that depose the law by replacing it as it has been duly transformed. Sorel is a violent thinker when he considers justice to be something that may be uttered or articulated, that someone may promote or sanction but also appropriate and arrogate to themselves, install, and stipulate through the actions that lead to it.

Above all, Sorel is a violent thinker because his *Reflections* respond to a theological and productivist understanding of justice, of socialism as justice, as an *oeuvre*, work to be realized: "I have already called attention to the terrifying nature of the revolution as conceived by Marx and the syndicalists and I have said that it is very important that its character of absolute and irrevocable transformation should be preserved, because it contributes powerfully to giving socialism its high educational value[, which is] the profoundly serious work which is being carried on by the proletariat."[5]

With the *myth of the workers' general strike*, the *Reflections* propose an interruption of bourgeois violence without, however, considering the *performative* question as to how the technologies in which these *reflections* and this *myth* are configured and organized within bourgeois technologies of violence. The destruction of the empirical manifestations of transcendental contracts is proposed, which, nevertheless, not being thematically reflected upon in the *Reflections* themselves, remain the unsuspected given in which they are thematized. While Sorel's writing experiments with an ideological solidarity with the revolution that will destroy the sovereign frame, the technical configuration of his text functions as sovereign possibility. Sorel has satisfied revolutionary conditions only at the level of the mind and the will but has failed to consider that revolutionary possibility is only to be found in the detailed consideration of the way in which the social relations expressed in his writing—and the technologies in which the latter are deployed—are present *in* the mediations that it produces and reproduces, without interrupting (as far as this is possible) the historical context in which they are written. This is because it is not just a matter of having a progressive or revolutionary attitude toward existing relations of production, but rather of how one's critical technologies are present in said relations. And in their avant-gardist attitude and gestures, Sorel's *Reflections* are possessed by— and blindly active within—the very frame that they intend to destroy.

In itself, it is of little or no relevance for the text that Sorel is a violent thinker. It is relevant that Sorel's thought, the preunderstandings in which his notable *Reflections* unfold, constitutes one of the key international models of language in which many of the turn-of-the-century anarchist, libertarian, socialist, syndicalist, and workers' movements expressed themselves. References to his text thus function here like a mirror for a fragmentary reading of the discursive technologies that cut across a significant part of the anarchist movement.

As noted, rather than questioning the violent conditions of existence of its own scene, the *myth of the general strike* inhabits them as it reintroduces into the conceptual technologies in which it is figured, the same technologies that it wants to interrupt, above all, as it believes that "overcoming" them is equivalent to simply interrupting them. The dialectics of "overcoming," as anticapitalist as it may be, is the reflux of capital in epic-revolutionary key: a slogan, a successful commodity. In the most triumphal of cases, this key produces a simple inversion of the relations of domination—its positions—while conserving their structure. Reflecting *on violence* is a technical matter, not a militant epic or knight's charge. And Sorel's *Reflections* are epic-like, which is why they think of violence in the way that violence thinks of them. The event of *pantoporos*—that "all paths are open"—which the *myth of the general strike* supposedly activates and in which it is consumed as an event, rather than producing a suspension of the historical violence into which it erupts, feeds it, thus crowning the *factum* that "all paths are closed"—especially by way of the fetish of "overcoming" (that is, the fetish of the opening and closing of paths along which Western sovereign violence moves): that functionary of *aporos*.

When Sorel expressly declares that the *workers' general strike* does not aspire to found political constitutions, or parliaments, or new hierarchies, parties, or tribunes, or rights of man,[6] and when he stresses that it should not be confused with the moderately socialist *general political strike* (for which the strike is a means of founding the dictatorship of the proletariat and installing a centralized disciplinary violence that, through organized commissars who will impose silence and decree their own lies as nature,[7] swaps the power of one privileged class for that of another), seeming thus to escape foundationalism, it is in fact appropriated by the foundationalist schema, by the aestheticism and productivism of the great work and the epic of victory. The myth of the *proletarian general strike*, preunderstood from the perspective of the technology of victory,[8] transforms revolution into a fetish of capital. The technology of violence that harnesses the *myth of the general strike* is a productivist philosophy of history—and like every productivist philosophy, it is at the same time a philosophy of the result, of the end, of the foundation of a work, of the aestheticization of politics.

Victory arrogates to itself the meaning and justification of all that it undertakes, however disproportionate, big or small. It is not frightened by the most difficult, because it is the most difficult of the difficult—its fanatically brandished *idea*. No passion or value surpasses it. The paranoid talent that it possesses in abundance convincingly justifies anything, beginning with the defeats and its own dead, which it instrumentalizes as the banners and icons of its new battles. Victory must defeat all that it confronts since retreat is prohibited from it. It dies if it stops winning: the *production of production*, said Marx; *the will of will*, said Nietzsche. Victory does not focus on singular points of view. These only find significance within it as the ash that cements its document of culture. The monument to victory is built on the erasure of the small perspectives that make it possible. Violence is the midwife of victory. From the point of view of victory, the violence that singular experience suffers constitutes an optical illusion until it has achieved the perspective of triumph. This suffering is the *cunning* of victory, the instrument of its technology, the means of the realization of its cathedrals.

"Whoever draws up a programme for the future is a reactionary."[9] "There is no process by which the future can be predicted . . . nor even one which enables us to discuss whether one hypothesis about it is better than another. . . . The greatest men have committed prodigious errors in thus desiring to make predictions about even the least distant futures."[10]

Strikes do not admit of either futurologies or utopianism. But Sorel is interested in the performative forces that such representations can unleash. Utopias are

> the framing of the future in some indeterminate time. . . . When it is done in a certain way, [it can] be very effective. . . . [It entails] myths, in which are found all the strongest inclinations of a people, of a party or of a class, inclinations which recur to the mind with the insistence of instincts in all the circumstances of life, and which give an aspect of complete reality to the hopes of immediate action upon which the reform of the will is founded. . . . Christian thought profited so greatly from the apocalyptic myth. . . . The hopes that Luther and Calvin had formed of the religious exaltation of Europe were by no means realized. . . . Must we for that reason deny the immense result that came from their dreams of Christian renovation? We can readily admit that the real developments of the [French] Revolution did not in any way resemble the enchanting pictures which created the enthusiasm of its first adherents; but without those pictures would the Revolution have been victorious? The myth was heavily mixed up with utopias.[11]

And if for Sorel utopianism constituted the "opium of the people," then that opium has a performative effectivity that was independent from its figurative predications. Rather than on account of their contents, utopias and myths "must be judged as a means of acting on the present,"[12] for their historical effectiveness. Christianity amassed its planetary capital with the rituals, metaphorizations, and slogans of nothingness.

Utopianism is not to be found in Sorel, but foundationalism is: the instrumentalization of the performative force of myth in the outbreak of the revolutionary general strike as an instrument of socialism. He understands the general

strike as one sole act that, within the present, breaks with it, inaugurating another. The instant of

> the transition from one world to the other . . . of the men ["enslaved producers,"
> in the Spanish-language version—Trans.] of today into the free producers of tomor-
> row working in workshops where there are no masters. . . .[13] More than one social-
> ist writer . . . cannot arrive at an understanding of such *anarchist madness*; they ask
> themselves what might come after the general strike: all that will be possible is a soci-
> ety organized according to the plan of production itself, that is, a socialist society. . . .
> Those who support the general strike aspire to the disappearance of everything that
> had concerned the old liberals. . . . Has not socialism insisted that it wanted to create a
> society that is entirely new?[14]

In the first instance, Sorel would seem to understand the general strike in a
monadological register: "The general strike is indeed . . . the myth in which socialism is wholly comprised."[15] Rather than substantive, this myth seems to be of
a spectral order, being composed of quotations from many myths: those of "the
general strike of the syndicalists and Marx's catastrophic revolution," "myths . . .
constructed by primitive Christianity, by the Reformation, by the [French] Revolution, and by the followers of Mazzini."[16] Each myth that makes up the *myth of
the general strike* appeals to a multitude of images that evoke all of the revolutions and strikes throughout history, opening itself up to an expressive fragmen-
tariness that resists being reduced to one phrase or ideology. As in the monad,
in the Sorelian myth we find testimony to the ways in which revolutions and
strikes throughout history have unfolded, the resonances and rumors of revolt
in society itself (or of societies both near and far in space and time).

In this way, myth appears in Sorel as a patchwork whose fragments do not
compose a finished whole but rather a totality that is multiplied according to
the ways in which it is predicated in each case from the perspective of each fragment: "Appeal must be made to collections of images which, taken together and
through intuition alone, before any considered analyses are made, are capable of
evoking the mass of sentiments which correspond to the different manifestations
of the war undertaken by socialism against modern society."[17]

Thus, there does not seem to be a unique source or unity to the *myth of the
general strike*, its form adopting the irregular *maniera* (style) of its elements.
Nor would the latter constitute simple substantive units that a meticulous decomposition might discover. Each element is also a monad. It thus also (cor)re-
sponds to singularity rather than to identity; like demons and phantasms, it is

plural and a-centric. And its predicates lack any focal point that is not virtual: "Only the shadows are actualized. . . . Myths are anonymous."[18]

But Sorel turns such citational dissemination, heterochronism, atopic temporality, the becoming of predicates in each element of the myth, and instrumentalizes it in function of an agglutinating principle that is instantly captured. The

> body of images capable of evoking instinctively all the sentiments which correspond to the different manifestations . . . engendered in the proletariat the noblest, the deepest and the most moving sentiments that they possess. . . . The general strike groups them all in a coordinated picture and, by bringing them together, gives to each one of them its maximum intensity. . . . It colours with an intense life all the details of the composition presented to consciousness. . . .[19] We do not obtain an intuition of reality, that is, an intellectual sympathy with the most intimate part of it, unless we have won its confidence by a long fellowship with its superficial manifestations. . . . So immense a mass of facts must be accumulated and fused together that in this fusion all the preconceived and premature ideas which observers may unwittingly have put into their observations will be certain to neutralize each other. Only in this way can the bare materiality of the known facts be exposed to view. . . .[20] Their reason, their hopes and their ways of looking at particular facts seem to make [in myth] but one indivisible unity. . . .[21] The general strike must be considered as an undivided whole [that thus admits of no analysis]. . . . There is always a danger of losing something of this understanding if an attempt is made to split up this whole into parts. . . .[22] They should be taken as a whole, as historical forces, and . . . we should be especially careful not to make any comparison between the outcomes and the pictures people have formed for themselves before the action. . . .[23] The perfection of this method of representation would vanish in a moment if any attempt were made to resolve the general strike into a sum of historical details.[24]

But more than a synthetic representational unity, it is a question of the unity of a conatus as one gesture or performative intuition that "we obtain . . . as a whole . . . instantaneously."[25] The unity of the myth is not something that propositional language can express in clear and distinct terms: "It must be taken as an undivided whole and the passage from capitalism to socialism conceived as a catastrophe whose development defies description."[26] It is rather an unpronounceable that performatively interrupts with clarity: "It does not in the least prevent us picturing the proletarian movement in a way that is exact, complete and striking, and this may be achieved by the aid of that powerful construction which the proletarian mind has conceived in the course of social conflicts and which is called the general strike,"[27] one act or present alone that destroys as it founds.

Rather than opening itself up to citation and testification, to heterochronicity and the coexistence of times, the *myth of the general strike* subsumes its citations to the technology of the instant, understood as a performative present that destroys the blocking of pathways, leaving open the paths to another present— as the work of the outbreak itself. Rather than expressing itself in dispersion, anachronistic testification is instrumentalized in function of one conatus alone. For Sorel, spectral, contemplative, fragmentary, purely destructive, melancholic dispersion is intolerable. Such fragmentation is the ruin of instrumentality, the teleology into which Sorel always arranges all testimony. Instead of exposing himself in the unworking tense, indecisive, paralysis of its decentered citations and testimony, the *myth of the general strike* rushes headlong to a single action in which it synthetically presents all anachronisms. There is no indecisiveness or vacillation in the general strike—"revolutionary syndicalism . . . endeavours to leave nothing in a state of indecision"[28]—nor is it disorganized: "Marx wishes us to understand that the whole preparation of the proletariat depends solely upon the organization of a stubborn, increasing and passionate resistance to the present order of things. . . ."[29] I have already called attention to the terrifying nature of the revolution as conceived by Marx and the syndicalists and I have said that it is very important that its character of absolute and irrevocable transformation should be preserved."[30]

Every time that it presents itself as a *means toward an end*, as an instrument that founds and produces the work of socialism, the *myth of the strike* inscribes itself *in* production, *as* production. This is why, technically, Sorel's *myth of the general strike* is unable to suspend the productivist economy, the ontotheology of *poiesis*. The strike is thought of as work, as the propedeutics of a horizon of a *production without masters*. It is part of the "social war, for which the proletariat ceaselessly prepares itself in the *syndicats* [so as to] engender the elements of a new civilization suited to a people of producers. . . ."[31] The idea of the general strike, engendered by the practice of violent strikes, entails the conception of an irrevocable overthrow. There is something terrifying with this—which will appear more and more terrifying as violence takes a greater place in the mind of the proletarians. But, in undertaking a serious, formidable and sublime work, the socialists rise themselves above our frivolous society and make themselves worthy of pointing out new roads to the world."[32]

The *general strike* thus constitutes a working toward a product rather than a strike defined as *essential unoccupancy* or as an instance *radically without work (argos)*.

Sorel's general strike does not constitute that time without labor or production, an instance that is unattached from all finalities and tasks, from the time of the gift, of sacrifice, of the mystical life that Bataille suggests as "equivalents,"[33] opening onto the eternity of the stars that never belabored anyone: *star dust, divinity of the night, myriad stars* that are not subordinated to employment[34]— and in the midst of which *works and days*, the wars of production, the accumulative massacres *in a distant corner of the glittering universe*, constitute further examples of explosions of unproductive expenditure "in which the human is added to the useless games of the starry skies."[35]

Sorel's *proletarian general strike* concludes in a humanism of the production and reproduction of life, as the production of the repression of the night. It buries its head in the productive chain of labor—which the earth demands from all so that they may free themselves from its inclemency—subtracting it from the general uselessness that contains it: "Like a flea that ignores the wild running of the child it infects,"[36] the productivist general strike forgets heaven's absolute strike, "so that men may fight as bravely for slavery as for safety."[37] Under the guise of the interruption of work, Sorel's general strike works for work and for its progress. Just as negativity provides the energy for the spirit in process that is always at work—because, as Hegel might say, the labor of spirit never ceases— the founding strike provides the energy of surplus value. Insofar as it is tied to the sovereign principle of foundation, Sorel's general strike will be disposed in order to defend what it founds so as to conserve and nourish it.

34

BENJAMIN: PURE STRIKE AND CRITIQUE

According to Benjamin, Sorel has the merit of having distinguished between two essentially different kinds of strike for the first time—the *general political strike* and the *general proletarian strike*[1]—and at the same time of having differentiated between two kinds of violence: foundational violence and purely destructive violence. The *general political strike*, working according to a *means-ends* rationale, destroys by founding, it establishes the law, encourages reform, looks for improvements, *feeds* the matrix of exception as the rule in which progress as historical norm is lived—a strike that establishes as it exposes itself must protect and conserve what it founds, replenishing the apparatus of immunization. This strike is violent in its *expropriating-founding* moment, and in the moment of its *normalization* and *promotion* it remains so. In contrast, the *proletarian general strike* as, Benjamin explains, may be found in Sorel, "sets itself the sole task of destroying state power. . . . 'The basis of the existence of the ruling group, who in all their enterprising benefit from the burden borne by the public . . . announces its indifference toward material gain through conquest' [and] rejects every kind of programme . . . of law-making . . . in the determination to resume only a wholly transformed work . . . [that] as a pure means [that is, without intention or teleological ends] is non-violent."[2]

Rather than foregrounding an essential difference between the *political strike* and the *proletarian strike*—a subtle affair—I have instead suggested the identity of the matrix in which they may be related. If, in Sorel, *the proletarian general strike* is not utopian and blocks any instrumentalization as either reformism or the dictatorship of the proletariat, reproducing state violence under the imperium of other rulers, then it remains understood in a foundational key, as a strike that suspends an epoch, "overcomes" a general present to inaugurate, instantly, a socialist present or "work without masters." Sorel endows *proletarian general strike* with an "edifying destruction" a "founding," "establishing," "intentional," "progressive" character. In doing so, he in essence moves close to the idea of a *political general strike* while essentially distancing himself from what Benjamin thinks under the name of *pure strike* and *pure violence* as the interruption of the violence of the *means-ends* schema.

Far from Sorel's *proletarian strike*, Benjamin's *pure strike* (or *pure violence*) does not privilege or negate temporal vectors, does not impugn a "now" to affirm an after, and does not jump from one homogeneous present to another. It rather suspends them all affirmatively, opening up their mosaic, persevering in the clashes of many, in their zone of reciprocal interruption, as a *moment of awakening*. This *awakening* remains hesitant, tense, within the clashing of vectors: without alienating itself in any, and without remaining outside of the many, nor least of all locate itself in a space that transcends them all. *Awakening* is not located or established; it stutters, oscillates, far from each one but crossed, infected by some, destabilizing the terms of their homogeneity, their identity and intentionality. This tense coimplication of elements, each infected by the others, but most of all the complication of each of their borders with and by the others, breaks down identities, domains, contracts, juridical dialectics, the stenciling and containing mechanisms that are sustained by the intentionality of regulating, founding violence. The Benjaminian *pure strike* is not constituted as the simple passage from one world to another, nor as simple nonpassage—nor as the straightforward jump from slave labor to a work without masters—from an economy of production to the essential inoccupation of stardust. The pure strike makes a place for the vectors in their uneasy constellation, challenging their one-sidedness, their fixity, the finalities of each, interrupting their order and intentionality, making their blindness evident.

Benjamin cites Sorel's proletarian strike against the grain of what we are discovering is Sorel's foundationalism:[3] quotation as a pure *anarchist* strike in the destructive *performance* of (the) "Critique of Violence," a purely destructive *performance*, which in the text figures the *pure strike* in a sense that is analogous to what is inscribed there as *pure violence* and in others as *pure language* (or *langue*),[4] or real *state of emergency*.[5] "Critique of Violence" deploys less of an enunciative, discursive, argumentative, judicative mode of violence than a performative mode of "installation" (atlas, mosaic, constellation), of the quotation of discursive positions on violence. The text arranges such positions and arguments on violence in a *literary montage* that makes them clash with one other, interrupting them, breaking down their intentionality or contention, making way for a *testimony*[6] that exceeds testimony, discourse, containment as well as each of their arguments, as if the editor-director, now just one more piece of the montage of interruptions, were to unwork the intentionality of the positions from within, infected by many but, at the same time, keeping distant from them all, neither identifying nor becoming ill because of any—and suspending any dialectic that would resolve the tension between the quoted (installed) positions into a sentence, a judgment, a discourse, a conclusive, stabilizing general story. There is *"nothing to say"* about *language, violence,* the *pure strike*, nothing to *formulate*, nothing to judge or to agree on, to contract—each time that it is the arguments, the contracts, the agreements, the judgments that they (the *language,* the *violence,* the *pure strike*) suspend. What does, however, go with these positions, arguments, intentions—if one were tempted to interrupt their gesture, their violence—is *to do them justice in the only way possible: showing them, using them,*[7] *citing them à l'ordre du jour.* This use, this *showing* or quotation that tensely arranges the clashing positions, unworking them—such a testification and montage that an utterance makes without dying, such a *performance*, and no other—is *pure violence,* the *pure strike*.

35

THE DESTRUCTION OF THEATER

In the same way in which the *metaphysics of representation* and the *metaphysics of right* name the performance of a same theater, the destruction of the *metaphysics of right* is at the same time the destruction of the *metaphysics of representation*. This *destruction* will thus involve the destruction of metaphysical theater, of Western theater, insofar as it is a metaphysics of right and of representation. Strikes and progressive, foundational revolutionary movements have happened and left the marks of both critique and crisis on such a theater, whose basic topology has already been outlined: that is, the tripartition of stage/pit/stalls, author/work/spectator, thought/speech/writing, subject/difference/object. Such strikes and movements, however, figuratively rising up against representation, have nourished the abstract principle of representation, its oppositional dialectic, the topos, dynamic and transferential economy between stage and stalls, state and people, without unworking it.

What is always involved in destruction, in the Benjaminian *pure strike*, however, is the unworking of said theater as well as of the fetish of revolution and sovereign strikes whose evangelist version of the extinction of bourgeois theater—the extinction of the state (Lenin)—has in fact constituted its ratification in the negative—that is, its disavowal.

If, as noted, both the strike and critique often located themselves in this theater at one of its poles in tension, then where might destruction locate itself? What would the place of the *pure strike* be? How does it locate itself with regard to *metaphysical theater* and with respect to traditional critique? In the theater? Outside of the theater?

Benjamin locates destruction within the theater, not in a periphery with regard to a center, and not in a center with regard to a periphery, but in the very pit that makes the theatrical topography of stage/stalls possible as well as its hierarchies and transferences, the economy and dynamics of its parts. And not by reaffirming the pit, which sustains this theater, its places, and their transferences, although not by exhausting the arrangement itself either, but rather by weakening it and by making it tremble.

Destruction is the *pure strike* of the pit and of the fetish that it sustains. In large measure, this destruction had already been happening over half a century, according to Benjamin, and can now be seen. We quoted him on this above: "The

abyss which separates the players from the audience . . . has steadily decreased
in significance. The stage is still raised, but it no longer rises from an unfathomable depth."[1]

To insist: *destruction* would not thus be the leveling of the pit and theater but
rather its "uneasing" through the "systematic" illumination of its fetish, its de-
substantivization, rather than its absolute extinguishing. It is not for nothing that
the tropology of the spark, the sparkle, the clash, the interruption, the lightning
with which Benjamin alludes to destruction also suggests a threshold, a kind of
pit, a scission or dividing line, a limit, a ray, a *flash*, an incandescent and dazzling marker, of sight and blindness, an *in between*, a blinking that is essentially
distant from itself and that cannot acquiesce within any topology or identity but
that is trembling and turbulent, an unlocalizable virtual topos.[2] (Instead of lightning, sparks, and rays, Deleuze offers us a metaphorics of streams, erosion, and
herpes, and rhizomes, cascades, foam, manes, intervals, and curves).

And what can such a thing be? How to represent to ourselves such a quasi
theater in which the pit has become both erosion and lightning? What might
such a theater be—that of the pure strike of the pit, in which its places, its categorial conventions, its fetish and its zones of intention, have ceased to work
significantly, depotentializing its effects of truth and naturalness, the illusion
of the "first" and "second degree,"[3] the hierarchies and subordinations that it
produces?

The eloquence necessary for the explanation of this (non)theater, of the pit's
"real state of emergency," is lacking. And it is lacking because, among other
things, it is this eloquence that *destruction* erodes. There is no eloquence or representation for this nontheater, for the lightning flash of the *dialectical image*.
And it is lacking because there is so much. *Destruction* will always lack representation, because representation is what (it) destroys.

It is thus necessary to insist on the materiality of theaters, the figure of their
resources, distances, and pathos, their rituals (shamanic and religious, their feast
and sacrifice, their carnival)—to insist on its juridical frameworks and the relations with which it uses them so as to maintain politics, strikes, revolution, war,
violence, terror, and life. It is necessary to insist equally on the efficiencies of
Western theater, the juridical and representational metaphysics in which life and
its movements as *mere life*—in a variety of ways—is produced and reproduced,
and to insist on the disciplinary efficiencies of the Aristotelean theater of final-
ized virtues and passions, as well as on the pathetic, predeconstructive, even
avant-gardist efficiencies of the *pestiferous theater of cruelty* (Artaud)—that, in
launching its alchemic virus not into the stalls, not onto the stage, not at the

script, but into the *pit*, unleashes a kind of generalized incontinence or general strike of the pose, of the ends of individual and social movements and passions, activating shadows that no apparatus of subjection (medical, political, ideological) is able to govern, because it is these same apparatuses that are the first to be contaminated by the *cruelty* of expanding, astringent, repulsive, vibrating, cloning[4] movements (ruled more by the shock of a *nervous system in flames, burning, crackling and moving without destination*[5] than by the habits of a disciplinary theater that is concerned with the script, story, and dénouement, its ancient inertia in whose *epokhé* the body is sustained, day by day, as *mere body* in the process of representation). And it is necessary to insist finally on the distances and pathos of the avant-garde theater as an assault by the stalls on the stage, the melodramatic politicization of the stage—or, inversely, of the fascist assault by the stage on the stalls, as the pathetic aestheticization of the stalls (the mass matrix of monstrous marches and rallies, "efforts to render politics aesthetic culminat[ing] in one thing: war,"[6] the kind of war that gives direction and meaning "for mass movements on the largest scale while respecting the traditional [the auratic conditions of the] property system,"[7] the First or Second World War, or the Cold War). It is necessary to insist—desistently—on all this.

When Benjamin undertakes the "technical—not chivalrous"[8]—analysis of the work of art, the artisanal actor, and theater in their clash with photography, the film actor, and cinema, opening up a moment of legibility or a differend between the auratic-theatrical mode of production of the political—its stage and its organicist categories—and mass industrial-photographic and cinematographic politics, the de-auratized, photo-montaged, or cinematically constructed personality of the charismatic strongman (*caudillo*) and film star, the mass-matrix of the serial form whose cathexis is so subjectively interned as to de-differentiate it from the "immense collection of commodities,"[9] the "immense accumulation of spectacles"[10] of the brothel principle, the metaphoricity, or unlimited interexchangeability of the *everything is for sale*; that is, when Benjamin undertakes the analysis of "The Work of Art in the Age of Mechanical Reproduction," "the 'great transformation' . . . toward the state of the integrated spectacle (Debord), and toward capitalist-parliamentarianism" (Badiou) or business-finance banditry (Lacoue-Labarthe) "that is driving the kingdoms of the Earth (republics and monarchies, tyrannies and democracies, federations and national states),"[11] all these events had begun to disturb the established relations "between earth, terra, territory, and terror."[12]

And just as at the height of the industrial revolution there was a demand, according to Benjamin, to "brush aside a number of outmoded concepts . . . whose uncontrolled (and at present almost uncontrollable) application would lead to a processing of data in the Fascist sense,"[13] the height of postindustrial capitalism will also devalue the system of interpretation, the axiomatics, the logic, the rhetoric, the categories, and evaluations that, it is supposed, the industrial system of understanding or representation—analogic, centralized, and centralizing—maintained, despite everything. The categories of property and locality, power's modalities of action (ideology, repression), of subordination and the determination in the last instance, of the law as the privileged site of the expression of power,[14] the concepts of sovereignty, right, nation, people, democracy, general will, "have to be abandoned, or at least, to be thought all over again"[15] or desisted from, insisting on said desistence so as to unwork dogmatic dreams—as if the demand, now, is not to invent new categories but rather to desist categorial insistence.

The paradox of sovereignty (that in the midst of *exception* embodied the proposition that there "is nothing outside of the law,"[16] nothing outside the sovereign theater and its categories), becomes readable now in the proposition that "there is no within the law because all laws are outside of the law."[17] There are no facts within the law. There are no facts outside of the law. The fetish of an essential difference, of a significant pit between questions of law and questions of fact, breaks down before the gradual legibility of the legal order as a question of fact and vice versa: "Everywhere, in Europe as well as Asia, in the industrialized as well as in Third World countries democratic or totalitarian, traditional or revolutionary power has entered into a crisis of legitimacy in which the *state of exception*, which was the hidden ground of the system, has come to light."[18] The pit, the autonomous sites that it founded and sustained through repression and containment "in . . . its psychoanalytical sense and its political sense—whether it be through the police, the military, or the economy—ends up producing, reproducing, and regenerating the very thing it seeks to disarm,"[19] de-differentiating what its theater differentiated, introducing "semantic instability, irreducible trouble spots on the border between concepts, in the very concept of the border"[20] between war and peace,[21] war and state terrorism, and war and antistate terrorism, between national and international terrorism,[22] between the law and violence, between making death and letting live,[23] making life and letting die.

These sites have become diffuse, to say the least, and because of this all the more manipulable in legitimated dogmatic ways—in each and every case—for their opportunistic use. It is not that the curtains have raised to reveal a new scenario before our very eyes. The theater has become visible, or redistributed within the *felt*,[24] without stage, without stalls, without pit, without allocated places. We thus momentarily experience its lack, the lack of places, of organicity, of hierarchies, of fetishes and clichés. We experience its lack in the same way we experience its excess.

If under the effects of theater, of the sovereign frame, mere life was fetishized as well as reduced to the peripheries—the peripheral belts, the encampments, the wired fences, the zero-income ghettos lacking the minimal capital to be included as subjects of the law and sovereignty, reduced to inclusion as targets at which sovereignty or the police take aim and shoot, grey zones against which democracy, dictatorship, and postdemocracy measure their modernization, their high and low indices of vulnerability or social cohesion according to the requirements of business investment—then, under the destruction or defetishization of the sovereign theater, it becomes evident that mere life extends throughout the *felt*: through the ghettos that the police protect, the education that disciplines, the biopolitics that lets live and the sovereignty that lets die, always far from "a dog's life," "the better, invisible part of the human," the "just life"[25]—all terms that do not name life *beyond* (or that transcends) the verisimilar that populates the *felt* but that rather constitutes the name of just another coexisting verisimilitude.

THOUGHT IS INSEPARABLE FROM A CRITIQUE

Thought, creation, "is inseparable from *a* critique,"[1] writes Deleuze, with all of the precautions that the indefinite article underlines (we shall return to this). There are, he continues, two ways of criticizing. One way stresses beliefs, knowledges, determinate principles, which may be judged false in counterposition to others that are judged to be true. This mode criticizes knowledge, beliefs, determinate principles while leaving the genre of knowledge, the genre of principle, the genre of belief, and the genre of critique untouched. True critique, he continues, would be that of the *genres* themselves.[2] But the latter returns us to the understanding of critique as a negative activity, as *critique of . . .* , presupposing an *object of critique*, a genre, on which its activity falls, negating it—and more than negating it, disavowing it upon repositing and structurally affirming it while pretending to overcome it as it moves to another place (*topos*), another genre, turning itself into the means of its *continuum*. It takes us back to the performance of critique as founding negation, to the sovereign technology of critique, of critique as a nihilistic activity.

But Deleuzian critique, as it unfolds within the constellation of *desire, life*, and *becoming*, explicitly *desists* from such an understanding. If the nihilist logic of critique is linked to negativity, overcoming, the breaking of ties and censure—guerrilla struggles *against* the obstacles that prevent the unfolding, the expression, the manifestation of certain forces, the *battles to* improve circumstances, the *desire to* prosper—then what is critical in Deleuze is never an action or reaction *against . . .* or in *support of . . .* given states of things, be they *relations of production*, structurally understood, or modes of the understanding. It does not sanction the liquidation or overcoming of a material presupposition, a point of view that *weighs on the mind of the living* and that must be overcome. It does not negate a previous form's advancing toward a new one according to reasons that are foundational, letting a previous referent burn, constituting itself as *a turning point that makes history insofar as it breaks with prehistory*.[3] It does not declare the exception or a state of siege of the old in order to install itself as foundation. It is not activated as a *departing from. . . .* It lacks a point of departure. It erodes through the middle (or by means of the middle), without anteriority (presupposition) or posterity—without establishing a beginning with which it breaks, with respect to an after that it inaugurates. It does not react or progress; it does not mourn or triumph, it does not negate or found. Like desire, becoming, and life—which in Deleuze is never *desire of . . .* , the *becoming of . . .* , the *life of . . .*[4]—critique will never be a critique *of . . . or* a "symptom" that expresses previous histories, needs, insufficiencies, saturations, excesses. It lacks referents. It does not allow itself to be regulated by antecedents or principles, and cannot be reduced to established norms of observance. In each of these cases, its *positivity* is blocked and reduced to negations, reactions, intentions, discharges. Critique happens as a *minor becoming*, as a becoming *minus* a point of departure, negativity, direction, genre, modes of action, the determination in the last or first instance. It *opens fissures in blocks of sense*, erodes shores, beds, borders, hard divisions, and significant cuts, the posed, the presupposed, and the deposed, breaking open enclosures and frames, *clearing*, and *making space*. The notion of *middle* (*growing through the middle*)—and also of *interval* and *between*—measures their potentiality, diluting the notions of *origin, beginning, ground, negativity, direction, centrality, opposition*.

Deleuze links becoming, desire, and critique to *construction, a* construction that does not found, does not build, does not work, but that does not simply defound or destroy, either, but rather, as in a montage, an installation, arranges simultaneous vacillations that coexist in multiple strata and levels of intensity.

Thought is inseparable from a critique, we said with Deleuze, considering the multiple precautions that the indefinite article brings to bear. A critique is something other than *the* critique, in the same sense in which *a* life is different from *the* life. So that life—*the* life (la vie)—reveal itself and become a substantive fact, it must have transcended the existing field or plane of immanence, the frame or mode of production of appearing and witnessing. But Deleuze's philosophy of immanence has desisted from any form of transcendence and substantivization. Because it escapes transcendence, absolute immanence is not immanent to anything else but itself.[5] Absolute immanence is not immanent *to* something, nor is it subject to predicates in the same way in which given qualities may belong to a subject. Immanence is not the subject or predicate *of* . . . , "is not immanence *to* substance; rather substance and modes are in immanence. . . . Immanence is not related to Some Thing as a unity superior to all things or to a Subject as an act that brings about a synthesis of things: it is only when immanence is no longer immanence to anything other than itself that we can speak of a plane of immanence."[6]

When a subject is considered to have fallen outside of a field of immanence and is taken as a universal or substantive principle to which immanence is attributed, or of which it is a predicate, then a denaturalization of the plane of immanence occurs, a denaturalization that doubles the plane of immanence by introducing a deformation that makes it the content of a substance, or a transcendent subject,[7] or by making it the support of predicates.

So that *critique* reveal itself, make itself visible, and become a substantive act, it must transcend the *plane of immanence*. But such transcendence does not constitute itself anywhere other than in the field of immanence. Transcendence is always a fold of immanence that is fetishized into verticality, substance, centrality. All transcendence is a fold that feeds the multiplicity of immanence, within immanence. And when *critique* understands itself nihilistically as the critique *of* . . . , as a subject that is distanced *from* a frame or object, such an understanding of critique similarly belongs to the virtuality of the immanent.

Deleuze speaks of *a critique*—philosophy is inseparable from a critique, he writes—in the same sense in which he speaks of *a life*. And just as he gave his "last" writing the title of *Pure Immanence: Essays on a Life*, it may be possible to formulate a parallel: pure immanence, a critique. Never *the* critique, but *a* critique. *A* critique is never a subject that transcends the field of immanence but a fold within it, "immanence of immanence," writes Deleuze, "absolute immanence . . . whose very activity no longer refers to a being [that is, a substance or subject] but is ceaselessly posed in a life":[8] an *impersonal critique* without subject, although singular, that erodes the plane opening up virtualities within the closely woven density of blockages and contracts.

NOTES

TRANSLATION HAS ALWAYS ALREADY BEGUN:
TRANSLATOR'S INTRODUCTION

1. See Hullot-Kentor, R., "Translator's Introduction," in Adorno, T., *Aesthetic Theory*, Bloomsbury, London, 2017, p. viii; and Benjamin, W., "The Task of the Translator," in *Illuminations*, Zohn, H. (trans.), Fontana, London, 1979, p. 71.

2. See Benjamin, W., "The Task of the Translator," p. 81; and Schleiermacher, F., "On the Different Methods of Translation" (1813), trans. by Bartscht, W., in *Theories of Translation: An Anthology of Essays from Dryden to Derrida*, Schulte, R., and Biguenet, J. (eds.), University of Chicago Press, Chicago, 1992, pp. 36–54. For secret cargo, see Benjamin, W., "Surrealism: The Last Snapshot of the European Intelligentsia," in *One-Way Street and Other Writings*, Jephcott, E., and Shorter, K. (trans.), New Left Books, London, 1979, pp. 231. See also Macherey, P., *A Theory of Literary Production*, trans. by Wall, G., Routledge, London, 2006.

3. Homi Bhabha's critique of colonial self-assurance still remains one of the most powerful in this respect. See Bhabha, H., *The Location of Culture*, Routledge, London, 1994. For the transculturation of imperial acculturation, see Kraniauskas, J., "El 'trabajo' de la transculturación: Cultivar, traducir, acumular," in *Políticas culturales: Acumulación, desarrollo y crítica cultural*, FLACSO, Mexico City, 2015, pp. 69–85.

4. This critical scene has also included many writers and critics from outside Chile, especially in the United States. These include Alberto Moreiras and Idelber Avelar (referenced in the endnotes), among others. Willy Thayer's other publications include: *La crisis no moderna de la universidad moderna (epílogo del conflicto de facultades)*, Editorial Cuarto Propio, Santiago de Chile, 1996; and *El fragmento repetido: Escritos en estado de excepción*, Ediciones Metales Pesado, Santiago de Chile, 2006. See in particular "El Golpe como consumación de la vanguardia" and "Crítica, nihilismo e interrupción: La *avanzada* después de *Márgenes e Instituciones*," Thayer's critique of the Chilean artistic avant-garde as historicized by Nelly Richard; and, among his Benjaminian essays, the important "Aura serial" (which, in retrospect, may be considered a possible precursor of *Tecnologías de la crítica*), in El fragmento repetido, pp. 15–94, 249–325. He is currently completing a book on the Chilean filmmaker Raúl Ruiz.

5. Williams, R., *Keywords: A Vocabulary of Culture and Society*, Fontana, London, 1983, pp. 85–86. For a more recent use of the term "criticism" (a criticism of Williams's vacating of the politics of its use as judgment), see North, J., *Literary Criticism: A Concise Political History*, Harvard University Press, Cambridge, 2017.

6. See in particular Thayer's account of "destruction," specifically the "Benjaminian destruction" of exception and sovereignty. "Hovering" also echoes Benjamin's own splendid image of the "constellation of awakening" for critique—as mentioned in an account of surrealism that seeks "the dissolution of 'mythology' into the space of history." See Benjamin, W., "Konvolut N [On the Theory of Knowledge, Theory of Progress]," in *The Arcades Project*, trans. by Eiland, H., and McLaughlin, K., Belknap Press, Cambridge, 1999, p. 458. Thayer deploys the image of "awakening" especially in Fragments 25 and 34, below.

7. As modeled on Deleuze's notion of "a life," rather than just "life" as such (which is where Thayer—against Georg Lukács—begins his account in his first fragment, below, titled "Critique and Life"). See Deleuze, G., *Pure Immanence: Essays on a Life*, trans. by Boyman, A., Zone Books, New York, 2001.

8. This is in addition to my own decision to provide fuller references—specifically, to provide the page numbers of works quoted, paraphrased, or otherwise referred to in the endnotes (although not so for references made in the main text). Arguably, this may make the present version a more "academic" one, in contrast to the more essayistic aspects of the Spanish-language publication (my hope, however, is that—following Adorno's reflection on the essay as form—such additions might add to this quality, the text's own poetic of "hovering montage"). See Adorno, T., "The Essay as Form," in *Notes to Literature*, vol. 1, trans. by Weber Nicholsen, S., Columbia University Press, New York, 1991, pp. 3–23.

9. For the Derrida quotation, see "The 'World' of the Enlightenment to Come (Exception, Calculation, and Sovereignty)," in *Rogues: Two Essays on Reason*, trans. by Brault, P.-A., and Naas, M., Stanford University Press, Stanford, 2005, p. 142.

10. Although not—and this is important—in its baroque form. See Thayer, W., "Aura serial," pp. 255–256—the segment titled "Singularidad barroca" ("Baroque Singularity").

11. Sorel rather "looms" and decides militantly. See Laclau, E., "Articulation and the Limits of Metaphor," in *The Rhetorical Foundations of Society*, Verso, London, 2014, pp. 53–78. Interestingly, in these new versions, a brief criticism of Derrida's own critique of Benjamin's account of Sorel—and its own supposed violence—is edited out.

12. In the process of production of this English-language version of Thayer's text, another change has been made to further stall its flow-effect: the continuous sequence of endnotes (from 1 to 389) is here reconfigured such that it rather recommences at 1 at the beginning of each and every fragment, thus further slowing down the toboggan ride. In addition, as a result of copyright issues, the following reproductions have not been included in this version of the text: the illustration of developments in the

painting of Manet and Mondrian, Malevich's *Black Square*, and a pictorial illustration of historical developments of the spinning Jenny.

1. CRITIQUE AND LIFE

1. Here we consider that, in general, signatures are far from homogeneous. Their singularity responds to a constellation of positions that are neither uniform nor centered. In each case, to do them justice is to obey the heteroclite dictate of such positions in the peculiarity of their gradation, to be absorbed into the detail of their testimony, registering moments that are diverse and dispersed, unsystematic, and nonunifiable into a homogeneous whole, and doing so without, however, reducing the constellation of the signature to the position that the citation particularly adopts. In this sense, we do not do justice to the signatures we cite. We rather bring them to bear according to the interests of the writing that hosts and intentionally arranges them in a new setting, accosting the semantic virtuality that the latter refer to in the enclaves of their provenance. They thus appear more or less apocryphal, more or less closed in the transposition that recreates them. This injustice is more fatal than intentional. If a passage, a work, a signature—things which we only believe in as singularities and constellations—is the future of its reading (Borges), the becoming of its citation and rewriting (and never, therefore, the progress of its identity in a journey of conquest), then there is no way in which to do justice to citations except by using them, in each case, in the knowledge that every version that takes itself as "proper" (beginning with the hypothetically "original" one) is made to suffer, destroying the supposed identity or self-sameness of its point of departure, *making appear that which, in the intentionality of the original, had not been written, as if with invisible ink* (see Benjamin, W., Konvolut N11.3, in *The Arcades Project*, trans. by Eiland, H., and McLaughlin, K., Belknap Press, Cambridge, 1999, p. 476)—like a *book of sand* (Borges). Citations, writes Benjamin, "are like wayside robbers who leap out armed and relieve the stroller of his conviction" (Benjamin, W., "One-Way Street," in *One-Way Street and Other Writings*, New Left Books, Jephcott, E., and Shorter, K. [trans.], London, 1979, p. 95). They host the other in the same. Nevertheless, it is not a question of making Saturnine incursions with regard to the citation, as in the judgment of commissars, but of attending to the frictions and crossings immanent to the material mediations of their performance.

2. Pure affirmation and pure becoming are never the affirmation or becoming *of* something, nor the passing of something from one state to another. Pure becoming without being, in its own moment, does not occur in a present either, in a specific place (*topos*) in time that jumps into another present. To conceive it as such would be to return it to a vulgar understanding of time as a succession of points in space. Becoming is not succession but rather the coexistence of planes and, in this sense, montage. (We will return to this.)

3. See Fragment 4n20.

4. See Lukács, G., *The Destruction of Reason*, trans. by Palmer, P., Merlin Press, London, 1980.

5. Lukács, G., *Destruction*, especially the chapter "Vitalism (*Lebensphilosophie*) in Imperialist Germany," pp. 403–582.

6. For Lukács, the horizon of the *philosophy of life*'s influence extended beyond that of a specific school or current of thought such as neo-Kantianism or phenomenology, infiltrating nearly all other schools; the social sciences; psychology; sociology; historiography; the history of art, the bourgeois literature concerned with the state of the world; as well as influencing the most well-known: for example, the influence of Nietzsche on writers, the repercussion of Dilthey on Weineger, of Simmel on Rathenau, and of both on Stefan Georg's school of poetry after the First World War, of Bergson in France, of James and pragmatism in the Anglo-Saxon world. The social mission of Nietzsche's philosophy, according to Lukács—whom we are paraphrasing here—consists in *saving* a kind of bourgeois intellectual for whom any serious conflict with the bourgeoisie was unnecessary, accentuating the agreeable feeling of being a true rebel by counterposing to a superficial and purely external social revolution another deeper one, a cosmic, vital, biological revolution directed against socialism, endowing the fear that, egoistically, the elites feel concerning the loss of their privileges with both a pathetic as well as an aggressive dimension. In *The Destruction of Reason*, Lukács proposes "to trace in its main phases the development . . . ultimately leading, in its consequences, to 'Nationalist Socialist philosophy.' Of course, the line we are tracing does not mean that German fascism drew its ideas from this source exclusively; quite the contrary. . . . But for a 'philosophy' with so little foundation or coherence, so profoundly unscientific and coarsely dilettantish to become prevalent, what was needed were a specific philosophical mood, a disintegration of confidence in understanding and reason . . . and credulity towards irrationalism, myth and mysticism. And vitalism created just this philosophical mood. . . . The key to all these difficulties, it was thought, could be located in the concept of 'life,' especially if this was identified, as always in vitalism, with 'experience.' Experience, with intuition as its organon and the irrational as its 'natural' object. . . . The appeal to the richness of life and experience, as opposed to the barren poverty of the understanding, permitted philosophy to counter the materialist inferences from social and scientific developments in the name of a natural science, biology. . . . But as we shall see, vitalism's relationship to biology was very loose, metaphysical rather than concrete, and never a philosophical assessment of concrete problems of biological science. . . . It would be absurd to regard Dilthey or Simmel as writing forerunners of fascism. . . . Here, however, we are concerned not with a psychological analysis of intentions, but with the objective dialectics of the development itself. And in the objective sense, every thinker whom we have discussed contributed to the creation of the aforesaid mood in philosophy." (Lukács, G., *Destruction*, pp. 416, 412, 417).

7. Karmy, R., *Políticas de la excarnación: Para una genealogía teológica de la biopolítica*, Editorial Universitaria UNIPE, Buenos Aires, 2014, p. 15.

8. Furthermore, what might a life free from all closures, institutions, contracts, particular distributions *be*, a life outside of all frames, forms, or technologies? Would not such a life in general constitute just one more of the many comprehensive technologies of life, one more of life's virtualities, and one that extends itself vulgarly as if it were life itself, life as such, substantive, free of mediations, of categories or the crossing of categories, or of frames of understanding? Life itself, in itself, as such, would at any rate be the status that any technology of life that behaves incautiously with respect to its own closure or condition might acquire. Any plausible technology of life constitutes (and is constituted in) a regime of truth that essentializes, universalizes, or naturalizes itself, in the same measure that it forgets itself as a particular regime, as a system of limits and conditions, and projects itself imperially as without condition. All regimes or technologies of life will affirm their universal and natural character as they forget their genealogy, their originary accumulation—and, for the most part, they *will* forget.

9. To paraphrase Horace as cited by Freud: "*Vita furca expellas, tamen usque recurret*" (the original refers to *Naturam*—Nature—rather than *Vita*—Life). See Freud, S., "Delusions and Dreams in Jensen's *Gradiva*," in *Writings on Art and Literature*, Stanford University Press, Stanford, 1997, p. 30. "Painting is full of images of God. My question is: is it sufficient to say that this is an inevitable constraint in this era? . . . The philosopher and philosophy don't escape either. . . . Could we not make up another hypothesis, namely that painting in this era has so much need of God that the divine, far from being a constraint for the painter, is the site of his maximum emancipation? . . . God is directly invested by painting, by a kind of flow of painting, and at this level painting will find a kind of freedom for itself that it would never have found otherwise. At the limit, the most pious painter and the one who does painting and who, in a certain way, is the most impious, are not opposed to each other. [For example, the paintings of] el Greco . . . could only be achieved on the basis of Christian figures. Then it's true that, at a certain level, constraints acted on them, and at another level the artist is the one who Bergson said this about the living thing (vivant), he said that the living thing is what turns obstacles into means. This would be a good definition of the artist. . . . Forms are unleashed. They embark upon a kind of Sabbath, a very pure dance, the lines and colors lose all necessity to be verisimilar, to be exact, to resemble something. It's the great enfranchisement of lines and colors which is done thanks to the outward show: the subordination of painting to the demands of Christianity." (*Lectures by Gilles Deleuze: On Spinoza*, http://deleuzelectures.blogspot .co.uk/2007/02/on-spinoza.html, accessed June 13, 2012). "Life becomes resistance to power when power takes life as its object. . . . The two operations belong to the same horizon." (Deleuze, G., *Foucault*, trans. by Hand, S., University of Minnesota Press, Minneapolis, 1990, p. 92). "Where there is power, there is resistance. . . . These points of resistance are present everywhere in the power network. . . . They are the odd term in relations of power, they are inscribed in the latter as an irreducible opposite. . . . The forces that resisted relied for support on the very thing it invested,

that is, on life and man as a living being. . . . Life as a political object was in a sense
taken at face value and turned back against the system that was bent on controlling
it." (Foucault, M., *The Will to Knowledge: The History of Sexuality, Volume 1*, trans. by
Hurley, R., Penguin Books, London, 1990, p. 95–96, 144–145). It is as if the agency of
potentiation and of life were at the same time the patient of mortification and blockage, the agent of mortification and blockage, the patient of life and potentiation, both
arranged as the threshold of a spectral indistinction. Agamben, who also quotes some
of the above passages from Deleuze and Foucault (see Agamben, G., "Absolute Immanence," in *Potentialities: Collected Essays in Philosophy*, trans. by Heller-Roazen, D.,
Stanford University Press, Stanford, 1999, pp. 220–239), also refers to Spinoza and
the Stoics in order to present the infinite vacillation between agent and patient.
Spinoza, in the footsteps of the Stoics, used the old Sephardic Spanish (Ladino) verb
pasearse (to take oneself for a stroll, or to take oneself for a walk—translation revised
[JK]) because in it the agent-cause of the stroll is immanent to its own patient effect
(that is, when "agent and patient are one and the same person"). Perhaps the walk
in the prison yard, or in the cell, the concerned stroll anywhere—stressful roving—is
the best expression of that undecidable, undiscernible instant between the agent and
patient of mortification and potentialization of life, the indiscernible moment that, although immanent to them, does not belong to any subject or machine at all. Spinoza
and the Stoic's *paseo* may be translated into the activity of conversation, understood
in Benjamin's sense, as going for a stroll in language. According to his essay "The
Storyteller," in conversation, in the histories that emerge among the workers in an
artisan's workshop, from within the loose threads of stories without either judgments
or ulterior motives, life affirmed its potency amid the mortification and blockages of a
labor subordinated to needs, as well as amid the pitchforks of syntax and grammar, of
saying and conversing. This is because conversation is immanent to the total institution of language (*langue*), an institution that Nietzsche, Artaud, and more recently
Blanchot, Deleuze, and others—including Barthes—denounced as a place in which
the blocking and containing regiments have their springtime. It is also because language is an iron syntax of genres and species, subjects and predicates, compliments
and copula at the very moment when it seems to let speak as if it were a smooth plain
along which you may freely stroll.

10. The expression is Benjamin's: "Then we shall clearly realize that it is our task
to bring about a real state of emergency" (*wirklichen Ausnahmezustand*). (Benjamin, W., "Theses on the Philosophy of History," in *Illuminations*, Zohn, H. (trans.),
Fontana/Collins, London, 1979, p. 259). Here Benjamin alludes to an *emergency* [or
an "*exception*," as in the Spanish-language translation—Trans.] *without sovereignty*,
to a suspension of the rule, of the law, no longer as the constitutive means through
which a sovereign juridical order conserves, founds, or refounds the law, but rather as
a nonjuridical, nonjudicative power that suspends and is unconditionally open to an
event without frame. Developments of the expression *real state of emergency* can be
found in Fragments 9, 22, 23, 24, 25, and 28 of Benjamin's own notes to "Theses on

the Philosophy of History" as edited and translated into the Spanish by Pablo Oyarzún in *La dialéctica en suspenso*, LOM ediciones, Santiago de Chile, 2009.

11. "Montage . . . was already everywhere. . . . It proceeds the filming, in the choice of material, that is, the portions of matter which are to enter into interaction. . . . It enters into the filming, in the intervals occupied by the camera-eye (the cameraman who follows, runs, enters, exits: in short, life in film). It comes after the filming, in the editing-room, where material and filming are evaluated against one another (the life of the film), and in the audience, who compare life in the film and life as it is. These are the three levels which are explicitly shown to coexist in *Man with a Movie-Camera*, but which had already inspired all his [Vertov's] previous work." (Deleuze, G., *Cinema 1: The Movement-Image*, trans. by Tomlinson, H., and Habberjam, B., Athlone Press, London, 1986, p. 40). "Death achieves a dazzling montage of our life." (Pier Paolo Pasolini, quoted in Deleuze, G., *Cinema 2: The Time-Image*, trans. by Tomlinson, H., and Galeta, R., Athlone Press, London, 1989, p. 35).

12. Deleuze, G., The Fold: Leibniz and the Baroque, trans. by Conley, T., Athlone Press, London, 1993, pp. 27–38.

13. Deleuze, G., *Fold*, pp. 30, 15, 17. The unfolding of the inflection is not its attenuation but the continuation of its act toward the limit of the frame, always exceeding it: "The fold is divided into folds, which are tucked inside and which spill onto the outside. . . . The fold affects all materials [to] become expressive matter, with different scales, speeds and different vectors." Thus, "every contour is blurred to give definition to the formal powers of the raw material, which rise up to the surface and are put forward as so many detours and supplementary folds . . . end[ing] only in watery froth or in a flowing mane," discontinuous series without depth or verticality. Their only depth is endless surface. Landscape becomes an installation with no end: clothes, body, rock; the waters, the earth, the lines; the mountains, the fabric, the living tissue, the brain—the illusion of a canvas whose horizon is never ending, towards the infinitesimal folds in each inflection of the landscape, as in "a virtuality that never stops dividing itself . . . that must go as far as indiscernability" (Deleuze, G., *Fold*, pp. 35, 34, 17, 35). As Benjamin writes, "an eddy in the stream of becoming" (Benjamin, W., *The Origin of German Tragic Drama*, trans. by Osborne, J., New Left Books, 1977, p. 45).

14. Karmy, R., *Políticas*, p. 117.

15. Nietzsche, F., *Fragmentos póstumos (1885–1889), Volumen IV*, Editorial Tecnos, Madrid, 2008, p. 297, quoted in Karmy, R., Políticas, p. 117.

2. CRITIQUE AND WORK

1. "Pygmalion, the sculptor who becomes so enamoured of his creation as to wish that it belonged no longer to art but to life." (Agamben, G., *The Man without Content*, trans. by Albert, G., Stanford University Press, Stanford, 1999, p. 2). "Life can only be rendered good, beautiful, and happy at the level of art." (Keyserling, H., *The Art of Life*, Selwyn and Blount Books, London, 1935, quoted in Michaud, E.,

The Cult of Art in Nazi Germany, Stanford University Press, Stanford, 2004, p. 1).
When discussing "the living work of art," Hegel notes that performance, the festival,
constitutes a higher art than sculpture. In the festival, "man thus puts himself in the
place of the statue as the shape that has been raised and fashioned for perfectly free
movement, just as the statue is perfectly free repose . . . and on him is bestowed, as
a reward for his strength, the decoration with which the statue was honoured, and
the honour of being, in place of the god in stone, the highest bodily representation
among his people of their essence" (Hegel, G. W. F., The *Phenomenology of Spirit*,
Oxford University Press, Oxford, 1977, p. 438). "God, the subject, disappears, because
he is no longer distinct. The other mode is the unity of God and of the world. The
incarnation among the Indians, in Greek art, belong to it, as does, in a much purer
sense, the Christian religion, in which the unity of human and divine natures is
manifest in Christ. This is an incarnation that is not exposed in an anthropomorphic
mode, unworthy of the Divine, but rather in such a way as to lead to the true idea of
God." (Hegel, G. W. F., *Lecciones sobre la filosofía de la historia universal*, trans. by
Gaos, J., Alianza Editorial, Madrid, 1999, pp. 111–112 [my translation direct from this
Spanish-language edition—Trans.]). Thus, the highest merges with the lowest, and
vice versa. The history of the (in)*carnation* in painting seems to remit to this model.
According to Vasari, sculptors believed sculpture to be the mother of the arts, not because of the number of genres that she herself contained (carving, relief, works made
of clay, of wax, of plaster and wood, metal cast, engravings of various kinds, precious
stones, painting), but because God had created human beings from a clay sculpture, or because he himself was incarnated as man (of dual nature: a ready-made of
heaven–earth). Painters would have responded in a similar vein, affirming their own
art: that before sculpture, God made a drawing (*plastikos*) of man, and that this drawing is the mother of the arts. (Vasari, G., *The Lives of the Artists*, Oxford University
Press, Oxford, 1991, pp. 3–4). The motifs of the *living work* and of *life as work* could
be multiplied: not only Adam and Eve, Pygmalion's sculpture, Wang-fô's painting, the
picture of Dorian Gray, the living doll, the Golem, Pinocchio, the Tin Man, Frankenstein's monster, Descartes's reflections on the artificial man, *tableaux vivants*, the
theater, the chorus, the happening, Adolf Appia's *L'oeuvre d'art vivant*. Vilém Flusser
defends the idea that at present the most ancient conception of art is emerging once
more—what in Latin is referred to as *ars vivendi*, the art of life or of the knowledge of
how to live. Biotechnology holds the promise that soon it will be possible to program
life at the level of those genes that transmit information that concerns life. Until now,
all arts were limited to the more or less sophisticated manipulation of inanimate,
ephemeral, entropic matter. The novelty is that, as of now, it will be possible to make
information, to imprint it into living matter, and to make this information multiply
and preserve itself *ad infinitum*, at least while its conditions are produced and reproduced. Flusser adds that shortly, it will be possible not only to mime known forms of
life but also to create "alternative" ones, with nervous systems of another kind, even
with mental processes that are unknown to us. Since it will be possible to produce

living works capable of multiplying themselves as well as to create new ones, how can we remain content with inanimate and perishable objects? Given such a consideration, adds Flusser, "it is necessary for artists to participate in biotechnology. Currently, we have at our disposal an art (*techné*) that is able not only to create new living beings, but also forms of life with mental processes (spirits) that are new. We now possess an art able to create something that is unimagined and unimaginable which the creators themselves are unable to understand since they are grounded in genetic information that does not belong to them" (Flusser, V., "Curie's Children," in *De la pantalla al arte transgénico*, La Ferla, J. (ed.), Libros del Rojas, Buenos Aires, 2002, pp. 14–15).

2. As Blanchot suggests: "The writer belongs to the work, but what belongs to him is a . . . mute collection of sterile words, the most insignificant thing in the world. The writer who experiences this void believes only that the work is unfinished, and he thinks that a little more effort, along with some propitious moments, will permit him and him alone to finish it. So he goes back to work. But what he wants to finish by himself remains interminable. . . . That the work is infinite means, for him, that the artist, though unable to finish it, can nevertheless make it the delimited site of an endless task. . . . At a certain moment, circumstances—that is, history, in the person of the publisher or in the guise of financial exigencies, social duties—pronounce the missing end, and the artist, freed by a dénouement of pure constraint, pursues the unfinished matter elsewhere. . . . This is what is meant by the observation that the writer, since he only finishes his work at the moment he dies, never knows of his work" (Blanchot, M., *The Space of Literature*, trans. by Smock, A., University of Nebraska Press, Lincoln, 1989, pp. 23, 21–22, 23). "The idea of a definitive text belongs only to either religion or weariness." (Borges, J. L., "Las versions homéricas," in *Discusión* (*Obras Completas*, vol. 1), Editorial Emecé, Buenos Aires, 2001, pp. 94–95.

3. For example, if "the lifework is preserved in this work and at the same time cancelled," in a way that is analogous to how "in the life work, the era," and "in the era, the entire course of history" (Benjamin, W., "Theses on the Philosophy of History," in *Illuminations*, Zohn, H. (trans.), Fontana/Collins, London, 1979, p. 265).

4. To become a work—an *ópera* as "organism" (see Fragment 4)—*qua* "technology" and not just a mere juxtaposition of elements, it must gather and return its materials and testimony to itself from its hyperboles, journeys, and expansions, and preserve and capitalize on itself, articulating its dispersions into an equation, incorporating the exterior that runs through it. Similarly, this presupposes an organizing principle that it must satisfy if it is to constitute itself, end and preserve itself.

5. Referring thus to the work, we would seem to be speaking of life in opposition to inanimate matter, as an autonomous organism that grows and develops in every case according to an internal program of sustainability and homeostasis with its environment, permanently gathering and returning to itself the energies, movements, and exteriorities that compose it. Life has not only been elevated as work's ideal, but the work has also been elevated as an ideal of life. "The fact that life must be a work of art, because it is mortal, is an important theme." (Foucault, M., *Dits et écrits*, vol. 4, Galli-

mard, Paris, 1994, p. 615, quoted in Castro, E., *El vocabulario de Michel Foucault: Un recorrido alfabético por sus temas, conceptos y autores*, Universidad Nacional de Quilmes, Buenos Aires, 2005, np.

6. Derrida himself sets out in detail the distance between Heideggerian *destruktion* and deconstruction: see Derrida, J., *Rogues: Two Essays on Reason*, trans. by Brault, P.-A., and Naas, M., Stanford University Press, Stanford, 2005.

7. Here we should also consider Derrida's *animots* (animal-words) and *neither alive nor dead*, Foucault's *care of the self*, Deleuze's *body without organs*, and Benjamin's *real state of emergency* or justice as life.

8. See Fragment 1n11.

9. Aristotle, "De Anima (On the Soul)," in *The Basic Works of Aristotle*, McKeon, R. (ed.), Random House, New York, 1941, 413a, pp. 556–557.

10. If this took place, if a particular regime of work, of life, were imposed, subsuming the constellation of frames within a general one, then the hypertrophy of one and the atrophy of many would take place. The tension between them would weaken, too, to become distended into the continuum of only one regime. And insofar as tension is the source of heterogeneity and virtuality, the latter would end up ceding its potentiality and possibility to homogeneity's characteristic depotentialization. If this does happen, however, homogeneity would become one more tension within the immanence of the constellation.

11. Immanent emanation.

12. There are two words in the Greek for the Spanish *arco* [which in English is captured by the words *arc*, *arch*, and *bow*, for example, into which it may be translated—Trans.]: *toxos* and *biós*. The term *bíos* (life) is echoed—homophonically, in the Greek—in *biós* (arc[h/bow]). The phonic difference between *bíos* (life) and *biós* (arc[h]/bow) lies only in the accent. The sentence of Heraclitus to which we refer—"*tói oún tóxoi ónoma bíos, érgon dè thánatos*" (Freeman, K., *Ancilla to the Pre-Socratic Philosophers: A Complete Translation of the Fragments in Diels, Fragmente der Vorsokratiker*, Basil Blackwell, Oxford, 1971, Fragment 48)—does not, as can be seen, use the term *biós* (arc[h]/bow) for the term "arc[h]" but the term *toxos* (arc[h]). *Biós* is, in the Greek, implicit in *toxos* as both synonym (*toxos/biós*) and as the homophony between the terms *biós* (life) and *bíos* (life) as if it stated: "*The bow (biós) is called life (bíos), but its work is death.*" See Freeman, K., *Ancilla to the Pre-Socratic Philosophers*, p. 28.

13. "I do set my bow in the cloud, and it shall be for a token of a covenant between me and the earth." (Genesis 9:13).

14. Chantraine, P., *Dictionnaire étimologique de la langue Grecque: Histoire des mots*, Éditions Klincksieck, Paris, 1968, p. 402.

15. "Rather than just searching for life as a concept, we must look at analyses of movement. It is here that one finds the true thought of life." (López Petit, S., *El infinito y la nada*, Editorial Bellaterra, Barcelona, 2004, p. 17). We find movement—

before its "concept"—in the figure itself, in *bíos/biós* and in zoe. See Chantraine, P., *Dictionnaire étimologique*, p. 402.

3. THE *KRÍNO* CONSTELLATION

1. For example (without any particular order and with no pretension to exhaustivity): exegesis, anathema and excommunication, sacrilege, censorship, treason, the strike, revolution, ecstasy, destruction, deconstruction, irony, estrangement, reduction (*epokhé*), invective, reprobation, reparation and reproach, objection, rupture, analysis, evaluation, discrimination, commentary, reading, explication, opinion, condemnation, negation, and contestation.

2. Aristotle, "Politics," in *The Basic Works of Aristotle*, McKeon, R. (ed.), Random House, New York, 1941, 1253a, p. 1129.

3. See Koselleck, R., *Critique and Crisis: Enlightenment and the Pathogenesis of Modern Society*, MIT Press, Cambridge, 1988, pp. 30–31; and Koselleck, R., "Crisis," *Journal of the History of Ideas*, vol. 67, no. 2, April 2006, pp. 357–400.

4. Koselleck, R., *Critique and Crisis*, p. 127 and passim.

5. Pavis, P., *Dictionary of the Theatre: Terms, Concepts, and Analysis*, University of Toronto Press, Toronto, 1998, p. 83.

6. Blanquez Fraile, A., *Diccionario latino español*, Editorial Sopena, Barcelona, 1968, pp. 632, 213.

7. Koselleck's *Critique and Crisis* is the classic reference here, as is his essay "Crisis." See also the first chapter of Starobinski, J., *La relation critique*, Editions Gallimard (e-book), Paris, 2013, loc. 30–2604, which discusses the reception in France of both *krinein* and *cerno*.

4. TECHNOLOGIES OF CRITIQUE

1. Lalande, A., *Vocabulaire technique et critique de la philosophie, vol. 2 (N–Z)*, Editions Quadrige/Presses Universitaires de France, Paris, 1997, pp. 1031–1032.

2. Agamben, G., *The Man without Content*, trans. by Albert, G., Stanford University Press, Stanford, 1999, pp. 94–97.

3. Benjamin, W., "The Work of Art in the Age of Mechanical Reproduction," in *Illuminations*, Zohn, H. (trans.), Fontana/Collins, London, 1979, p. 224.

4. "The construction of its stories should clearly be like that in a drama; they should be based on a single action, one that is a complete whole in itself, with a beginning, middle, and end, so as to enable the work to produce its own proper pleasure with all the organic unity of a living creature. . . . We have laid it down that a tragedy is an imitation of an action that is complete in itself, as a whole of some magnitude. . . . Now a whole is that which has beginning, middle, and end. . . . A well-constructed Plot, therefore, cannot either begin or end at any point one likes. . . . To be beautiful, a living creature, and every whole made up of parts, must not only present a certain order in its arrangement of parts, but also be of a certain definite magnitude. Beauty is a mat-

ter of size and order." (Aristotle, "Poetics," in *The Basic Works of Aristotle*, McKeon, R. (ed.), Random House, New York, 1941, 1459a17–21, p. 1480, 1450b23–37, p. 1462).

5. By way of the theater in the sixteenth and seventeenth centuries (for example, through Chapelain, la Mesnardière, and D'Aubignac), the rule of the three unities becomes doctrine. This concerns the unity of action, the unity of place, and the unity of time amid the scattering of places, times, and actions in which the work unfolds. Boileau articulated the most celebrated definition of this doctrine along the following lines: *that in one place, on one day, over one event, the theater remains full to the end*. The average spectator who is preunderstood in the notions of organicity and unity would not tolerate two or three hours of scattered and unconnected actions, places, and times in which narrative continuum and unity, the (organic) life of the work, as well as its own are shattered. The paradox is that to preserve the unity of the work and the concentration that ensues, an editing technology is required that is far from everyday causality. The unity of the work is not acquired by obeying "real facts" but by way of a technical framework of rules and conventions. What is impossible is to ground unity in the mechanical facts of everyday life, which absolutely lacks any unity. The classical order demands an editing that is free of jumps in language, in time, in space, in genre, without excessive hyperbaton. And this order is broken when the narrator, which every spectator is, is assaulted by the disconnect of these elements. This unity is broken in the nineteenth century, with Büchner. From then, no kind of unity could hide the multiplicity of elements. Pirandello, Brecht, and Becket pulverize the fetish of unity. This does not mean, however, that unity absolutely ceases to hold. It continues, no longer as a general mediator but rather as a mediation among mediations, a technology among technologies. See Pavis, P., *Dictionary of the Theatre: Terms, Concepts, and Analysis*, University of Toronto Press, Toronto, 1998, pp. 273–274.

6. "Socrates: But surely you will admit at least this much: Every speech must be put together like a living creature, with a body of its own; it must be neither without head nor without legs; and it must take a middle and extremities that are fitting both to one another and to the whole work." (Plato, *Phaedrus*, trans. by Nehamas, A., and Woodruff, P., Hackett e-publishing, Indianapolis, 1995, 264c, p. 61).

7. "Our subject being Poetry, I propose to speak not only of the art in general but also of its species and their respective capacities; of the structure of the plot required for a good poem; of the number and nature of the constituent parts of a poem; and likewise of any other matters in the same line of inquiry. Let us follow the natural order and begin with the primary facts." (Aristotle, "Poetics," 1447a7–12, p. 1455).

8. "For the painter will not allow the figure to have a foot which, however beautiful, is not in proportion, nor will the ship-builder allow the stern or any other part of the vessel to be unduly large, any more than the chorus-master will allow anyone who sings louder or better than the rest to sing in the choir. . . . A city which produces numerous artisans and comparatively few soldiers cannot be great, for a great city is

not to be confounded with a populous one. . . . To the size of states there is a limit, as there is to other things, plants, animals, implements; for none of these retains their natural power when they are too large or too small, but they either wholly lose their nature, or are spoiled. . . . Further, the state is by nature prior to the family and to the individual, since the whole is by necessity prior to the part; for example, if the whole body be destroyed, there will be no foot or hand, except in an equivocal sense, as we might speak of a stone hand; for when destroyed the hand will be no better than that. But things are defined by their working and power; and we ought not to say they are the same when they no longer have their proper quality, but only that they have the same name. The proof that the state is a creation of nature and prior to the individual is that the individual, when isolated, is not self-sufficing, and therefore he is like a part in relation to the whole. But he who is unable to live in society, or has no need because he is sufficient for himself, must be either a beast or a god. . . . The state is a creation of nature, and that man is by nature a political ["social" in the Spanish version—Trans.] animal. And he who by nature and not by mere accident is without a state is either a bad man or above humanity; he is like the 'tribeless, lawless, heartless one' whom Homer denounces. . . . For, inasmuch as every family is a part of the state, and these relationships are the parts of a family, and the virtue of the part must have regard to the virtue of the whole." (Aristotle, "Politics," in *The Basic Works of Aristotle*, McKeon, R. (ed.), Random House, New York, 1941, 1284b7–13, pp. 1196–1197, 1326a22–40, p. 1283, 1253a19–29, pp. 1129–1130, 1253a1–6, p. 1129, 1260b13–15, p. 1145).

9. "A nose which varies from the ideal of greatness to a hook or a snub may still be of good shape and agreeable to the eye, but if the excess be very great, all symmetry is lost, and the nose at least ceases to be a nose at all on account of some excess in one direction or defect in the other, and this is true of every other part of the human body. The same law of proportion equally holds in states." (Aristotle, "Politics," 1309b23–31, p. 1250).

10. "The various qualities of men are clearly the reason why there are various kinds of states ["city" in the Spanish version—Trans.]. . . . As in other departments of science, so in politics, the compound should always be resolved into the simple elements or least parts of the whole. We must therefore look at the elements of which the state is composed in order that we may see in what the different kinds of rule differ from one another, and whether any scientific result can be attained about each one of them. . . . We must see also how many things are indispensable to the existence of a state, for what we call parts of a state will be found among the indispensable. Let us then enumerate the functions of a state, and we shall easily elicit what we want: first, there must be food; secondly, arts, for life requires many instruments; thirdly, there must be arms, for the members of a community have need of them, and in their own hands, too, in order to maintain authority both against disobedient subjects and against external assailants; fourthly, there must be a certain amount of revenue, both

for internal needs, and for the purpose of war; fifthly, or rather first, there must be a care of religion, which is commonly called worship; sixthly, and most necessary of all, there must be a power of deciding what is for the public interest and what is just in men's dealing with one another. These are the services which every state may be said to need. For a state is not a mere aggregate of persons, but a union of them sufficing for the purposes of life; and if any of these things be wanting, it is as we maintain impossible that the community can be absolutely self-sufficing." (Aristotle, "Politics," 1328a39, p. 1287, 1252a20–24, p. 1127, 1328b2–18, pp. 1287–1288).

11. "In virtue of this reasoning, when he framed the universe, he fashioned reason within soul and soul within body, to the end that the work he accomplished might be by nature as excellent and perfect as possible. This, then, is how we must say, according to the likely account, that this world came to be, by the god's providence, in very truth a living creature with soul and reason. . . . For that embraces and contains within itself all the intelligible living creatures, just as this world contains ourselves and all other creatures that have been formed as things visible. For the god, wishing to make this world most nearly like that intelligible thing which is best and in every way complete, fashioned it as a single visible living creature, containing within itself all living things whose nature is of the same order. Have we, then, been right to call it one Heaven [universo in the Spanish-language version—Trans.], or would it have been true rather to speak of many and indeed of an infinite number? One we must call it, if we are to hold that it was made according to its pattern [modelo in the Spanish-language version—Trans.]. For that which embraces all the intelligible living creatures that there are cannot be one of a pair, for then there would have to be yet another Living Creature embracing those two, and they would be parts of it, and thus our world would be more truly described as a likeness, not of them, but of that other which would embrace them. Accordingly, to the end that this world may be like the complete Living Creature in respect of its uniqueness, for that reason its maker did not make two worlds nor yet an indefinite number; but this Heaven has come to be and is and shall be hereafter one and unique." (Cornford, F., *Plato's Cosmology: The Timaeus of Plato*, Hackett, Indianapolis, 1997, 30b–31a, pp. 33–42).

12. In the Aristotelian structure, not only are members coupled to other members but different kinds of organisms are related, too. The whole universe is linked to everything through precise relations governed by an unmoved mover that moves toward its virtue. Parts and things are defined by the function for which they are arranged. This implies an idea of the universe as an adjusted structure in which, thanks to their function, parts are centered according to principles, centers, or first or final causes. The definition of each element or thing depends on the form of finality that governs it—the actuality of the whole: "We must consider also in which of two ways the nature of the universe contains the good and the highest good ["sovereign good" in the Spanish version—Trans.], whether as something separate and by itself or as the order of the parts—probably in both ways as an army does, for its good is found both

in its order and in its leader ["general" in the Spanish original—Trans.], and more in
the latter, for he does not depend on the order, but it depends on him. And all things
are ordered together somehow, but not all alike—both fishes and fowls and plants,
and the world is not such that one thing has nothing to do with another, but they are
connected. For all are ordered together to one end, but it is as in a house, where the
freemen are least at liberty to act at random, but all things or most things are already
ordained for them. . . . For this is the sort of principle that constitutes the nature of
each. . . . For it is not a hand in any and every state that is a part of man, but only
when it can work, and therefore only when it is alive; if it is not alive, it is not a part."
(Aristotle, "Metaphysica," in *The Basic Works of Aristotle*, McKeon, R. (ed.), Random
House, New York, 1941, 1075a, pp. 885–886, 1036b30, p. 801).

13. "If, ever since the Twelfth Century, *universitas* refers to the administrative
gathering of persons of the same guild rather than of knowledges and techniques, the
idea of bringing together all of the disciplines, the utopia of a complete encyclopedia
of knowledges and the wise has long been desired (see Durkheim, E., *L'evolution
pedagogique en France*, Presses Universitaires de France, Paris, 1990, p. 131). It
constituted one of the teleological principles of the university, its metanarrative of
unity and life. One might say that the university always demanded of itself that it be
a total system that should structure and arrange the diversity of languages, points of
view, inventions, discourses and codes, methods and techniques according to a single
criterion. A diversity of mobile and unstable activities, states of knowledge that the
university should organize and arrange both within and without, above and below the
scholarly institution. The university has been represented to us as a living, malleable
organism that digests, expels, impels, locates, and dislocates knowledges and tasks
dispersed in a variety of traditions, knowledges and tasks which before the consideration and verdict of the university wander loose, barbarous and pagan, in languages
and territories. The university looks to itself as a system of the heterogeneous, as a
reunion of the diverse, a version of versions or 'knowledge of knowledges' (Kant, I.,
The Conflict of the Faculties, Abaris Books, New York, 1979, p. 45)—as expressed
in the 'uni' of university. The university has looked to itself as 'God's mind' (Leibniz, G., "The Principle of Philosophy Known as Monadology," trans. by Bennett, J.,
http://www.earlymoderntexts.com, p. 8, accessed May 10, 2018), the 'absolute Idea'
(Hegel, G. W. F., The *Phenomenology of Spirit*, Oxford University Press, Oxford,
1977, p. 479), 'capital' (see Marx, K., *Capital*, vol. 1, Penguin Books, Harmondsworth,
1976). When a crisis in the university is referred to, what is meant is a crisis in its life,
its soul, of its functional unity. What is actually in crisis would be the organic unity of
knowledge, a unity that Husserl had intended to re-establish (Husserl, E., *The Crisis
of European Sciences and Transcendental Phenomenology*, Northwestern University
Press, Evanston, 1970, p. 3). What is mainly declared to be broken is the inquiry into
the unity, of its principle, of the foundation itself. Actual knowledge would thus be
dispersed. This does not mean that, when articulated, different specialisms have no

contact with each other and are self-enclosed atomistically without doors or windows, lacking all preestablished harmony that guarantees their communicability. Dispersal would rather suggest that the organic ideal of the systematic unity of knowledges in a functional totality was no longer programmatically accomplished: one life, one soul. Nor was the reflexive principle that, refusing to embed itself in any one discipline, included them all in a questioning of a 'knowledge of knowledges.' The unity of the university can no longer be thought as such. A unitary knowledge which, open to events, might gather and guide the university whilst submerged in their midst is no longer possible—a knowledge that, furthermore, would provide it with an autonomous path through contingency. In turn, the fracture of the programmatic principle of reunion given in the name 'university,' that breakup of the university as a uni-version of possible worlds, constitutes at the same time the crisis of its systematic-disciplinary organization. Under the authority of a variety of stories and renowned signatures modernity conjugated the eagerness to divide up and classify the real with the will to systematize everything within one single account (ratio)—such as, to paraphrase Descartes: 'the light of the sun illuminates all objects from the same clarity' (see Descartes, R., "Règles pour la direction de l'esprit," in *Oeuvres et lettres,* Bridoux, A. (ed.), NRF, Bibliothèque de la Pléiade, Paris, 1963). The character of the actual crisis lies in the impossibility of a 'new,' more modern and progressive 'organic' replacement. In this sense, the actual crisis should be referred to as a 'crisis' of organic crisis as it had been occurring until now. Now more than ever, however, in a context forcefully shaped by digital telematics, diversity appears gathered within the luminous flow of a virtual nomenclature. The eagerness to gather and archive what exists thoroughly will be accomplished digitally, which seems to be emerging as the technological culmination of the teleological encyclopedic project of the modern university: the university as informatics, as the electronic re-union of diversity. But what does 'reunion' mean here? What kind of unity is given in the indefinite flow of electricity? It might be that the electrical logic of the information market, which compels all objects and subjects to present themselves in communicational mode, multiplies perspectives concerning the real, giving the word (and not the power) to a growing number of cultures and aspects that, not having been historical actors, now are—which would gradually dissolve points of view that are centred and totalizing in a way that reverses what Adorno, Horkheimer and McLuhan (the latter, more optimistically) foresaw with regarding the globalizing effects of the explosion/implosion of the *mass media* industries. Presented as 'subjects'—if this were the case—many dialects and subcultures which had been passively presented as objects of university representations, studies and pedagogy, would break open the representational unity of the world, disseminating it to as many corners as points of view emerge. And if a metanarrative fold that transcendentally articulates the totality of active reflections of the world within a unitary world appears impossible within digital telecommunication—a meta-reader is a datum that is always given within it—it becomes itself the *de facto* support of a heteroclite scattering of things, one beside another, connected by an 'and': the 'and' as that last place, a place immanent to the meta-story." (Thayer, W., *La crisis no moderna de la universidad moderna*, Editorial Cuarto Propio, Santiago de Chile, 1996, pp. 23–39).

14. "And God, the author of Nature, was able to carry out this divine and infinitely marvelous artifice because every portion of matter is not only divisible to infinity, as the ancients realized, but is actually sub-divided without end, every part divided into smaller parts, each one of which has some motion of its own rather than having only such motion as it gets from the motion of some larger lump of which it is a part. Without this infinite dividedness it would be impossible for each portion of matter to express the whole universe. And from this we can see that there is a world of creatures—of living things and animals, entelechies and souls—in the smallest fragment of matter. Every portion of matter can be thought of as a garden full of plants or a pond full of fish. But every branch of the plant, every part of the animal (every drop of its vital fluids even) is another such garden or pond. And although the earth and air separating the plants in the garden and the water separating the fish in the pond are not themselves plants or fish, they contain other organisms, but usually ones that are too small for us to perceive them. Thus there is nothing barren, sterile, dead in the universe; nothing chaotic, nothing confused except in appearance. Here is an example of that: If you see a pond from a certain distance, you may see the swirling of the fish without being able to pick out any individual fish; it may seem to you that you are seeing confused movements of the fish, but really nothing is confused in itself—what's happening here is that you are perceiving confusedly. We can see from this that every living body has one dominant entelechy, which in an animal is its soul; but the parts of that living body are full of other living things, plants, animals, each of which also has its entelechy or dominant soul." (Leibniz, G., "The Principle of Philosophy," p. 10).

15. Liddel, H., and Scott, R., *Greek-English Lexicon* (1883), Harper and Bros., New York, 1997, p. 664.

16. See Starobinski, J., *La relation critique*, Editions Gallimard (e-book), Paris, 2013, loc. 120 [my translation—Trans.]

17. Inside the aporias concerning the *birth* of the *theatron*, there also appear the aporias of the *birth* of history. The winding path taken by Pavis's *Dictionary* is not sufficient to erode the myth of a first stage, before a second stage, which is before a third, etc. The ripples of his text sink into a founding myth and are insufficient to preserve the immanence of places. Nor are they sufficient to dissolve its progressive schematization or to arrange themselves into a montage in and from which it (once the myth of self-foundation is dissolved) may speak, without origin, of prototheatrical elements as posttheatrical ones, supposing not the *crisis of origin* but the *crisis of montage*, which, assembling positions, interrupts them, making possible a pause that is far from any of them but at the crossing of many. See Pavis, P., *Dictionary of the Theatre*, p. 387 and passim.

18. Pavis, P., *Dictionary of the Theatre*, p. 316.

19. The notion of singularity is one piece within a constellation of other pieces such as *virus* (Deleuze), *parasite* (Serres), *fossil* (Benjamin), *specter* (Derrida), *fold* (Deleuze), *ready-made* (Duchamp), *collage, patchwork, multiplicity, becoming, desire* (Deleuze and Guattari), among others—and all irreducible to each other. These are notions that allude to a plane of vacillations and turbulence that breaks down centering or transcendental functions, the general principle of composition, totality, the functions of teleology and organicity, as well as the soul and the aura of structure.

20. In contrast to structure as a community or as a functional set of organic or mechanical elements and positions that maintain significant relations with each other (biunivocal, dichotomous, multilateral)—which block their disseminating of hyperbola through recapitulation, rather than escaping through them, and that root powers of dispersion by way of functions and hierarchies that center and contain—*singularity* does not figure unities, specificities, places—be they univocal or biunivocal. It is not stabilized into totalities or functions; it *grows through the middle* in interregna of multiple dimensions that do not synthesize elements, in a potential of difference that does not *come from* nor is it *en route to*. It does not develop or evolve. It does not depart from, arrive at, or trace an itinerary. It ceaselessly interrupts recognition and erodes all origin, goal, course, or containment. Its deterritorialization (deconstruction or destruction) counters not only organic structure but also the simple decomposition and unilateral decompensation characteristic of the *agregatum*. Simple decomposition is a possibility of the structure, an inclination that feeds its dynamic and its economy.

21. Aristotle, "Physics," in *The Basic Works of Aristotle*, McKeon, R. (ed.), Random House, New York, 1941, 192a32, p. 235.

5. THE WORD "CRITIQUE"

1. Indeed, the dictionary removes words that are no longer in use. As of October 2007, the electronic version (http://www.rae.es) includes 4,618 modifications approved by the corporation between June 24, 2004, and December 13, 2006. Among these, for example, 350 exclusions and 1,331 additions are considered. The exclusion and inclusion of meanings are decided upon as follows: "Proposals . . . for removal or emendation come mainly from stable academic commissions that suggest amendments. The Institute of Lexicography documents the proposed changes with material from the following sources: (1) the Spanish Language Data Bank, which has more than 400 million records in its synchronic (the CREA—*Corpus de Referencia del Español Actual*) and diachronic (the CORDE—*Corpus Diacrónico del Español*) stores; (2) the Academy's historical file, with its more than 14 million lexical and lexico-graphical index cards; (3) the relevant monographic studies and works of reference; (4) consultation with academics and other recognized experts in the relevant fields. Once the proposals are put together, they are sent to the Plenary" (Real Academia Española, http://www.rae.es).

2. The twenty-third online edition is permanently updated, realizing the idealist-historicist dream of an isomorphic simultaneity between "living language" and the dictionary, such that the variation of the former has its own correlate on the web. One might then expect that the twenty-third edition were both the last and at the same time the first edition of a dictionary in permanent change, the same and not the same, like Heraclitus's river, symmetrically readjusting itself to the displacements in the living language.

3. I am using three editions: the eighteenth of 1956; the twenty-first of 1992–2005; and the present, online edition (http://www.rae.es), whose eyes are on the twenty-second online edition of 2005 and the work-in-progress of the twenty-third, and the first edition of 1780.

4. In 1780, the present is still that of the Inquisition, which re-posed "the question" as an *investigation of the truth*.

5. "Critique (from the Greek *kritiké*). Art of judging the goodness, truth and beauty of things; any judgment made of a work of literature or art"; "Censure of the actions or the conduct of a person; the set of opinions expressed about a matter; murmur." (*Diccionario RAE*, 1958). According to Koselleck, the expressions *critike*, *criticism*, and *critics* had become naturalized into the national languages of France and England, from the Greek and through Latin, by around 1600. Critique was understood as *the art of judgment adequate to its object*, be this an ancient text, a work of art or literature, a people, or person, according to Starobinski, in French critique, "begun by designating 'the art of judging a work of the spirit.' On the basis of implicit or explicit criteria, critique recognized beauty and disapproved of defects. It is a faculty of discernment that is exercised here. As this art was more often used to condemn defects than to praise beauty, critique was seen to be something negative and understood only as disapproval. To criticize was 'to censure, to find something to condemn.' . . . The critic was a 'censor.' . . . The erudite Jean Le Clerc defined it as 'the art of understanding the ancient authors, whether in verse or in prose, the art of discerning those of their writings that are authentic from those that are apocryphal, and also to discriminate those that conform to the rules of art and those which do not.' . . . . But," continues Starobinski, "in the succession of meanings given up until the twentieth century the main one has been that of the act of judgment" (Starobinski, J., *La relation critique*, Editions Gallimard (e-book), Paris, 2013, loc. 93–100).

6. The privileging of the understanding of *critique* as *judgment* is also present in one of the most ambitious current projects of creating a Greek–Spanish dictionary undertaken by the Department of Greco-Latin Philology of the Instituto de Filología (of the Consejo Superior de Investigación, Madrid), directed by Francisco R. Adrados and Elvira Gangutia. The first reference that this online dictionary gives for the word *kritiké* is *juicio* (judgment). In doing so, it refers primarlity to Nicosia, S., "Sul concetto di 'giudizio' (krisis) in Grecia: Un approccio linguistico," in *Il giudizio. Filosofia, teologia, diritto, estetica*, Nicosia, S., (ed.), Carocci Editori, Roma, 2000, pp. 55–68.

7. This is a figure of critique that exists in tension with another that understands it as "something constructive or reconstructive, insofar as it attends to the institution's (academic, cultural, social, political) demand for meaning" (Oyarzún, P., "Regreso y derrota: Diálogo sobre el 'gran poema,' el estar y el exilio," in *La letra volada: Ensayos sobre literatura*, Ediciones Universidad Diego Portales, Santiago de Chile, 2009, p. 241).

8. *Díke, prós díkes, ben díke, katá díken*: justly, with justice, according to justice.

9. A general question that emerges laterally is that the constellation of *diké* as judicative justice, tends discursively toward definition, reunion, conclusion, site. In contrast, the constellation of *kríno* tends to separation, to dissemination within the detail.

10. Artaud, A., "To Have Done with the Judgement of God" (1947), http:// surrealism-plays.com, accessed December 15, 2017.

11. "Critic (from the Latin *criticus*, which is from the Greek *kritikós*). (1) adj. Belonging or related to critique. (2) adj. Said of the state, moment, point, etc., in which this is produced: a critical day, a critical age, critical pressure, critical point, critical temperature. . . . (4) adj. Said of a point, of an occasion, of a time, etc., which being the most opportune should be taken notice or advantage of. (5) adj. phys. Said regarding the conditions with which a nuclear chain reaction begins. (6) Person who exercises critique. (7) Colloquial. Person who speaks well, with affectation. (8) Examination and judgment of someone or something, particularly those who expresses themselves in public about a spectacle, a book, a work of art, etc. (9) Set of public judgments concerning a work, a concert, a spectacle, etc. (10) Set of persons who, on the basis of the same specialization, exercise criticism in the broadcasting media: 'critics did not attend the comedy's premiere.' (11) Murmur. (12) Censure (disapproval)" (Real Academia Española, http://www.rae.es, accessed December 2009).

12. See Fragment 5n11.

13. Koselleck, R., "Crisis," *Journal of the History of Ideas*, vol. 67, no. 2, April 2006, p. 358.

6. MARX'S CRITICAL TURN

1. Marx, K., "A Contribution to the Critique of Hegel's Philosophy of Right: Introduction," in *Early Writings*, Penguin Books, Harmondsworth, 1977, p. 244.

2. Marx, K., and Engels, F., *The German Ideology*, ed. by Arthur, C. J., Lawrence and Wishart, London, 1977, pp. 58–59.

3. Marx, K., "Contribution to the Critique," p. 247.

4. Marx, K., "Contribution to the Critique," p. 247.

5. Marx, K., "The Eighteenth Brumaire of Louis Bonaparte," in *Surveys from Exile: Political Writings, Vol. 2*, Penguin Books, Harmondsworth, 1977, p. 146.

6. *Anachronisms* does not refer to coexistences such as those of "an ancient tradition with the most recent cinematographic, radiophonic, and theatrical techniques of montage," as suggested by Bertolt Brecht (see Didi-Huberman, G., *Quand les images prennent position: L'oeil de l'histoire, 1*, Editions Minuit, Paris, 2009, p. 61), a coexistence that presupposes strong topologies, somewhat like a *timerose* (rather than a windrose or Rose of the Winds) that fixes and substantiates an anterior with regard to a posterior. *Anachronisms* refers here to a mode of coexistence without a *timerose* that stabilizes places and directions, in which technologies are reciprocally anachronic and heterochronic with respect to each other in a context in which the assignation of anteriority and posteriority lacks a principle or center on the basis of which order may be established. In such a case, no technology is contemporary with another. Rather, each one is anachronic with regard to others insofar as the time of each technology is a predicate of its figure and not a general order of inscription or *portmanteau* (estuche). Similarly, the notion of *obsolescence* is not restricted so as to refer to technologies that have been "overcome" by others that are more modern, but amplified so as to designate the reciprocal obsolescence of technologies with respect to each other insofar as their "time"—again—is the predicate of their weave, their figure.

7. The concept of critique that characterizes Bourriaud's book *Relational Aesthetics* falls within this framework or technology. According to Bourriaud, with regard to critique, we see in Marx "the stance of the 'critical' artist, when this position consists in judging the world as if he were excluded from it . . . and played no part in it. This idealistic attitude can be contrasted with . . . Marx's idea that explains that real criticism is the criticism of reality that exists through criticism itself. For there is no mental space where the artist might exclude himself from the world he represents" (Bourriaud, N., *Relational Aesthetics*, trans. by Pleasance, S., and Woods, F., Les Presses du Reel, Dijon, 2002, p. 110).

7. CRISIS AND AVANT-GARDE

1. Marx, K., "The Eighteenth Brumaire of Louis Bonaparte," in *Surveys from Exile: Political Writings*, Vol. 2, Penguin Books, Harmondsworth, 1977.

2. Habermas, J., "Modernity versus Postmodernity," *New German Critique*, 22, Winter, 1981, p. 4.

3. Oyarzún, P., "Un fragmento sobre la crítica," in *El rabo del ojo: Ejercicios y conatos de crítica*, Ediciones Universidad ARCIS, Santiago de Chile, 2003, p. 239.

4. Hughes, R., *Nothing If Not Critical: Selected Essays of Art and Artists*, Harvill Press, Glasgow, 1991, p. 13.

5. Pérez Villalobos, C., *Primer manifiesto surrealista (1924) de Breton*, unpublished manuscript.

6. Marx, K., "A Contribution to the Critique of Hegel's Philosophy of Right: Introduction," in *Early Writings*, Penguin Books, Harmondsworth, 1977, p. 250.

7. Borges, J.L., *Borges profesor: Curso de literatura inglesa en la Universidad de Buenos Aires*, Editorial Emecé, Buenos Aires, 2000, p. 110

8. Schmitt, C., "Appropriation/Distribution/Production: Towards a Proper Formulation of Basic Questions of Any Social and Economic Order (1953)," *Telos*, March 20, 1993, pp. 52–64.

9. See Nietzsche, F., *The Will to Power*, ed. and trans. by Kaufman, W., Vintage, New York, 1968, pp. 3–4; and Nietzsche, F., *Ecce Homo: How to Become What You Are*, trans. by Large, D., Oxford University Press, Oxford, 2007, p. 3.

10. Marchant, P., *Sobre árboles y madres*, Editorial La Cebra, Buenos Aires, 2009, p. 115.

11. For example, as in the surrealist statement: "Caesar, shot with a Browning," representing all that should be avoided. "Every epoch forges its own universe mentally. . . . It does so according to its own gifts, its specific ingenuity, its qualities, its own curiosity, with all that distinguishes it from preceding epochs. . . . The problem is to establish with exactitude the precautions to be taken, the prescriptions to be observed in order to avoid the sin of all sins—the most unpardonable sin of all: the anachronism." (Febvre, L., *Le problème de l'incroyance au XVI siècle: La religion de Rabelais*, Albin Michel, Paris, 1968, pp. 12, 15, quoted in Didi-Huberman, G., *Devant le temps: Histoire de l'art et anachronisme des images*, Les Éditions de Minuit, Paris, 2000, pp. 29–30).

12. See Derrida, J., "Structure, Sign and Play in the Discourse of the Human Sciences," in *Writing and Difference*, Bass, A. (trans.), Routledge, London, 1990, p. 279.

13. See Derrida, J., *Writing and Difference*, Bass, A. (trans.), Routledge, London, 1990, pp. 279–280, 36.

14. See Mellado, J. P., "Ensayo de interpretación de la coyuntura plástica," in *Cuadernos de/para el Análisis*, 1, Centro de Documentación Artes Visuales, Santiago de Chile, 1983, p. 18.

15. See Oyarzún, P., "Arte en Chile de veinte, treinta años," in *Arte, visualidad e historia*, Editorial La Blanca Montaña, Santiago de Chile, 1999, p. 234 and passim.

16. Descartes, R., "Recherche de la vérité," in *Oeuvres*, vol. 10, Adam, C., and Tannery, P. (eds.), Léopold Cerf Editeur, Paris, 1908, p. 508.

17. Descartes, R., "Discours de la méthode," in *Oeuvres*, vol. 6, Adam, C., and Tannery, P. (eds.), Léopold Cerf Editeur, Paris, 1902, p. 11.

8. CRITICAL ATTITUDE

1. The Spanish *principio* can be translated into the English as both "beginning" and "principle," and frequently means both in Thayer's reflections on particular kinds of order. In both languages, of course, the figure of the "prince" is also evoked in this regard (as we shall see below).—Trans.

2. Foucault, M., "What Is Critique?," in *The Politics of Truth*, Semiotext(e), Los Angeles, 2007, p. 26

3. But the *Christian pastoral* introduces innovation and deviation with regard to Greco-Roman sovereignty. In contrast to Schmitt, Foucault traces a radical discontinuity between Plato and Christian pastoral power. For Foucault, the power of the pastor is not exercised in a polis as sovereignty over a territory but over a flock or multitude as it wanders. If the Greco-Roman god personifies the territorial polis, then the Jewish god accompanies its flock through territories. It is a question not of territorial sovereignty but of securing the life of individuals and the group. The shepherd "gathers, guards, and leads" its flock with an eye on the herd or pack as well as on each of the sheep. Insofar as the shepherd must ensure the salvation of each and every one, it presents itself as a "benevolent" power that foments life. It is precisely for its "benevolence" that pastoral power is considered by Foucault as an antecedent of the modern doctor who promotes the health of the individual and the population, of the individual body, and of the social body. Unlike the judge who lets die or lets live, the sovereign who decides on the antichrist, the pastor is the chief medic and public-health worker who makes life, who permanently cares for one and all in order to "improve" their lives. Seeing the affirmation of life as their main concern, it is understandable why for Foucault the pastoral is the antecedent of biopolitics, which works according to the same strategies of making life and letting die, of promoting and governing populations. Since they belong to different technologies of power, for Foucault, government and sovereignty are technical concepts that must not be confused (see Karmy, R., *Políticas de la excarnación: Para una genealogía teológica de la biopolítica*, Editorial Universitaria UNIPE, Buenos Aires, 2014, p. 19).

4. Foucault, M., "What Is Critique?," p. 27.

5. Foucault, M., "What Is Critique?," p. 28.

6. Descartes, R., "Discours de la méthode," in *Oeuvres*, vol. 6, Adam, C., and Tannery, P. (eds.), Léopold Cerf Editeur, Paris, 1902, pp. 32–33.

7. Descartes, R., "Meditations," in *Oeuvres*, vol. 9, Adam, C., and Tannery, P. (eds.), Léopold Cerf Editeur, Paris, 1904, p. 19.9.

9. SOVEREIGN CRITIQUE I

1. Common usage of the word "method" refers to a number of things: an ordered way of doing and saying; the steps that must be followed with regard to certain kinds of paperwork (*tramitación*); a way of stalking and surrounding a prey; a system of rules to obtain certain ends; a set of habits; and, in some cases, a compulsion. In all of these is echoed a philosophy of method conceived as a *knowledge of first principles* (*arkhai*) from which things may follow (but without their following any).

2. See Descartes, R., "Au P. Mesland, Leyde, 2 Mai, 1644[?]," in *Oeuvres et lettres*, Bridoux, A. (ed.), NRF, Bibliothèque de la Pléiade, Paris, 1963, p. 1167; Descartes, R., "Correspondance Avril 1622 à Février 1638," in *Oeuvres*, vol. 1, Adam, C., and Tannery, P. (eds.), Léopold Cerf Editeur, Paris, 1897, pp. 145–146. See also Descartes, R., "Correspondance mai 1647 à février 1650," in *Oeuvres*, vol. 5, Adam, C., and Tan-

nery, P. (eds.), Léopold Cerf Editeur, Paris, 1903, p. 224. This also resounds with a philosophy of rule—that is, of the prince—for whoever possesses the principles (or the "theory") will be the guide, the chief, the architect (*arkhitecton*) who "know[s] the 'why' and the cause. Hence we also think that the master-workers in each craft are more honourable and know in a truer sense and are wiser than the manual workers, because they know the causes of the things that are done" (Aristotle, "Metaphysica," in *The Basic Works of Aristotle*, McKeon, R. (ed.), Random House, New York, 1941, 981a29–981b2, p. 690).

10. HYPERBOLE

1. The Spanish pronoun *yo* ("I," in English) is also the word for "ego" in psychoanalysis.—Trans.

2. Descartes, R., "Principia philosophiae," in *Oeuvres*, vol. 8, Adam, C., and Tannery, P. (eds.), Léopold Cerf Editeur, Paris, 1905, pp. 18–19.

3. Descartes, R., "Letter of the Author," in *The Principles of Philosophy*, trans. by Veitch, J., Blackmask Online, 2002, p. 2, https://pdfs.semanticscholar.org/7220/3dc200335bebc4a7fa987ae61f3275b2f1d8.pdf, accessed March 7, 2018.

4. "To Styx and the other Fates . . . to dark forces or spirits from before." (See Descartes, R., "Correspondance Avril 1622 à Février 1638," in *Oeuvres*, vol. 1, Adam, C., and Tannery, P. (eds.), Léopold Cerf Editeur, Paris, 1897, p. 145).

5. Descartes, R., "Discours de la méthode," in *Oeuvres*, vol. 6, Adam, C., and Tannery, P. (eds.), Léopold Cerf Editeur, Paris, 1902, p. 22.

6. Descartes, R., "Recherche de la vérité," in *Oeuvres*, vol. 10, Adam, C., and Tannery, P. (eds.), Léopold Cerf Editeur, Paris, 1908, p. 508. See also Descartes, R., "Meditationes de prima philosophia," in *Oeuvres*, vol. 7, Adam, C., and Tannery, P. (eds.), Léopold Cerf Editeur, Paris, 1904, p. 17.

7. Descartes, R., "Discours de la méthode," p. 11.

8. Descartes, R., "Discours de la méthode," p. 11.

9. Descartes, R., "Recherche de la vérité," p. 508.

10. Descartes, R., "Correspondance Avril 1622 à Février 1638," p. 145–146.

11. Descartes, R., "Correspondance Avril 1622 à Février 1638," p. 152. See also Descartes, R., "Correspondance Mai 1647 à Février 1650," in *Oeuvres*, vol. 5, Adam, C., and Tannery, P. (eds.), Léopold Cerf Editeur, Paris, 1903, p. 224.

12. Descartes, R., "Correspondance Avril 1622 à Février 1638," p. 146.

13. More than a set of rules and procedures in function of determinate ends, method is a suspending machine that guarantees the sovereignty or unconditionality of the decision contained in the principles: *methodical doubt*. As the suspension of the prejudgment [*prejuicio* in the Spanish as "prejudice"—Trans.] of the judgment that guarantees the unconditionality of the principle—that is, of the decision concerning the principle—*methodical doubt*, the quintessence of method, is staged in Descartes's first meditation (in *Meditations on First Philosophy*) as an exhaus-

tive series of reductions (*epokbés*) that, in their hyperbole (evil genius), result in the suspension of the possibility of judgment (as well as its conditions) to open on to *the moment of* decision.

14. For a countersecular account of this analogy that is present throughout exceptionalism in modern philosophy from Hobbes to Kelsen, see Schmitt, C., *Political Theology*, University of Chicago Press, Chicago, 2005.

15. "'Sovereignty only rules over what it is capable of interiorizing,' or 'confining.' It is the system that "designates itself as exterior to itself." (Giorgio Agamben quoting Gilles Deleuze and Félix Guattari and Michel Foucault and Maurice Blanchot, in Agamben, G., *Homo Sacer: Sovereign Power and Bare Life*, Stanford University Press, Stanford, 1998, p. 18).

16. Like someone who "composes worlds according to their whim, without principles that oblige, in total indifference" (Descartes, R., "Correspondance Avril 1622 à Février 1638," p. 145–146. See Descartes, R., "Correspondance Mai 1647 à Février 1650," p. 224; and Descartes, R., "Correspondance Juillet 1643 à Avril 1647," in *Oeuvres*, vol. 4, Adam, C., and Tannery, P. (eds.), Léopold Cerf Editeur, Paris, 1901, p. 118).

11. SOVEREIGN CRITIQUE II

1. Schmitt. C., *Dictatorship: From the Origin of the Modern Concept of Sovereignty to Proletarian Class Struggle*, Polity Press, Cambridge, 2014, p. 231n2. "In particular, the obvious difference between the older republican dictatorships and the later ones of Sulla and Caesar might have suggested a much closer examination of the concept of dictatorship[,] the contradiction between commissary and sovereign dictatorship." (Schmitt. C., *Dictatorship*, p. 2).

2. "The ignominy of such an authority . . . lies in the fact that in this authority the separation of law-making and law-preserving violence is suspended. If the first is required to prove its worth in victory, the second is subject to the restriction that it may not set itself new ends. Police violence is emancipated from both conditions. It is law-making . . . and law-preserving, because it is at the disposal of these ends. The assertion that the ends of police violence are always identical or even connected to those of general law is entirely untrue. Rather, the 'law' of the police really marks the point at which the state, whether from impotence or because of the immanent connections within any legal system, can no longer guarantee through the legal system the empirical ends that it desires at any price to attain. Therefore the police intervene 'for security reasons' in countless cases where no clear legal situation exists, when they are not merely, without the slightest relation to legal ends, accompanying the citizen as a brutal encumbrance through a life regulated by ordinances, or simply supervising him. Unlike law, which acknowledges in the 'decision' determined by place and time a metaphysical category that give it a claim to critical evaluation, a consideration of the police institution encounters nothing essential at all. Its power

is formless, like its nowhere tangible, all-pervasive, ghostly presence in the life of civilized states. And though the police may, in particulars, everywhere appear the same, it cannot finally be denied that their spirit is less devastating where they represent, in absolute monarchy, the power of a ruler in which legislative and executive supremacy are united, than in democracies where their existence, elevated by no such relation, bears witness to the greatest conceivable degeneration of violence." (Benjamin, W., "Critique of Violence," in *One-Way Street and Other Writings*, Jephcott, E., and Shorter, K. (trans.), New Left Books, London, 1979, pp. 141–142).

3. Bayle's *Dictionnaire*, quoted in Koselleck, R., *Critique and Crisis: Enlightenment and the Pathogenesis of Modern Society*, MIT Press, Cambridge, 1988, p. 110.

4. Koselleck, R. *Critique and Crisis*, p. 109.

12. THE EPOCH OF CRITIQUE

1. Kant, I., *Critique of Pure Reason*, Cambridge University Press, Cambridge, 1998, pp. 100–101.

2. Benjamin, W., "One-Way Street," in *One-Way Street and Other Writings*, Jephcott, E., and Shorter, K. (trans.), New Left Books, London, 1979, p. 89.

3. See Kant, I., *Critique of Pure Reason*, p. 99.

4. "Yet by this I do not understand a critique of books and systems." (Kant, I. *Critique of Pure Reason*, p. 101).

5. Miguel Valderrama (*Modernismos historiográficos*, Editorial Palinodia, Santiago de Chile, 2008) sets out the relation between critique and frame (*parergon*), critique and work (*ergon*), work (*ergon*) and frame (*parergon*). Beginning with the question of power and the possibility of the work, Valderrama's essay proposes to destabilize those readings which in one way or another, from one side or another, have intended to fix the relation between work (*ergon*) and frame (*parergon*), "stabilizing it in (a determined) meaning," belittling thus the unstable route of the unresolved. "Desisting" from such stabilization, the essay reflects upon an "infinite resistance" that would "insistently" overturn it. But this would not only be a question of shaking the intention with which "critical readings" and historiographical texts make us work in framing them. Insofar as the critical or historiographical texts are recognized as such, they are so because they, in their turn, also respond to a stabilizing frame that makes them recognizable. Valderrama thus proposes to specially exercise that "infinite resistance" with regard to the frame of the critical or historiographical frame, to reverberate insistently upon the tympanum of this second frame so as to destabilize it. The essay names such an operation as a "metacommentary." Its more general purpose is to convey a liminal (parergonal) writing concerning that which, as a possibility, remains irreducible to the power of the work, of the frame, and the power of the frame of the frame, a possibility that insists "between" them, as undecidable vacillation.

6. See Barthes, R. "Lecture in Inauguration of the Chair of Literary Semiology,

College de France, January 7, 1977," trans. by Howard, R., *October*, vol. 8, Spring, 1979, p. 3.

7. Montaigne, M. de, "Judgement on God's Ordinances Must Be Embarked upon with Prudence," in *The Complete Essays*, Penguin Books, London, 1991, p. 242.

8. See Benjamin's discussion of Nietzsche's *The Birth of Tragedy* in Benjamin, W., *The Origin of German Tragic Drama*, trans. by Osborne, J., New Left Books, 1977, p. 103.

9. According to Foucault, "Kant gives three examples: we are in a state of 'immaturity' when a book takes the place of our understanding, when a spiritual director takes the place of our conscience, when a doctor decides for us what our diet is to be" (Foucault, M., "What Is Enlightenment?," in *The Foucault Reader*, ed. Rabinow, P., Pantheon Books, New York, 1984, p. 34.

13. CRITIQUE WITHIN THE FRAME, CRITIQUE OF THE FRAME

1. Aristotle, "De Partibus Animalium (On the Parts of Animals)," Book 1, in *The Basic Works of Aristotle*, McKeon, R. (ed.), Random House, New York, 1941, 639a, p. 643.

2. According to Sergio Rojas, "critique is to be found in the spilling over (desborde)," but not as a going "beyond the limit," but rather "as the experience of the limit itself" (Rojas, S., "De la expectativa moderna de un arte crítico contemporáneo," paper presented at the *Imágenes, imaginarios e imaginación crítica* conference, Santiago de Chile, 2010). The *experience of the limit itself* can be assumed in at least two or three ways, according to two or three ways of understanding and locating the limit: first, as the *experience of the limit* as *general framework, condition of possibility*, or as the *relations of production and understanding* of experience itself; then as the *experience of the limit of experience*, which makes the condition of experiencing itself, experienceable, interrupting the naturalized contract in which experience unfolds, *denaturalizing the real* (Rojas, S., "De la expectative," 2010). In this first sense, it seems to me, critique, conceived as the *experience of the limit as the experience of the frame, as the experience of the general condition of possibility of experience*, is outlined in Rojas's text. The second, which I set out below from Fragment 16 on, critique, the *experience of the limit*, will be understood not so much as the experience of the condition, the general framework, of the general relations of production and understanding, understood as frame. It will understand critique considered rather as *collage* or *patchwork*, a singular position *in the midst* of the multiple immanence of the given without frame, without horizon, without condition or general limit. A third is provided by Sergio Villalobos-Ruminott in his essay "Modernismo y desistencia." Here, we find critique "oscillating between everything considered as modernist, critical and rupturist, and a certain desistance . . . on the margin between . . . *modernism and desistence*." Beyond the Derridean reference, which Villalobos-Ruminott makes explicit,

"*desistence* does not refer to an intentional use (which returns all to the plane of decision), but rather to the imbalance of all decision as an opening to that which cannot be decided. . . . On the other hand, it is important to note a relation between desistence and *abdication* (relevant if we consider the latter as also being implicated in the question of the *interregnum*), which we think here as indetermination or even exception, as if we might say: we are not interested in sovereign abdication, but rather in the (unintended) effect of the interregnum" (Villalobos-Ruminott, S., "Modernismo y desistencia: Formas de leer la neo-vanguardia," *Archivos: Revista de Filosofía*, 6–7, 2011–2012, pp. 553–588).

3. The faculties of theology, law, and medicine (see Kant, I., *The Conflict of the Faculties*, Abaris Books, New York, 1979, p. 31).

4. The English-language version of Benjamin's phrase reads, unlike the Spanish (verdadero estado de excepción), rather as "real state of *emergency*" (emphasis added).—Trans.

5. Heidegger, M., *Observaciones relativas al arte: La plástica, el espacio*, Editorial Universidad Pública de Navarra, Pamplona, 2003, pp. 85, 87.

14. MANET: THE KANT OF PAINTING

1. Danto, A. C., *After the End of Art: Contemporary Art and the Pale of History*, Princeton University Press, Princeton, 1997, p. 7. "Using the history of philosophy as a 'collage' (already an old technique in painting) . . . would be better than 'selections' [fragmentos escogidos in the Spanish version—Trans.], but it would require particular techniques. You would need some Max Ernsts in philosophy." (Deleuze, G., "On Nietzsche and the Image of Thought," in *Desert Islands and Other Texts 1953–1974*, Taormina, M. (trans.), Semiotext(e), New York, 2004, p. 141).

2. Danto, A. C., *After the End of Art*, p. 7.

3. See also Foucault, M., *Manet and the Object of Painting*, Tate Publishing, London, 2009, p. 42.

4. Groys, B., *The Total Art of Stalinism: Avant-Garde, Aesthetic Dictatorship, and Beyond*, trans. by Rougle, C., Verso, London, 2001, pp. 15–16.

15. HEIDEGGER'S DEMAND

1. Heidegger, M., *Being and Time*, trans. by Macquarrie, J., and Robinson, E., Blackwell, Oxford, 1997, p. 29 (emphasis added).

2. Heidegger indicates that he moves far from Kant: "Philosophy, even when it becomes 'critical' through Descartes and Kant, always follows the course of metaphysical representation" (Heidegger, M., "Letter on Humanism," in *Basic Writings*, Farrell Krell, D., (ed.), Routledge, London, 1993, p. 234).

3. For a panoramic view of the collateral effects of the putting into crisis of the basic concepts, see Kuhn, T., *The Structure of Scientific Revolutions*, University of Chicago Press, Chicago, 1962.

4. Heidegger, M., *Being and Time*, p. 67.

5. "Laying the foundations, as we have described it, is rather a productive logic—in the sense that it leaps ahead, as it were, into some area of Being, discloses it for the first time in the constitution of its Being, and, after thus arriving at the structures within it, makes these available to the positive sciences as transparent assignments for their inquiry. To give an example, what is philosophically primary is neither a theory of the concept-formation of historiology nor the theory of historiological knowledge, nor yet the theory of history as the Object of historiology; what is primary is rather the Interpretation of authentically historical entities as regards their historicality. Similarly, the positive outcome of Kant's *Critique of Pure Reason* lies in what it has contributed towards the working out of what belongs to any Nature whatsoever, not in a 'theory' of knowledge. His transcendental logic is an *a priori* logic for the subject-matter of that area of Being called 'Nature.' But such an inquiry itself—ontology taken in the widest sense without favouring any particular ontological directions or tendencies— requires a further clue. Ontological inquiry is indeed more primordial, as over against the ontical inquiry of the positive sciences. But it remains itself naïve and opaque if in its research into the Being of entities it fails to discuss the meaning of Being in general. And even the ontological task of constructing a non-deductive genealogy of the different possible ways of Being requires that we first come to an understanding of 'what we really mean by this expression 'Being.' The question of Being aims therefore at ascertaining the *a priori* conditions not only for the possibility of the sciences which examine entities as entities of such and such a type, and, in doing so, already operate with an understanding of Being, but also for the possibility of those ontologies themselves which are prior to the ontical sciences and which provide their foundations." (Heidegger, M., *Being and Time*, 1997, p. 30–31).

6. Heidegger, M., *What Is That—Philosophy?*, trans. by Brann, E. T. H., St. John's College, Annapolis, 1991, pp. 9, 12, 11.

7. Heidegger's affirmation that "science does not think" is well known (Heidegger, M., *What Is Called Thinking*, trans. by Glenn Gray, J., Harper and Row, New York, 1968, p. 8). Science develops thanks to an unthought that makes it possible. Science is possible thanks only to a first forgetting: the forgetting of the preunderstanding of being that prethinks it. Without said forgetting there would be no science, there would be no West as the technical closure of thought. Science "does not think, and cannot think—which is its good fortune, here meaning the assurance of its own appointed course" (Heidegger, M., *What Is Called Thinking*, p. 8). On the other hand, "without science there would be no modern university today." If modern science— which is the condition of the modern university—does not think, if there is no modern university without modern science, then neither does the modern university think. According to Heidegger, there is a great danger in universities of a misunderstanding concerning thinking, especially in those research centers and teaching institutes in which science is referred to most (Heidegger, M., *Der Satz vom Grund*,

G. Neske, Pfullingen, 1957, p. 49). Not only does the university not think, Heidegger tells us, but especially its departments of philosophy—they too, emplotted into the growing phantasmagoria that results from the forgetting of being—do not think. It is thanks to such forgetting that, among other things, there are departments of philosophy. But also, it must be said, the teaching of philosophy in high schools as well as the portentous division of university knowledge into degree programs and professions, and the portentous technical division of labor. In departments of philosophy there exists "commendable efforts in the investigation of the history of philosophy. These are useful and worthy tasks, and only the best talents are good enough for them, especially when they present to us models of great thinking. But even if we have devoted many years to the intensive study of the treatises and writings of the great thinkers, the fact is still no guarantee that we ourselves are thinking, or even ready to learn thinking. On the contrary—preoccupation with philosophy more than anything else may give us the stubborn illusion that we are thinking just because we are incessantly 'philosophizing'" (Heidegger, M., *What Is Called Thinking*, p. 5). Not only do departments of philosophy, insofar as they are dedicated to the history of philosophy, not think. Ontology does not think. It does not think what it must think, that which only is "worthy" of thought. In order to make room for thought, not only is it unnecessary to take a course in metaphysics but, perhaps, it is necessary not to do so. Avoid the course, on the one hand, and destroy the history of Western understanding on the other, a history that has produced, as the epitome of its fetish, the Chair of Metaphysics and the History of Philosophy as the backbone of departments of philosophy: "This hardened tradition must be loosened up, and the concealments which it has brought about must be dissolved" (Heidegger, M., *Being and Time*, p. 44). It is necessary not only to go behind the disciplines, the technical division of university knowledge but also behind the "understanding of Being" (Heidegger, M., *Being and Time*, p. 31) in which the "sciences which examine entities of such and such a type, and, in so doing, already operate with an understanding of Being" (Heidegger, M., *Being and Time*, p. 31). Moreover, it is necessary to go behind the ontologies themselves, "which are prior to the ontical sciences and which provide their foundation" (Heidegger, M., *Being and Time*, p. 31). It is necessary to go to the condition of possibility of these ontologies, "an understanding of being" in which they "already operate," for "all ontology, no matter how rich and firmly compacted a system of categories it has at its disposal, remains blind and perverted from its ownmost aim, if it has not first adequately clarified the meaning of Being, and conceived this clarification as its fundamental task" (Heidegger, M., *Being and Time*, p. 31).

8. Danto, A. C., *After the End of Art: Contemporary Art and the Pale of History*, Princeton University Press, Princeton, 1997, p. 67.

9. An analogous operation, in another terminological context, is announced by Marx. A general theory of history, a science of the commodity, is not possible without a particular theory of capitalism as the *basic ontology* of the capitalist mode

of production on the basis of which a general theory of history and a science of the commodity may be elaborated. For this reason, Marx's *Capital* is prior to any general theory of history and science of the commodity.

16. CRITIQUE AND FIGURE

1. Deleuze, G., *Proust and Signs: The Complete Text*, trans. by Howard, R., University of Minnesota Press, Minneapolis, 2000, pp. 101, 108; Deleuze, G., "On Nietzsche and the Image of Thought," in *Desert Islands and Other Texts 1953–1974*, Taormina, M. (trans.), Semiotext(e), New York, 2004, p. 140.

2. Agamben, G., "Absolute Immanence," in *Potentialities: Collected Essays in Philosophy*, trans. by Heller-Roazen, D., Stanford University Press, Stanford, 1999, pp. 220–239.

3. Deleuze, G., *Cinema 2: The Time-Image*, trans. by Tomlinson, H., and Galeta, R., Athlone Press, London, 1989, p. 141.

4. See Benjamin, W., *The Arcades Project*, trans. by Eiland, H., and McLaughlin, K., Belknap Press, Cambridge, 1999, p. 460.

5. "To Martin Buber," in *The Correspondence of Walter Benjamin*, Scholem, G., and Adorno, T. W. (eds.), Jacobsen, M. R., and Jacobsen, E. M. (trans.), University of Chicago Press, Chicago, 1994, p. 313.

6. Allegory is never "avowedly chosen to express a concept" (Benjamin quoting Schopenhauer), nor is it "an expression of the particular" that might exemplify "the general" (Benjamin quoting Goethe), nor "a conventional relationship between an illustrative image and its abstract meaning" or a "writing" indebted to a "conventional system of signs" in which a substitution takes place (Benjamin, W., *The Origin of German Tragic Drama*, trans. by Osborne, J., New Left Books, 1977, pp. 161–162).

7. Benjamin, W., *Origin of German Tragic Drama*, p. 45.

17. THOUGHT AND FIGURE

1. See Didi-Huberman, G., *Devant le temps: Histoire de l'art et anachronisme des images*, Les Éditions de Minuit, Paris, 2000, p. 10.

2. Benjamin, W., "The Work of Art in the Age of Mechanical Reproduction," in *Illuminations*, Zohn, H. (trans.), Fontana/Collins, London, 1979, pp. 223, 225.

3. "For Antiquity, the imagination . . . was the supreme medium of knowledge." (Agamben, G., *Infancy and History: Essays on the Destruction of Experience*, trans. by Heron, L., Verso, London, 1993, p. 24).

4. See Deleuze, G., and Guattari, F., *What Is Philosophy?*, Verso, London, 1994, pp. 15–16.

5. See Deleuze, G., "Trois questions sur *Six fois deux* (Godard)," *Pourparlers*, Les Éditions de Minuit, Paris, 1990, pp. 64–65. See also Deleuze, G., and Guattari, F., *A Thousand Plateaus: Capitalism and Schizophrenia*, trans. by Massumi, B., Athlone Press, London, 1988, pp. 25, 98.

6. Benjamin, W., *The Origin of German Tragic Drama*, trans. by Osborne, J., New Left Books, 1977, p. 187.

7. Bertold Brecht's *Journals 1934–1955*, ed. by Willet, J., trans. by Rorrison, H. B., Routledge, New York, 1993, bring together figures of thought, photomontages and montages (even if to contradict each other) to underline the immanence of thought to the figure.

8. Benjamin, W., "The Storyteller," *Illuminations*, p. 90.

9. Benjamin, W., *Origin of German Tragic Drama*, pp. 45–46. See also Benjamin, W., *The Arcades Project*, trans. by Eiland, H., and McLaughlin, K., Belknap Press, Cambridge, 1999, p. 482 (Benjamin is quoting André Monglond's *Le préromantisme français*, vol. 1, Grenoble, 1930, p. xii).

18. THE LEVELING OF THE PIT

1. "After these tearings with the pincers, Damiens, who cried out profusely, though without swearing, raised his head and looked at himself." (From the description of the torture of the regicide described in Foucault, M., *Discipline and Punish*, Penguin Books, London, 1991, p. 4).

2. Oyarzún, *Arte, visualidad e historia*, Editorial La Blanca Montaña, Santiago de Chile, 1999, p. 24.

3. Benjamin, W., "One-Way Street," in *One-Way Street and Other Writings*, Jephcott, E., and Shorter, K. (trans.), New Left Books, London, 1979, p. 89.

4. Benjamin, W., "What Is Epic Theater?," *Illuminations*, p. 156.

5. Benjamin, W., "The Work of Art in the Age of Mechanical Reproduction," in *Illuminations*, Zohn, H. (trans.), Fontana/Collins, London, 1979, p. 244.

6. "The masses have a right to change property relations; Fascism seeks to give them expression while preserving property. The logical result of Fascism is the introduction of aesthetics into political life. The violation of the masses, whom Fascism, with its Führer cult, forces to their knees, has its counterpart in the violation of an apparatus which is pressed into the production of ritual values." (Benjamin, W., "Work of Art," p. 243.)

7. "By means of its technical structure, the film has taken the physical shock effect out of the wrappers in which Dadaism had, as it were, kept it inside the moral shock effect." (Benjamin, W., "Work of Art," 1979, p. 240).

8. Benjamin, W., "One-Way Street," 1979, pp. 45–104.

9. Benjamin, W., "Work of Art," p. 225.

19. THE CLASH OF FILM AND THEATER

1. Rilke, R. M., *The Notebooks of Malte Laurids Brigge*, trans. by Pike, B., Dalkey Archive Press, Champaign, p. 5.

2. Benjamin, W., "The Work of Art in the Age of Mechanical Reproduction," in *Illuminations*, Zohn, H. (trans.), Fontana/Collins, London, 1979, p. 225.

3. Benjamin, W., "Work of Art," p. 240.
4. Benjamin, W., "Work of Art," p. 252.
5. Benjamin, W., "Work of Art," p. 240.
6. Benjamin, W., "Work of Art," p. 240.
7. Benjamin, W., "Work of Art," p. 241.
8. Duhamel, quoted in Benjamin, W., "Work of Art," p. 240.
9. Benjamin, W., "Work of Art," p. 251n17.
10. Benjamin, W., "One-Way Street," in *One-Way Street and Other Writings*, Jephcott, E., and Shorter, K. (trans.), New Left Books, London, 1979, p. 45.
11. Valery, quoted in Benjamin, W., "Work of Art," 221.
12. The images collected by someone walking in the streets work against the grain of both idealist literary language and psychologism. For Benjamin, this world of reified images and phantasmagoria has the status of a dream in which the masses are effectively constituted in their everyday alienation. Their enclosure in such a contrivance takes its strength from the dialectics of the image that synthetically and unwarily returns the aura of the singular object back to it, aestheticizing the artificial paradise in the form of an absolute site or nature. See Buck-Moors, S., *The Dialectics of Seeing: Walter Benjamin and the Arcades Project*, MIT Press, Cambridge, 1991, p. 27.
13. Pirandello, quoted in Benjamin, W., "Work of Art," pp. 231–233.
14. Benjamin, W., "One-Way Street," p. 89.

20. CRITIQUE'S LOSS OF AURA

1. Marx, K., and Engels, F., "Manifesto of the Communist Party," in Marx, K., *The Revolutions of 1848: Political Writings, Vol. 1*, Penguin Books, Harmondsworth, 1981, p. 70.
2. Baudelaire, C., "Lost Halo," in *Paris Spleen*, trans. by Waldrop, K., Wesleyan University Press, Middletown, 2009, p. 88.
3. Benjamin, W., "One-Way Street," in *One-Way Street and Other Writings*, Jephcott, E., and Shorter, K. (trans.), New Left Books, London, 1979, pp. 89–90.
4. Marx, K., "Results of the Immediate Process of Production," *Capital*, vol. 1, trans. by Fowkes, B., Penguin Books, Harmondsworth, 1976, p. 1040.
5. Marx, K., "Results of the Immediate Process," pp. 1039–1040.
6. Jameson, F., "Postmodernism, or the Cultural Logic of Late Capitalism," *New Left Review*, 146, July–August, 1984, p. 57.

21. CRITIQUE AND MASS

1. Benjamin, W., "One-Way Street," in *One-Way Street and Other Writings*, Jephcott, E., and Shorter, K. (trans.), New Left Books, London, 1979, p. 89.
2. Benjamin, W., "The Work of Art in the Age of Mechanical Reproduction," in *Illuminations*, Zohn, H. (trans.), Fontana/Collins, London, 1979, p. 242.
3. Lyotard, J. F., "Pequeña perspectiva de la decadencia y de algunos combates

minoritarios por entablar allí," in *Políticas de la filosofía*, Grisoni, D. (ed.), Fondo de Cultura Económica, Mexico City, 1982, p. 135.

4. Lyotard, J. F., "Pequeña perspectiva," p. 135.

5. Benjamin, W., "One-Way Street," p. 89.

6. Benjamin, W., "Work of Art," p. 225.

7. "The desire of contemporary masses [is] to bring things 'closer' spatially and humanly, which is just as ardent as their bent toward overcoming the uniqueness of every reality by accepting its reproduction. Every day the urge grows stronger to get hold of an object at very close range by way of its likeness, its reproduction. . . . To pry an object from its shell, to destroy its aura, is the mark of a perception whose 'sense of the universal equality of things' has increased to such a degree that it extracts it even from a unique object by means of reproduction." (Benjamin, W., "Work of Art," p. 225).

8. Effects of dominance, not in the sense of *the most advanced and new with respect to the most backward and old* but in the ways in which the reciprocally anachronic or obsolete coexist in an actuality in which each interface testifies according to its weave, its figure, its predicates, its singular rhythm, its immanent time, without relation to any general, transcendental, common inclusive *portmanteau* (estuche) of time. It is rather a matter of the effects of reciprocity within a *patchwork* of polychronisms without *timerose*.

9. Benjamin, W., "Work of Art," pp. 236, 233, 230–231.

10. See Benjamin, W., *The Origin of German Tragic Drama*, trans. by Osborne, J., New Left Books, 1977, p. 28.

11. Benjamin, W., *Origin of German Tragic Drama*, p. 45.

12. See Benjamin, W., *The Arcades Project*, trans. by Eiland, H., and McLaughlin, K., Belknap Press, Cambridge, 1999, p. 476; and Benjamin, W., "The Task of the Translator," in *Illuminations*, Zohn, H. (trans.), Fontana, London, 1979, pp. 73–82.

13. Benjamin, W., "One-Way Street," p. 95.

14. See Serres, M., *The Parasite*, trans. by Schehr, L. R., Johns Hopkins University Press, Baltimore, 1982.

15. Benjamin, W., "Apuntes sobre el concepto de historia," in *La dialéctica en suspenso*, Oyarzún, P. (ed. and trans.), LOM ediciones, Santiago de Chile, 2009, pp. 55–56. Oyarzún also provides an introduction to "Apuntes" in that volume. Benjamin refers here to Henri Focillon's, *Life of Form in Art* (1934), Zone Books, New York, 1992.

22. NIHIL AND PHILOSOPHY

1. Heidegger, M., *Nietzsche (Volume IV): "Nihilism,"* ed. by Krell, D. F., trans. by Capuzzi, F. A., Harper Collins, New York, 1991, pp. 4–5. As in other cases, this translation has been corrected according to my convenience.

2. Heidegger, M., "'Only a God Can Save Us': *Der Spiegel*'s Interview with Martin

Heidegger," trans. by Alter, M. P., and Caputo, J. D., in *The Heidegger Controversy: A Critical Reader*, Wolin, R. (ed.), Stambaugh, J. (trans.), MIT Press, Cambridge, 1993, pp. 91–116.

3. Nietzsche, F., "On Truth and Lies in a Nonmoral Sense," in *The Nietzsche Reader*, Ansell Pearson, K., and Large, D. (eds.), Blackwell, Oxford, 2006, p. 115.

4. Engels, F., "The English Constitution," quoted in Schmitt, C., *Political Theology*, Schwab, G. (trans.), MIT Press, Cambridge, 1985, p. 51.

5. Blanchot, M., *The Infinite Conversation*, trans. by Hanson, S., University of Minnesota Press, Minneapolis, 1993, p. 144.

6. Whether it be called water, idea, valorization of value, eternal return of the same, mode of production, homogeneous empty time, metatecnics, etc.

7. The other version, that of *active nihilism*, produces a detranscendentalization that opens onto the immanence of the multiple singular and not onto homogeneous transcendental facticity.

8. See Jacobo Muñoz's discussion of Heidegger in Muñoz, J., "Solo un dios puede salvarnos," in *Heidegger o el final de la filosofía*, Navarro Cordón, J. M., and Rodríguez, R., (eds.), Editorial Complutense, Madrid, 1997, pp. 127–138.

9. Nietzsche, F., *Philosophy in the Tragic Age of the Greeks*, trans. by Cowan, M., Regnery Publishing, Washington, 1962, p. 41. "Greek philosophy seems to begin with an absurd notion, with the proposition that *water* is the primal origin and the womb of all things. Is it really necessary for us to take serious notice of this proposition? It is, and for three reasons. First, because it tells something about the primal origin of all things; second, because it does so in language devoid of image or fable; and finally, because contained in it, if only embryonically, is the thought, 'all things are one.' . . . The third makes him [Thales] the first Greek philosopher. . . . By presenting his unity-concept in the form of his water-hypothesis, Thales did not, it is true, overcome the low level of empiric insight prevalent in his time. What he did was to pass over its horizon. The sparse and unordered observations of an empirical nature which he made regarding . . . water (more specifically, of moisture) would have allowed . . . no such gigantic generalization. What drove him to it was a metaphysical conviction. . . . We meet it in every philosophy, together with ever-renewed attempts at a more suitable expression, this proposition that 'all things are one'." (Nietzsche, F., *Philosophy in the Tragic Age of the Greeks*, trans. by Cowan, M., Regnery Publishing, Washington, 1962, pp. 38–39).

23. JENNY

1. The passage from the simple tool to the complex machine-tool is not given in the shift in motor from the power of the human motor to that of an external motor, be it sea, wind, or mule. If this were the case, then there would have been machine-tools since Adam and Eve ploughed with mules in paradise. The machine-tool is different from the mere tool, not because of what its motor force is (be it horse or human) but

rather because the number of terminals that the machine-tool can operate simultaneously exceeds the direct operating possibilities of the human body. This difference
introduces transformations that are historical rather than physical. What changes with
the Jenny is the historical understanding of the virtuality of work and of the body.

2. Marx, K., *Capital*, vol. 1, Penguin Books, Harmondsworth, 1976, pp. 492–508.

3. Marx, K., *Grundrisse*, trans. by Nicolaus, B., Penguin, Harmondsworth, 1973,
pp. 817–831.

4. Marx, K., *Capital*. [The English-language version does not give "machine-
tool" here, which would be the direct translation of the Spanish-language version
of "máquina herramienta," but "tool" or "working machine." I will thus, following
Thayer's argument, translate his use of the Spanish-language version as "machine-
tool"—Trans.]

5. "These men will be composed, as we are, of a soul and a body. And I must
describe for you first the body on its own; and then the soul, again on its own; and
finally I must show you how these two natures would have to be joined and united
so as to constitute men resembling us." (Descartes, R., "The *Treatise on Man*," in
The World and Other Writings, Gaukroger, S. (trans.), Cambridge University Press,
Cambridge, 2004, p. 99)

6. Descartes, R., "Règles pour la direction de l'esprit," in *Oeuvres et lettres*,
Bridoux, A. (ed.), NRF, Bibliothèque de la Pléiade, Paris, 1963, p. 37.

7. According to Descartes, the compositional regime is governed from head to toe
by the imagination, conceived as a power to compose landscapes of various kinds:
physical and astrophysical, biological and anatomical, urban and peasant, of diverse
complexity and containing varied customs; portraits, anecdotal, or abstract paintings,
which are more or less colorful; illusions, memories, evocations according to moods
and passions of varied intensity; the more or less plausible echoes and specters of
dreams, daydreams, and artifice, etc. Whatever its task, as a faculty for composing
landscapes the imagination constitutes a finite power of infinite composition. It
makes on the basis of what it does not have, and which it has been given. It requires
materials and compositional principles. More than an interest in the varied universe of
composition, however, Descartes is attracted by the order of elements, the principles
and materials of which composition is composed. They attract him because in these
elements reside power and the possibility of composition, as well as composition and
the possibility of power. Whosoever controls the principles of world composition also
governs not only the worlds, but their very possibility. It is a question then, in a first
moment, of suspending the universe of compositions or imaginings so as to unearth
in them the elements and mechanisms from which they are made and function. The
strategy of their unearthing would consist in looking for what in them, without being
composed, constitutes the basis of their composition: the principles and materials
from which the imagination composed them—the principles and materials that condition the power of the imagination as a possible maker of worlds. Once the principles

and elements of the imagination are revealed as part of an analytics that moves from the composed to the noncomposed within the composed, the scene of the conditions of the imagination become, so to speak, visible. These conditions would not be the product of the imagination, but, on the contrary, their law, their limit, the prescription on whose basis the imagination is free to produce however many compositions it wants—infinite in number, probably—but always subject to the principles that govern it, without governing them itself. The freedom of the imagination thus lacks sovereignty. It would not be able to declare the *state of exception* of the principles that prescribe it, nor could it decide on its own principles. It is not its own constituent power but rather a constituent principle whose own bases are constituted principles, a kind of *commissarial consul*. Those principles that condition the imagination are commonly referred to as the principles of the understanding. Insofar as they are imagined and composed from here, as we have noted, such principles, in constituting the conditions of the imagination, cannot be imagined or composed by it. The imagination finds its limit in the understanding. And the understanding, is it sovereign with regard to its categories and principles? Can it declare the exception of its principles? Is it the constituent power of the principles that constitute it? Here, I believe, is the turbulence on which the question of the sovereignty of the principle [*principio*, which is also "beginning," thus establishing an important conjunction in Thayer's argument—Trans.], of the prince, of the evil-genius-machine, of the subject as subject without the subjection of subjection must be focused. The question of the sovereignty of the principles of the understanding opens up Descartes's text to the hyperbolic turbulence of sovereignty, of the possibility of a compositional principle or of an imagination that, over and above the understanding or of principles, whatever it may be, as a state of exception decides on the principles without principals, an imagination that without rules, without motive, without concern, without condition, with total indifference, and as pure *fiat* can unconditionally create, among other things, the principles and conditions of the understanding as the limits of an imagination without sovereignty, subject to another sovereignty. ("The mathematical truths that you call 'eternal' have been laid down by God and depend on him entirely, no less than the rest of his creation. To say that these truths are independent of God is to talk of him as if he were Jupiter or Saturn. . . . Don't hesitate to assert that and proclaim everywhere that it's God who has laid down these laws . . . just as a king lays down laws in his kingdom. . . . You may say: 'if God had established these truths he would have been able to change them, as a king changes his laws.' To this the answer is: 'He can change them, if his will can change. But I understand them to be eternal and unchangeable.' And so is God in my judgement. 'But his will is free.' Yes, but his power is beyond our grasp. In general we can say that God can do everything that we can grasp, but not that he can't do what is beyond our grasp. It would be rash to think that our imagination reaches as far as his power. . . . He was as free to make it not true that the radii of a circle are all equal as he was to not create the world.'. . . . 'I don't think we should ever say of anything that it can't be brought about by God. For since every basis of truth and goodness depends on his omnipotence, I wouldn't risk saying that God can't make an uphill without a downhill; or bring it about that 1 plus 2 does not equal 3. I merely say that he has given me a mind such that I can't conceive of an uphill without a downhill, or a sum of 1 and 2 that is not 3; such things involve a contradiction in my conception." Descartes, R., *Selected Correspondence of Descartes*, trans. by Bennet, J., pp. 15, 16, 18, 210, 2010–2017, http://www.earlymoderntexts .com/assets/pdfs/descartes1619_1.pdf, accessed May 20, 2018.)

8. "Value is constantly changing from one form into the other, without becoming lost in this movement; it thus becomes transformed into an automatic subject. If we pin down the specific forms of appearance assumed in turn by self-valorizing value in the course of its life, we reach the following elucidation: capital is money, capital is commodities. In truth, however, value is here the subject of a process in which, while constantly assuming the form in turn of money and commodities, it changes its own magnitude, throws off surplus-value from itself considered as original value, and thus valorizes itself independently. For the movement in the course of which it adds surplus-value is its own movement, [and] its valorization is therefore self-valorization. By virtue of being value, it has acquired the occult ability to add value to itself. It brings forth living offspring or at least lays golden eggs. . . . In simple circulation, the value of commodities attained at the most a form independent of their use-values, i.e. the form of money. But now, in the circulation M-C-M, value suddenly presents itself as a self-moving substance which passes through a process of its own, and for which commodities and money are both mere forms. But there is more to come: instead of simply representing the relations of commodities, it now enters into a private relationship with itself, as it were. It differentiates itself as original value from itself as surplus-value, just as God the Father differentiates himself from himself as God the Son, although both are of the same age and form, in fact one single person; for only by the surplus-value of £10 does the £100 originally advanced become capital, and as soon as this has happened, as soon as the son has been created and, through the son, the father, their difference vanishes again, and both become one, £110." (Marx. K., *Capital*, vol. 1, Penguin Books, Harmondsworth, 1976, pp. 255–256).

9. Technically, for Marx, the *lumpen* is what proliferates as a "remainder" *between* modes of production. To a large extent, the *lumpen* is a precise figure of becom-ing, of the *in between*, the *middle* (and *medium*), of the conflict between modes of production.

10. See Marx, K., *Capital*, pp. 500–503.

11. The cloaked form, the fetish character adopted by the instruments of direct production in which labor power is worn out in productive becoming, is abolished. Henceforth, it is according to capital itself, in growth without end (*a-telos*), that the undefined activities are exposed as fetishes of a unique abstract act in which specific labor terminals or working organs are revealed as pure abstraction: expanding value,

the use value of value in expansion (or expanding value, the use value of expanding value).

    12. Marx, K., *Grundrisse*, p. 110.

    13. Marx, K., *Grundrisse*, p. 311.

24. THE EPOCH OF NIHILISM. *NIHIL* AS EPOCH.

    1. See Heidegger, M., "The Question of Being (Letter to Ernst Jünger 'Concerning "The Line,"'" in *Philosophical and Political Writings*, Kluback, W., and Wilde, J. T. (trans.), Continuum, New York, 2003, pp. 120–151; Heidegger, M., *Nietzsche (Volume IV): "Nihilism,"* ed. by Krell, D. F., trans. by Capuzzi, F. A., Harper Collins, New York, 1991; and Heidegger, M., "Overcoming Metaphysics," in *The Heidegger Controversy: A Critical Reader*, Wolin, R. (ed.), Stambaugh, J. (trans.), MIT Press, Cambridge, 1993, pp. 67–90.

    2. Heidegger, M., "Overcoming Metaphysics," pp. 85–86.

    3. Heidegger, M., "Overcoming Metaphysics," pp. 74–75.

    4. The title of an article by Sergio Villalobos-Ruminott in *Archivos de Filosofía*, 1, 2007, pp. 180–196.

    5. Blanchot, M., *The Infinite Conversation*, trans. by Hanson, S., University of Minnesota Press, Minneapolis, 1993, p. 150.

    6. Heidegger, M., "Question of Being," 2003, pp. 125–126.

    7. For the Marx of *Theories of Surplus Value*, it still seemed possible to differentiate significantly between the *unproductive labor* of Milton as the writer of *Paradise Lost*, and the wage labor of Milton for the publisher that produces this work for a bookseller. In the same way, the unproductive labor of a silkworm that secretes the fiber that affirms its nature could be differentiated from the labor of the silkworm arranged in a textile farm as the producer of a raw material sold for x amount of pounds sterling. For Marx, this difference was becoming more and more insignificant as a mode of production based on manufacture passed into another based in industry, until all difference between *unproductive and productive labor* was completely extinguished under *capitalism in its specific sense*, the *real subsumption of labor to capital*, the extinguishing of all *use value* as the *use value of capital*.

    8. Heidegger, M., "Overcoming Metaphysics," pp. 82–83, 85, 86, 87–88.

    9. And others of the same kind (even though not homologous), notions that are expressly deployed by Deleuze as the *nihilization of the nihil* (to use Villalobos-Ruminott's formulation). This is especially the case in Deleuze, G., *Difference and Repetition*, trans. by Patton, P., Continuum, London, 2010, which programmatically presents itself as a kind of "settling of accounts" with the *nihil*, the universal, the transcendental, totality, identity, the self-sameness expressed in dogmatic *images of thought* such as "being and thinking are the same," "giving sufficient reasons," "the will to," "the desire of," "the immanence of," etc.

    10. Heidegger, M., "'Only a God Can Save Us': *Der Spiegel*'s Interview with Martin

Heidegger," trans. by Alter, M. P., and Caputo, J. D., in *The Heidegger Controversy: A Critical Reader*, Wolin, R. (ed.), Stambaugh, J. (trans.), MIT Press, Cambridge, 1993.

11. Deleuze, G., and Guattari, F., *A Thousand Plateaus: Capitalism and* Schizophrenia, trans. by Massumi, B., Athlone Press, London, 1988, p. 477.

25. THE EXHAUSTED AGE

1. Febvre, L., *The Problem of Unbelief in the Sixteenth Century: The Religion of Rabelais*, trans. by Gottlieb, B., Harvard University Press, Cambridge, 1982, p. 2.

2. See Foucualt, M., "What Is Enlightenment?," in *The Foucault Reader*, ed. Rabinow, P., Pantheon Books, New York, 1984, pp. 32–50.

3. Benjamin, W., "The Work of Art in the Age of Mechanical Reproduction," in *Illuminations*, Zohn, H. (trans.), Fontana/Collins, London, 1979.

4. Benjamin, W., *The Arcades Project*, trans. by Eiland, H., and McLaughlin, K., Belknap Press, Cambridge, 1999, pp. 543–544, 473. Elizabeth Collingwood-Selby comments on this statement as follows: "It assumes the liquidation of the aura provoked by mechanical reproduction, and recognizes in the debacle of singularity and the authenticity of the past the emergence of something unique and unrepeatable. To be clear: liquidated auratic singularity is singularity understood as an authentic original's identitarian presence to itself. Post-auratic singularity of the unique is that which emerges—to disappear in the instant that follows—as the effect of a particular montage—a constellation—of times, of forms of mediation, of modes of production, that is as a dialectical image . . . a matter of uniqueness where identity touches its limit. The 'genuinely unique' that the politicization of art and the politicization of history must recognize in any actual constellation is not the repeatable and conservable singularity of the ever same, but of that which in the moment of its actualization sparkles as loss, that is, for the first and last time" (Collingwood-Selby, *El filo de la historia*, Metales Pesados, Santiago de Chile, 2009, pp. 177–178).

5. The final judgment as "a citation *à la ordre du jour*" (Benjamin, W., "Theses on the Philosophy of History," in *Illuminations*, Zohn, H. (trans.), Fontana/Collins, London, 1979, p. 256.

26. THE COEXISTENCE OF TECHNOLOGIES: MARX

1. Marx, K., *Capital*, vol. 1, Penguin Books, Harmondsworth, 1976, pp. 95–98, 102–103. The coexistence and clash of modes of production is connected, also, to the juxtaposition of historical interfaces and the coexistence of anachronisms as proposed by Foucault toward the end of *Society Must Be Defended* as well as at the beginning of his courses *The Birth of Biopolitics* and *Security, Territory, Population*. Here he punctually sets out the coexistence and juxtaposition of three clashing interfaces: as (1) premodern technology that understands life as a natural, sacred, and creatural phenomenon as it unfolded in the ancien régime; and (2) the *rights of man* machine of the French Revolution—"all men are equal by nature and before the law," "govern-

ment is instituted in order to guarantee to man the enjoyment of his natural and imprescriptible rights" (La Fayette, among others)—in which the originary status of the life of all is constituted as the right to life as it is mediated by the sovereign state, which, just as it grants and guarantees the right to life, can take it away. In this interface, life and death are rights of the subject or citizen according to the sovereign will such that before the sovereign power, it is neither alive or dead, but rather *neutral*, with "no law, no home," "an isolated piece," "a beast or a god" (Aristotle, "Politics," in *The Basic Works of Aristotle*, McKeon, R. (ed.), Random House, New York, 1941, 1253a, p. 1130), a survivor in a state of exception. Originally inscribed as a right, life is at the same time deployed within the field of state performative and disciplinary interventions that train *bodily powers* into productive forces. The final interface is (3) the biopolitical machine, which is not centered on the individual body or on the organic apparatus of disciplinary normalization but directed at the control and prevention of risk within the multiplicity of the human as population ("living mass," "species"), aiming at the global homeostatic balance, regularization, administration, and security of group bioeconomic processes (infant mortality, longevity of the population, social health, public hygiene, endemic disease, savings, consumption, security). It occupies itself with the immunization of the population against the exogenous, the other of biology and life, so as *to make live by letting die* whatever endangers them: the population's other, or the other population. It is through this immunological principle that Foucault assembles sovereignty and governmentality, "making life" and "making death." Racism is what gives this assemblage its direction, not as a blind ideological passion, ethnic hate, or linguistic phobia but, more originally, as "the break between what must live and what must die," a break that conducts life to a condition of permanent war: exposure to death, confrontation between what must live and what should die so as to affirm superiority there, in fact, in terms of the survival of the strongest and the fittest (Foucault, M., *"Society Must Be Defended": Lectures at the Collège de France*, 1975–76, trans by Macey, D', Picador, New York, 2003, p. 254 and passim).

27. REFERENTIAL ILLUSION

1. See Benjamin, W., "The Work of Art in the Age of Mechanical Reproduction," in *Illuminations*, Zohn, H. (trans.), Fontana/Collins, London, 1979, p. 229.

2. Nietzsche, F., quoted in Blanchot, M., *The Infinite Conversation*, trans. by Hanson, S., University of Minnesota Press, Minneapolis, 1993, p. 154.

3. "This film is an experiment in cinematic communication of real events/Without the help of intertitles/Without the help of a story/Without the help of theatre/This experimental work aims at creating a truly international language of cinema based on its absolute separation from the language of theatre and literature." (Vertov, D., *Man with a Camera*, 1929).

4. "The Bororo myth [is] simply a transformation, to a greater or lesser extent,

of other myths originating either in the same society or in a neighboring or remote societies. I could, therefore, have legitimately taken as my starting point any one representative myth of the group." (Levi-Strauss, C., *The Raw and the Cooked*, quoted in Derrida, J., *Writing and Difference*, Bass, A. (trans.), Routledge, London, 1990, p. 286).

28. CRITIQUE AND INSTALLATION

1. Jameson, F., *The Seeds of Time*, Colombia University Press, New York, 1994, p. 79.

2. Badiou, quoted in Žižek, S., *Organs without Bodies: On Deleuze and Consequences*, Routledge, New York, 2004, p. 29.

3. Borges, J. L., "The Aleph," in *Collected Fictions*, Hurley, A. (trans.), Penguin Books, London, 1999, pp. 274–286.

4. Benjamin, W., "Theses on the Philosophy of History," in *Illuminations*, Zohn, H. (trans.), Fontana/Collins, London, 1979, p. 256.

5. Borges, J.L., "The Book of Sand," in *Collected Fictions*, Hurley, A. (trans.), Penguin Books, London, 1999, pp. 480–483.

6. I am paraphrasing Derrida, J., *The Truth in Painting*, trans. by Bennington, G., and McLeod, I., University of Chicago Press, Chicago, 1987, p. 18.

7. The fabric is constitutively closed by the weave. It may be longitudinally infinite, but it comes and goes at the extreme verticals, closing, centering space, wrapping the body, more sedentary than nomadic, more of the home and routine work than of the empty vectors *of open pathways*.

8. Danto, A. C., *After the End of Art: Contemporary Art and the Pale of History*, Princeton University Press, Princeton, 1997, p. 7.

9. "Anachronism emblematizes a concept and the use of time in which the latter absorbs the characteristics of its opposite, eternity, without a trace." (Didi-Huberman, G., *Devant le temps: Histoire de l'art et anachronisme des images*, Les Éditions de Minuit, Paris, 2000, p. 16.). "Anachronism would thus be, less a scientific error than a fault committed in the light of the conviviance of times." (Jacques Rancière, quoted in Didi-Huberman, G., *Devant le temps*, p. 38).

10. Didi-Huberman, G., *Devant le temps*, p. 122.

11. As formulated by Elizabeth Collingwood-Selby in *El filo de la historia*, Metales Pesados, Santiago de Chile, 2009.

12. Didi-Huberman, G., *Devant le temps*, p. 19.

13. Didi-Huberman, G., *Devant le temps*, p. 37.

14. See Blanqui, L.-A., *Eternity by the Stars: An Astronomical Hypothesis*, trans. by Chouraqui, F., Contra Mundum Press, New York, 2013.

15. See Benjamin, W., "Central Park," trans. by Spencer, L., *New German Critique*, 34, Spring, 1985, pp. 32–58.

16. The *nihil* speaks: "The universe is infinite in time and space, eternal, boundless and undivided. All physical bodies, animate and inanimate, solid, liquid and gaseous, are held together by the very thing that separates them. . . . If one removed the

celestial bodies, space would remain, absolutely empty . . . but still possessing all . . . dimensions" (Blanqui, L.-A., *Eternity by the Stars*, p. 66).

17. "The locus in which the Greek philosophers deal with the question of time is always *Physics*. Time is something objective and natural, which envelopes things that are 'inside' it as if in a sheath (*periechón*): as each thing inhabits a place, so it inhabits time." (Agamben, G., *Infancy and History: Essays on the Destruction of Experience*, trans. by Heron, L., Verso, London, 1993, p. 93). For Benjamin, in contrast, time is a material predicate (in that objective sense) of singularities and monads—and not a *portmanteau*.

18. Benjamin, W., quoted in Buck-Moors, S., *The Dialectics of Seeing: Walter Benjamin and the Arcades Project*, MIT Press, Cambridge, 1991, p. 23.

29. CRITIQUE AS THE UNWORKING OF THEATER

1. See Benjamin, W., "The Author as Producer," in *Understanding Brecht*, Bostock, A. (trans.), Verso, London, 1998, pp. 85–103.

2. Benjamin, W., "Author as Producer," p. 94.

3. See for example "The Philosophy of Composition," "Letter to B—," and "Marginalia" in *Edgar Allan Poe: Complete Essays, Literary Studies, Criticism, Cryptography and Autography, Translations, Letters and Other Non-Fiction Works*, e-artnow, 2017, loc. 64–258, 6445–6707, 7381–7491.

4. Blanchot, M., *The Infinite Conversation*, trans. by Hanson, S., University of Minnesota Press, Minneapolis, 1993, p. 361.

5. Blanchot, M., *Infinite Conversation*, p. 362.

6. Blanchot, M., *Infinite Conversation*, p. 361.

7. Brecht, B., "The Exception and the Rule," in *Measures Taken and Other Lehrstucke*, trans. by Manheim, R., Bloomsbury, London, http://www.dramaonlinelibrary.com, accessed June 6, 2018.

8. I am paraphrasing Blanchot here (*Infinite Conversation*, pp. 364–365).

9. Benjamin, W., *Understanding Brecht*, trans. by Bostock, A., Verso, London, 1998, p. 21.

10. Barthes, R., "Lecture in Inauguration of the Chair of Literary Semiology, College de France, January 7, 1977," trans. by Howard, R., *October*, vol. 8, Spring, 1979, p. 5.

11. Deleuze, G., and Parnet, C., *Dialogues*, Flammarion, Paris, 1996, p. 42.

12. Barthes, R., "Lecture in Inauguration," p. 6.

13. Barthes, R., "Lecture in Inauguration," p. 6.

14. "To supply a production apparatus without trying, within the limits of the possible, to change it, is a highly disputable activity even when the material supplied appears to be of a revolutionary nature." (Benjamin, W., "Author as Producer," p. 94).

15. Deleuze, G., *Essays Critical and Clinical*, trans. by Smith, D. W., and Greco, M. A., University of Minnesota Press, Minneapolis, 1997, p. lv.

30. DESTRUCTION

1. See also: "The Destructive Character," "Fate and Character," "Karl Krauss," "Critique of Violence" (all included in Benjamin, W., *One-Way Street and Other Writings*, Jephcott, E., and Shorter, K. (trans.), New Left Books, London, 1979), "The Task of the Translator," and "Theses on the Philosophy of History" (in Benjamin, W., *Illuminations*, Zohn, H. (trans.), Fontana, London, 1979), among others. In his reflection on the concept of "destruction," Federico Galende refers to these essays. What the idea of "destruction" sets in train, he suggests, is a critique of a model of representation deployed as a system throughout the history of Western thought. What destruction *destroys* is thus the *metaphysics of representation*, of the metaphysical Western theater. The topology of this theater may be schematized in the tripartitions *stage/pit/stalls*, *author/work/spectator*; *thought/speech (orality)/writing, subject/difference/object*. In it, critique has mainly placed itself, as we have noted above, far from the stage, in the stalls, in the periphery or margin with respect to a center. Insofar as Galende proposes "destruction" as a critique of the metaphysics of representation, he is also proposing "destruction" as a critique of *vulgar criticism* as a possibility that is exercised inside that very theater: the stalls criticizing the stage (see Galende, F., *Benjamin y la destrucción*, Metales Pesados, Santiago de Chile, 2009).

2. Brecht, too: "Puntilla means hardly anything to me, the war everything; about puntilla I can write virtually anything, about the war, nothing. And I don't just mean 'may,' but truly 'can'" (*Bertold Brecht Journals*, Willett, J., (ed.), trans. by Rorisson, H., Methuen, New York, 1993, p. 97). See Didi-Huberman, G., *Quand les images prennent position: L'oeil de l'histoire, 1*, Editions Minuit, Paris, 2009, p. 23). Hence his *Journals* as performance, installation, cut-up, and *collage*.

3. See Benjamin, W., *The Arcades Project*, trans. by Eiland, H., and McLaughlin, K., Belknap Press, Cambridge, 1999, p. 476; and Benjamin, W., "The Task of the Translator," in *Illuminations*, Zohn, H. (trans.), Fontana, London, 1979, p. 73.

4. In the same sense as *pure language, pure violence, pure destruction*.

5. "Melancholy speaks herself": "Nowhere do I find rest,/I must even quarrel with myself./I sit,/I lie,/I stand,/but am always in thought" (Andreas T., *Melancholy Speaks Herself*, quoted in Benjamin, W., *The Origin of German Tragic Drama*, trans. by Osborne, J., New Left Books, 1977, p. 138).

6. Focillon, quoted in Benjamin, W., *La dialéctica en suspenso*, ed. and trans. by Oyarzún, P., LOM ediciones, Santiago de Chile, 2009, p. 55.

7. Literally *lumpfen*, meaning "rag" or "cloth."

31. SOVEREIGN EXCEPTION, DESTRUCTIVE EXCEPTION

1. Benjamin, W., "Theses on the Philosophy of History," in *Illuminations*, Zohn, H. (trans.), Fontana/Collins, London, 1979, p. 259.

2. In other words: (1) the bourgeois regime of the representation of language as

proposition and means of communication; (2) the bourgeois regime of representation of right in its dual forms as natural and positive right; (3) the regime that reduces justice, truth, and thought to judgment, statement, and rule; (4) the bourgeois regime of knowledge founded on and guaranteed by a method that protects its own results rather than interesting itself in truth; (5) a vulgar understanding of time as homogeneous and continuous (instant); (6) the regime of subjectivity as self-founding consciousness and experience; (7) auratic-exhibitionary understanding of the structure of the work of art, of politics—stage/pit/spectator and their respective critiques.

3. I agree with Schmitt here, who specifically points out that the state of exception does not refer to a casuistic approach to modern representational sovereignty but rather to its structure, its condition.

4. Benjamin, W., "Theses on the Philosophy of History," p. 259.

5. Benjamin, W., "Theses on the Philosophy of History," p. 259.

6. See Löwy, M., *Fire Alarm: Reading Walter Benjamin's "On the Concept of History,"* Verso, London, 2005.

7. We witness this Calvary, says Hegel, from the perspective of "the res gestae themselves" as well as from that of "the narration of what has happened"—inseparable, given that they each are part of the other, since "we must suppose historical narrations to have appeared contemporaneously with historical deeds and events" (Hegel, G. W. F., *The Philosophy of History*, trans. by Sibree, J., Dover Publications, New York, 1956, p. 60).

8. Hegel, G. W. F., *Philosophy of History*, pp. 72, 21.

9. Hegel, G. W. F., *Lecciones sobre la filosofía de la historia universal*, trans. by Gaos, J., Alianza Editorial, Madrid, 1999, pp. 77–78. [I am translating here directly from the Spanish-language version of Hegel's text, which is very different from the English-language version, being both longer and organized very differently—Trans.]

10. Hegel, G. W. F., *Elements of the Philosophy of Right*, trans. by Nisbet, H. B., Cambridge University Press, Cambridge, 1996, p. 373.

11. Hegel, G. W. F., *Philosophy of History*, p. 36.

12. Hegel, G. W. F., *Philosophy of History*, pp. 456–457. See also Hegel, G. W. F., *Elements of the Philosophy of Right*, pp. 372–380.

13. *Hegel's Science of Logic*, trans. by Miller, A. V., Humanity Books, New York, 1969, p. 824.

14. The process of production of absolute recollection makes of the lacunary a booty of memory, in a way analogous to how the commodity dissolves unpaid labor into capital.

15. This is because it is in absolute recollection's movement of negativity that recollection, by virtue of its synthetic mediation, recovers the substantive richness of the multiplicity with which it is related, becoming the substance of recollection, the recollection of substance, recollective substance, and substantial recollection.

16. The translation responds to what is inscribed in Hegel rather than to what is written by him [the author is here playing with the echo of the English "erase" and the Spanish érase (it was). Erase *érase* (what was): history as erasure—Trans.]. Hegel's text regularly reiterates that absolute knowledge maintains a difference with itself, a difference that constitutes its relation to itself. Both the expression *"all was once"* as absolute testimony and historicism's "whore called *once upon a time"* (Benjamin, W., "Theses on the Philosophy of History," p. 264) reduce such difference and dampen vacillation, the disquiet of difference. Testimony understood as a knowledge without fissures is the utopia of vulgar testimony. The aspiration to testimony as homogeneous *presentational* plenitude reduces the *vacillation of the negative*. The Hegelian absolute presupposes the perseverance of something irreducible, *the imperfection that all perfection demands*. It is not for nothing that at the end of *Science of Logic*, in "The Absolute Idea," there abruptly emerges a reference to Diogenes as a (Lacanian) *petit objet "a."* The organic life of the system requires the irreducible as sovereign exception, in other words: within the absolute idea difference is not a being other but rather transparent to itself, and it remains different in such transparency (see *Hegel, Science of Logic*, pp. 824–844). The absolute is thus the most *unconditioned differentiation* (Heidegger, M., *Hegel*, trans. by Arel, J., and Feuerbahn, N., Indiana University Press, London, 2015, Kindle edition, loc. 725). In Hegel, there is a result (*ergon*) *in* and *through* the restlessness that serves restfulness as a principle of the relation *to self*.

17. Nietzsche, F., "On Truth and Lies in a Nonmoral Sense," in *The Nietzsche Reader*, Ansell Pearson, K., and Large, D. (eds.), Blackwell, Oxford, 2006, pp. 114–123.

18. Nietzsche, F., "On Truth and Lies in a Nonmoral Sense," pp. 119, 117.

19. "White mythology—metaphysics has erased within itself the fabulous scene that has produced it, the scene that nevertheless remains active and stirring, inscribed in white ink, an invisible design covered over in the palimpsest." (Derrida, J., "White Mythology," *Margins of Philosophy*, trans. by Bass, A., Harvester Wheatsheaf, New York, 1982, p. 213.

20. "But the other side of its Becoming, *History*, is a *conscious*, self-*mediating* process. . . . This Becoming presents a slow-moving succession of Spirits, a gallery of images, each of which, endowed with all the riches of Spirit, moves thus slowly just because the Self has to penetrate and digest this entire wealth of its substance. As its fulfillment consists in perfectly *knowing* what *it is*, in knowing its substance, this knowing is its *withdrawal into itself* in which it abandons its outer existence and gives its existential over to recollection. Thus absorbed in itself, it is sunk in the night of its self-consciousness; but in that night its vanished outer existence is preserved, and this transformed existence—the former one, but now reborn of the Spirit's knowledge—is the new existence, a new world and a new shape of Spirit. In the immediacy of this new existence the Spirit has to start afresh to bring itself to maturity as if, for it, all that proceeded were lost and it had learned nothing from the experi-

NOTES TO PAGE 90

ence of the earlier Spirits. But recollection, the *inwardizing*, of that experience, has preserved it and is the inner being, and in fact the higher form of the substance. So although this Spirit starts afresh and apparently from its own resources to bring itself to maturity, it is none the less on a higher level that it starts. The realm of Spirits which is formed in this way in the outer world constitutes a succession in Time in which one Spirit relieved another of its charge and each took over the empire of the world from its predecessor. Their goal is the revelation of the depth of Spirit, and this is the *absolute Concept*. . . . The *goal*, Absolute Knowing, or Spirit that knows itself as Spirit, has for its path the recollection of the Spirits as they are in themselves and as they accomplish the organization of their realm. Their preservation, regarded from the side of their free existence appearing in the form of contingency, is History; but regarded from the side of their philosophically comprehended organization, it is the Science of Knowing in the sphere of appearance: the two together, comprehended History, form alike the inwardizing and the Calvary of absolute Spirit, the actuality, truth, and certainty of his throne, without which he would be lifeless and alone. Only from the chalice of his realm of spirits foams forth for Him his own infinitude." (Hegel, G. W. F., *The Phenomenology of Spirit*, Oxford University Press, Oxford, 1977, pp. 492–493 [translation slightly emended to echo the Spanish-language version—Trans.]).

21. "The thousands of millions of unheard thoughts of women before the Women's Liberation Movement; the thousands of tragic, small acts of shame angrily suffered before the liberation movement, the millions of tiny rituals of encounter via mimicry (mímica) as well as the messages left on the walls of semipublic surfaces for homosexuals forbidden by society before the creation of the Homosexual Front; the thousands of millions of isolated or collective meetings of workers on factory floors and in offices—a materiality that does not become words in trade union discourse except when fetishized in negotiable demands." (Lyotard, J. F., "Pequeña perspectiva de la decadencia y de algunos combates minoritarios por entablar allí," in *Políticas de la filosofía*, Grisoni, D. (ed.), Fondo de Cultura Económica, Mexico City, 1982, pp. 137–138).

22. "As Hegel has written in the objective logic, 'passive substance therefore only receives its due through the action of another power'; he sees written on his body, like in the famous novel by Kafka, the sentence of the *Weltgericht*. But, essentially, the point of view that grasps violence is still limited, illusory. As Hegel writes in the subjective logic, it 'may be regarded as violence,' but as a violence that is illusory, limited by the standpoint such as the understanding of a faculty that would like to substantialize the particular moment without inserting it in the general frame of reality. The people suffering violence are in fact without spirit. . . . They have a form of phantasmatic, lifeless existence, the survivors of a *Zeitgeist* that has already passed in the course of world-history. Therefore, in suffering violence, these people are executing the sentence of the tribunal of world-history, in a way similar to that in which punishment reaffirms the negated law in the criminal." Morfino, V., "The Syntax of Violence:

Between Hegel and Marx," *Historical Materialism*, 17, 2008, pp. 90–91. See Hegel, *Elements of the Philosophy of Right*, pp. 126–127.

23. Morfino, V., "Syntax of Violence," p. 88 (quoting *Hegel's Science of Logic*, p. 748).

24. Benjamin, W., "Theses on the Philosophy of History."

25. It is important that the moment of violence intervene in the passage from the realm of necessity to the realm of freedom, from passive to active substance, from darkness to light—its function is precisely to set this darkness aside. Nevertheless, this violence only appears as such from a superficial standpoint, the birth of meaning only being possible by way of a violence that is only apparent, since in reality it is only apparently exercised on an immediate presupposition, upon a dark accident. In truth, this darkness has only been posited by the light of the concept itself so as to be transformed into freedom by the power (*potencia*) of necessity. Light makes use of the dark, giving it dignity, freeing it from the somber night of senselessness, to introduce it into the chiaroscuro of a world that gradually lets a hierarchical scale of determinations appear: violence is the black trace on the white paper, a violence that is only apparent because through it the paper is ennobled, becoming something that was destined to be—design, meaning. "Through violence, passive substance is only *posited* as what it is in truth, namely, to be only something posited, just because it is the simple positive, or immediate substance; what it is *before-hand* (*das Voraus*) as condition, is the illusory (*Schein*) immediacy which active causality (*wirkende Causalität*) strips off from it." (*Hegel's Science of Logic*, pp. 567–568, quoted by Morfino, V., "Syntax of Violence," p. 83). "But now in being posited in its positedness, or in *its own* determination, the outcome is not that it is sublated, but rather that it only *unites with its own self* and therefore *in being determined* is, in fact, *originative*. On the one hand, therefore, the passive substance is *preserved* or *posited* by the active substance, namely, in so far as the latter makes itself into a sublated substance; but, on the other hand, it is *the act of the passive substance itself* to unite with itself and thus to make itself into the originative and into *cause*. Its *being posited* by an other, and its own *becoming* are one and the same thing." (*Hegel's Science of Logic*, p. 568). "The movement of the end can now be expressed as having for its aim to sublate its presupposition (*Voraussetzung*), that is the immediacy of the object (*Unmittelbarkeit des Objects*), and to posit the object as determined by the Notion." (*Hegel's Science of Logic*, p. 742, quoted by Morfino, V., "Syntax of Violence," p. 86).

26. "In the modern epoch, the lands of the Atlantic, which once had a culture when they were discovered by the Europeans, lost it once entering into contact with them. The conquest of the country signaled the ruin of their culture, of which *we have information*, but which says no more than it was a natural culture *which must expire as soon as Spirit approached it*." (Hegel, G. W. F., *Lecciones sobre la filosofía de la historia universal*, trans. by Gaos, J., Alianza Editorial, Madrid, 1999, p. 171 [translation from Spanish-language translation, except for italicized phrases, which come from Hegel, G. W. F., *Philosophy of History*, p. 81—Trans.]).

27. See Morfino, V., "Syntax of Violence," p. 88.

28. Brecht, B., *The Threepenny Opera*, quoted by Benjamin. W., "Theses on the Philosophy of History," p. 258.

29.

Speaking to the *La nación domingo* newspaper in November 2003 during the process of the modernization of the Chilean military, which was carried out by the government of President Ricardo Lagos (2000–6), the commander in chief of the armed forces, General Emilio Cheyre, stated the following regarding the falsified list that was submitted by the Chilean army to the Rettig Commission concerning the Puerto Montt Operation (1974–76), which the newspaper had reported on their front page and others in some detail, about how, with the use of helicopters, airports, cars, and service personnel of the Chilean state, the Pinochet dictatorship had exterminated the bodies of four hundred political prisoners, blowing them up with dynamite in the desert, dropping them into rivers, lakes, or the sea, wired to iron rails, their bodies cut open to facilitate their sinking: "What surprises me is that the new information obtained by newspapers or the courts, and which *La nación domingo* calculates at 400 people; what does it prove? That the 151 which we submitted were part of a whole, the part we could put together. But there is no doubt that had we further information, we wouldn't have submitted it. Because if we had known that there were not 151, but 551, it is more logical that we would have submitted that information at the time" (Cheyre, E., *La nación domingo*, November 23, 2003).

30. Nevertheless, it does not appear that Benjamin aspires to a simple euthanasia of progress. If the death of intentions is one of the emblems with which he sets out his concept of history (in "Theses on the Philosophy of History"), the death of intentions does not amount to the extermination of any (including the intentionality of progress in any of its dogmatic forms). For Benjamin, it is rather a matter of the destruction of the principle of general mediation that aspires to subordinate intentional flows to total systems and, in this sense, of the destruction of the common understanding of time as a continuous instant, a destruction that requires such intention, not now,

however, as a general mediation that subsumes other vectors but as just another vector within their folds, as one of many doctrines that circulate within the heteroclite and unsublateable plane of an actuality without general mediation.

31. Benjamin, W., *La dialéctica en suspenso*, ed. and trans. by Oyarzún, P., LOM ediciones, Santiago de Chile, 2009, p. 58.

32. Benjamin, W., *Dialéctica en suspenso*, p. 59.

33. In a sense analogous to *pure language*.

34. *Dialectical image*, the *death of intentions*, and *revolutionary general strike*, among others.

35. Benjamin, W., *The Origin of German Tragic Drama*, trans. by Osborne, J., New Left Books, 1977, p. 65.

36. Benjamin, W., *Origin of German Tragic Drama*, p. 65. See also the discussion in Agamben, G., *State of Exception*, trans. by Attell, K., University of Chicago Press, Chicago, 2005, pp. 52–64.

37. Benjamin, W., *Origin of German Tragic Drama*, p. 71; Agamben, G., *State of Exception*, p. 56.

38. "Just as compositions with restful lighting are virtually unknown in mannerist painting, so it is that the theatrical figures of this epoch always appear in the harsh light of their changing resolve." (Benjamin, W., *Origin of German Tragic Drama*, p. 71).

39. See Benjamin, W., *Origin of German Tragic Drama*, pp. 28–29, 157–158.

40. Benjamin, W., *Origin of German Tragic Drama*, p. 98.

41. Borges, J. L., "The Garden of Forking Paths," in *Collected Fictions*, Hurley, A. (trans.), Penguin Books, London, 1999, pp. 119–128. "The idea of the Chinese philosopher being involved with the labyrinth is an idea of Leibniz's contemporaries. . . . Leibniz is fascinated by the Orient, and he often cites Confucius. Borges made a kind of copy that conformed to Leibniz's thought with an essential difference: for Leibniz, all the different worlds that might encompass an Adam sinning in a particular way, an Adam sinning in some other way, or an Adam not sinning at all[—]he excludes all this infinity of worlds from each other[. They] are incompossible with each other such that he conserves a very classical principle of disjunction[—]it's either this world or some other one[—whereas] Borges places all these incompossible series in the same world, allowing a multiplication of effects. Leibniz would never have allowed incompossibles to belong to a single world." (*Lectures by Gilles Deleuze: On Leibniz*, http://deleuzelectures.blogspot.co.uk/2007/02/on-leibniz.html, accessed October 1, 2017).

42. Benjamin, W., *The Arcades Project*, trans. by Eiland, H., and McLaughlin, K., Belknap Press, Cambridge, 1999, p. 456. See also Didi-Huberman, G., *Devant le temps: Histoire de l'art et anachronisme des images*, Les Éditions de Minuit, Paris, 2000, pp. 119–127.

43. Derrida, J., *Sur parole: Instantanés philosophiques*, Éditions de l'Aube, Paris, 1999, pp. 18–19.

44. Aumont, J., and Marie, M., *Diccionario teórico crítico del cine*, Ediciones La Marca, Madrid, 2006, p. 221.

45. Blanchot, M., *The Infinite Conversation*, trans. by Hanson, S., University of Minnesota Press, Minneapolis, 1993, p. 326.

46. For example, in Schmitt, C., *Political Theology*, University of Chicago Press, Chicago, 2005; Bataille, G., *El límite de lo útil*, Losada, Madrid, 2005; and Artaud, A., *The Theatre and Its Double*, Alma Classics, London, 2017.

32. THE ABSOLUTE DROUGHT OF CRITIQUE

1. "Most of the everyday discourses on, or analyses of, violence that we hear through the media circulate in the conviction that the exercise of violence, on the one hand, and the rule of law, on the other, are divided by a profound enmity. All would seem to suggest that violence is most properly combatted from the established order of rights, and that, in the last analysis, this is the place from which violence is proscribed. In his 'Critique of Violence,' Walter Benjamin attacks the very roots of this supposition, exposing a link that the civilizing state persistently puts all its energy into covering up: the systemic alliance between right and violence." (Collingwood-Selby, E., "Al filo de la historia: Para la crítica de la violencia de Walter Benjamin," *Revista de Filosofía*, 2–3, 2008, p. 65).

2. Collingwood-Selby, E., "Al filo de la historia," p. 67.

3. The constellation of *"critique"* and *"crisis"* does not find in judgment (*juicium*) its simple *condition of possibility*, but rather just one more possibility, as a *condition of critique* is only such within a specific technology of critique, the judicial-juridical technology of critique, rather than of critique as such. Indeed, a series of critical activities to which we refer in Fragment 2, a-pathetic activities proper to the theoretical-contemplative register of *krino*—activities that remit to a discernment that separates, distinguishes, selects, analyzes, observes differences in a frenzy in which it is taken up and disseminated according to aspects dictated by the object itself, according to the meticulous obedience of the researcher, the arbiter, the judge, the critic listening to and contemplating (*theorein*) the infinite details dictated—belongs to another critical opening, not that of either the *jus* or the *juicium*. Judgment as critique's condition is only that of judicial, sovereign critique, but not of critique as the *real state of exception*. In this sense, "Critique of Violence" effectively constitutes a critique of critique as a kind of critique of judicial critique. A critique of judicative critique that "frees" critique into a virtuality that unworks judgment's condition.

33. SOREL: SOVEREIGN CRITIQUE

1. "Today I do not hesitate to declare that socialism could not continue to exist without an apology for violence." (Sorel, G., *Reflections on Violence*, ed. by Jennings, J., Cambridge University Press, Cambridge, 2004, p. 279).

2. "To maintain the idea of war today, when so many efforts being made to oppose

socialism with social peace, seems more necessary than ever." (Sorel, G., "Sindicalismo revolucionario," *Último recurso*, http://pages.infinit.net/sociojmt, accessed
February 17, 2008, p. 8).

3. The "general" character of the strike means, for Sorel, that "capitalism cannot be
abolished piecemeal[,] . . . that socialism cannot be realized in stages. . . . No formula
that can satisfy the universal character of the revolution has ever been produced"
(Sorel, G., "Sindicalismo revolucionario," p. 7). "Every strike, however local it may be,
is a skirmish in the great battle named the general strike." (Sorel, G., "Sindicalismo
revolucionario," p. 8). Like Hegel's Spirit or Marx's capital, "the general strike . . .
drags into the revolutionary track everything it touches" (Sorel, G., *Reflections on
Violence*, p. 124).

4. See Sorel, G., *Reflections on Violence*, p. 238.

5. Sorel, G., *Reflections on Violence*, p. 154.

6. "The time of political revolutions has come to an end. . . . The proletariat
refuses to allow new hierarchies to be constituted. Such a formula knows nothing
about the rights of man, of absolute justice, of political constitutions and parliaments;
it does not just purely and simply negate the government of the capitalist bourgeoisie,
but also every hierarchy more or less analogous to it. Those who support the general
strike aspire to the disappearance of everything that had concerned the old liber-
als: the eloquence of the tribunals, the management of public opinion, the alliances
between political parties." (Sorel, G., "Sindicalismo revolucionario," p. 8).

7. See Sorel, G., *Reflections on Violence*, pp. 109–119.

8. Sorel elaborates on the victorious structure of his myth connecting the triumphalism of the general strike with the triumphalism of the "Catholics," who "have
never been discouraged even in the hardest trials, because they have pictured the
history of the Church as a series of battles between Satan and the hierarchy supported
by Christ: every new difficulty that arises is an episode in this war which must finally
end in the victory of Catholicism. . . . The revolutionary *syndicats* argue about socialist action in exactly the same way as the military writers argue about war; they enclose
the whole of socialism in the general strike; they look upon every combination as one
that should culminate in this fact; they see in each strike a model, a test, a preparation
for the great final upheaval" (Sorel, G., *Reflections on Violence*, pp. 20, 110).

9. Sorel, G., *Reflections on Violence*, p. 128.

10. Sorel, G., *Reflections on Violence*, pp. 114–115.

11. Sorel, G., *Reflections on Violence*, pp. 115–116.

12. Sorel, G., *Reflections on Violence*, p. 116.

13. Sorel, G., *Reflections on Violence*, p. 238.

14. Sorel, G., "Sindicalismo revolucionario," p. 7.

15. Sorel, G., *Reflections on Violence*, p. 119.

16. Sorel, G., *Reflections on Violence*, p. 20.

17. Sorel, G., *Reflections on Violence*, p. 113.

NOTES TO PAGES 102–106

18. Lévi-Strauss, C., *The Raw and the Cooked, Mythologiques Vol. 1*, trans. by Weightman, J., and Weightman, D., University of Chicago Press, Chicago, 1983, p. 18.

19. Sorel, G., *Reflections on Violence*, p. 118.

20. Sorel, G., *Reflections on Violence*, pp. 121–122 (quoting Bergson's "Introduction to Metaphysics").

21. Sorel, G., *Reflections on Violence*, p. 117.

22. Sorel, G., *Reflections on Violence*, p. 120.

23. Sorel, G., *Reflections on Violence*, p. 20.

24. Sorel, G., *Reflections on Violence*, p. 140.

25. Sorel, G., *Reflections on Violence*, p. 118.

26. Sorel, G., *Reflections on Violence*, p. 140.

27. Sorel, G., *Reflections on Violence*, p. 140.

28. Sorel, G., *Reflections on Violence*, p. 112.

29. Sorel, G., *Reflections on Violence*, p. 126.

30. Sorel, G., *Reflections on Violence*, p. 154.

31. Sorel, G., *Reflections on Violence*, p. 280.

32. Sorel, G., *Reflections on Violence*, p. 281.

33. Bataille, G., *El límite de lo útil*, Losada, Madrid, 2005, p. 107.

34. Bataille, G., *El límite de lo útil*, p. 21.

35. Bataille, G., *El límite de lo útil*, p. 107.

36. Bataille, G., *El límite de lo útil*, p. 22.

37. Spinoza, B., *A Theologic-Political Treatise and a Political Treatise*, trans. by Elwes, R. H. M., Dover Philosophical Classics, New York, 2004, p. 5.

34. BENJAMIN: PURE STRIKE AND CRITIQUE

1. See Sorel, G., *Reflections on Violence*, ed. by Jennings, J., Cambridge University Press, Cambridge, 2004, especially Chapters 5 and 4, respectively.

2. Benjamin, W., "Critique of Violence," in *One-Way Street and Other Writings*, Jephcott, E., and Shorter, K. (trans.), New Left Books, London, 1979, pp. 145–146.

3. "It 'nullifies all the ideological consequences of every possible social policy; its partisans see even the most popular reforms as bourgeois.' 'This general strike clearly announces its indifference toward material gain through conquest by declaring its intention to abolish the state; the state was really . . . the basis of the existence of the ruling group, who in all their enterprising benefit from the burden borne by the public.' . . . Taking up occasional statements by Marx, Sorel rejects every kind of programme, of utopia—in a word, of law-making. . . . 'With the general strike all these fine things disappear; the revolution appears as a clear, simple revolt, and no place is reserved for either the sociologists or for the elegant amateurs of social reforms or for the intellectuals who have made it their profession to think for the proletariat.'" (Benjamin, W., "Critique of Violence," pp. 145–146).

4. See Benjamin, W., "On Language as Such and on the Language of Man," in *One-*

Way Street and Other Writings, Jephcott, E., and Shorter, K. (trans.), New Left Books, London, 1979, pp. 111, 120.

5. Benjamin, W., "Theses on the Philosophy of History," in *Illuminations*, Zohn, H. (trans.), Fontana/Collins, London, 1979, p. 259.

6. Benjamin, W., "The Work of Art in the Age of Mechanical Reproduction," in *Illuminations*, Zohn, H. (trans.), Fontana/Collins, London, 1979, p. 223.

7. Benjamin, W., "Theses on the Philosophy of History," p. 242.

35. THE DESTRUCTION OF THEATER

1. Benjamin, W., "What Is Epic Theatre?," *Illuminations*, Zohn, H. (trans.), Fontana, London, 1979, p. 156.

2. "A brief minute of the full possession of forms presents itself . . . as good fortune, like the Greek *akme*: in which the pointer on the scales barely moves. What I hope for is not to see it bend again, least of all to reach that moment of absolute fixity, but rather that miraculous, vacillating immobility, the slight, imperceptible tremor that shows me it is alive." (Benjamin, W., *La dialéctica en suspenso*, ed. and trans. by Oyarzún, P., LOM ediciones, Santiago de Chile, 2009, p. 55).

3. Benjamin, W., "The Work of Art in the Age of Mechanical Reproduction," in *Illuminations*, Zohn, H. (trans.), Fontana/Collins, London, 1979, p. 235.

4. Artaud, A., *Mensajes revolucionarios: Cartas a la nación mexicana*, Editorial Fundamentos, Madrid, 1981, p. 30.

5. See Artaud, A., *The Theatre and Its Double*, Alma Classics, London, 2017.

6. Benjamin, W., "Work of Art," p. 243.

7. Benjamin, W., "Work of Art," p. 243.

8. Benjamin, W., "One-Way Street," in *One-Way Street and Other Writings*, Jephcott, E., and Shorter, K. (trans.), New Left Books, London, 1979, p. 80.

9. Marx, K., *Capital*, vol. 1, Penguin Books, Harmondsworth, 1976, p. 125.

10. Debord, G., *Society of the Spectacle*, trans. by Nicholson-Smith, D., Zone Books, New York, 1995, p. 12.

11. Agamben, G., *Means without End: Notes on Politics*, trans. by Binetti, V., and Casarino, C., University of Minnesota Press, Minneapolis, 2000, p. 108.

12. Derrida, quoted in Borradori, G., *Philosophy in a Time of Terror: Dialogues with Jürgen Habermas and Jacques Derrida*, University of Chicago Press, Chicago (e-book editon), 2003, p. 101.

13. Benjamin, W., "Work of Art," p. 220.

14. Foucault, M., *The Will to Knowledge: The History of Sexuality, Volume 1*, trans. by Hurley, R., Penguin Books, London, 1990, p. 92–102.

15. Agamben, G., *Means without End*, p. 111.

16. That systematized exception is the mechanism for the autoimmunization of the law, of the sovereign as law, such that the latter was exposed, as exception, outside the law so as to introject that outside against the outside.

17. Agamben, G., "The Messiah and the Sovereign: The Problem of Law in Walter Benjamin," in *Potentialities: Collected Essays in Philosophy*, quoted in Moreiras, A., *Línea de sombra, el no sujeto de la política*, Palinodia, Santiago de Chile, 2006, p. 230.

18. Agamben, G., "The Messiah and the Sovereign," quoted in Moreiras, A., *Línea de sombra*, p. 229.

19. Derrida, quoted in Borradori, G., *Philosophy in a Time of Terror*, p. 99.

20. Derrida, quoted in Borradori, G., *Philosophy in a Time of Terror*, p. 99.

21. "The question of when there will be peace cannot be answered not because the duration of war is unfathomable, but rather because the question already asks about something which no longer exists, since war is no longer anything which could terminate in peace. War has become a distortion of the consumption of beings which is continued in peace [the Spanish-language translation includes here the following: "The war has become a kind of usury"—Trans.]. . . . This long war in its length slowly eventuated not in a peace of a traditional kind, but rather in a condition in which warlike characteristics are no longer experienced as such at all and peaceful character-istics have become meaningless and without content." (Heidegger, M., "Overcoming Metaphysics," in *The Heidegger Controversy: A Critical Reader*, Wolin, R. (ed.), Stam-baugh, J. (trans.), MIT Press, Cambridge, 1993, pp. 84–85.

22. Derrida, quoted in Borradori, G., *Philosophy in a Time of Terror.*

23. "And does killing necessarily mean putting to death? Isn't it also 'letting die'? Can't 'letting die,' 'not wanting to know that one is letting others die'—hundreds of millions of human beings, from hunger, AIDS, lack of medical treatment, and so on—also be part of 'more or less' conscious and deliberate terrorist strategy?" (Derrida, quoted in Borradori, G., *Philosophy in a Time of Terror*, p. 108).

24. Felt is a cloth made without knitting or stitching, without mobile wefts or fixed warps, that agglutinates and sediments fleeces of hair or wool with the residues of cholesterol produced by the sebaceous glands through the application of dampness, pressure, and heat until an inextricable, structureless mat is formed. Felt "implies no separation of threads, no intertwining, only an entanglement of fibers," it is "in no way homogeneous: it is nevertheless smooth." In every grid, felt opens up in many different directions; it is continuously unfocused and associated with the stain or blot, permanent variation, the turbulence of the commonplace, and the obstinacy of the plain. "It has neither top nor bottom nor center," no restraints, and, lacking all memory, is related to ash. It is also referred to as a *primary cloth*, in contrast to fabric, which is secondary, striated, and related to agriculture. Felt adapts interior space to the open air, the desert, the sea, exile. It responds to a haptic perception of the atmospheres and intensities of the steppes, continuously varying its reference points and connections. It is also completely opposed to fabric as an organic space of measurements and properties, constituted by variable (the weaves) and immobile (the warps) elements that crisscross to form striated, agricultural surfaces. In contrast

to felt, fabric is constitutively closed by the warp. It may be infinite in its length but not in its width. It comes and goes bouncing off the extreme verticals, closing and centering space, wrapping around the body, sedentary rather than nomadic, associated more with pastorage, hunting, routine chores than with vectors that open out and break with the field. The fabric integrates both the body and the outside into its fold and stationary elasticity. While the fabric is focused on the stitch, felt bursts. Felt and fabric, the smooth and the striated have always confronted each other. According to Pierre Chaunu, the smooth and the striated confront each other at sea "during the course of which the striated progressively took hold" over the smooth and felt. Alongside a navigation that is woven from constellation points in the sky, measured exactly according to the stars and the rotation of the earth, the calculation of longitudes, latitudes, and satellite webs, there has also existed a nomadic, smooth navigation that feels its way, in which the winds, noise, color, the sounds of the sea or of the desert interfere with empirical postulates (see Deleuze, G., and Guattari, F., *A Thousand Plateaus: Capitalism and Schizophrenia*, trans. by Massumi, B., Athlone Press, London, 1988, pp. 475–479).

25. Galende, F., *Walter Benjamin y el problema de la destrucción*, doctoral thesis, Universidad Nacional de Rosario (Argentina), 2008, pp. 34, 45, 169–170.

36. THOUGHT IS INSEPARABLE FROM A CRITIQUE

1. The English-language version reads: "Philosophy is inseparable from 'critique'"— the missing indeterminate article "a," however, is fundamental to this book's entire argument, as we shall see below (see Deleuze, G., "On Nietzsche and the Image of Thought," in *Desert Islands and Other Texts 1953–1974*, Taormina, M. (trans.), Semiotext(e), New York, 2004, p. 138).—Trans.

2. "True critique is the criticism of true forms, not false contents. You don't criticize capitalism or imperialism by denouncing their 'mistakes.'" (Deleuze, G., "On Nietzsche and the Image of Thought," p. 138).

3. Oyarzún, P., "Un fragmento sobre la crítica," in *Arte, visualidad e historia*, La Blanca Montaña, Santiago de Chile, p. 239.

4. Deleuze, G., and Parnet, C., *Dialogues*, Flammarion, Paris, 1996, p. 1.

5. Deleuze, G., *Pure Immanence: Essays on a Life*, trans. by Boyman, A., Zone Books, New York, 2001.

6. Deleuze, G., *Pure Immanence*, pp. 26–27.

7. I am paraphrasing Deleuze, G., *Pure Immanence*.

8. Deleuze, G., *Pure Immanence*, p. 27.

INDEX

WILLY THAYER is Professor of Philosophy and Aesthetics at the Universidad Metropoli-
tana de Ciencias de la Educación, Santiago. He has also served three times as
Visiting Professor at Duke University and has taught at several other universities in
North America. He is the author of many books in Spanish.

JOHN KRANIAUSKAS is Professor of Latin American Studies at Birkbeck, University of
London. His most recent books are *Políticas culturales: acumulación, desarrollo
y crítica cultural* (FLACSO, 2015) and *Capitalism and Its Discontents: Power and
Accumulation in Latin-American Culture* (University of Wales Press, 2017). He is
the translator and editor of Carlos Monsiváis's *Mexican Postcards* (Verso, 1997).